D0961959

Untangling

My Chopsticks

Broadway Books

New York

Untangling My Chopsticks

A CULINARY SOJOURN IN KYOTO

Victoria Abbott Riccardi

PRINTED IN THE UNITED STATES OF AMERICA

BROADWAY BOOKS and its logo, a letter B bisected on the
diagonal, are trademarks of Random House, Inc.

Visit our website at www.broadwaybooks.com.

Book design by Maria Carella

Permission credits are on page 283

Library of Congress Cataloging-in-Publication Data
Riccardi, Victoria Abbott.
   Untangling my chopsticks : a culinary sojourn in Kyoto /
Victoria Abbott Riccardi.
      p. cm.
   Includes index.
   I. Cookery, Japanese.   I. Title.
TX724.5.J3 R49 2003
641.5952—dc21   2002034251

ISBN 0-7679-0851-I

I0 9 8 7 6 5 4 3 2 I

To Little Buddha

For lighting the way of love

To eternal bliss

Acknowledgments

Had it not been for my grandparents, Esther and Gordon Abbott (fondly referred to by their grandchildren as Gunga and Pama), the wonders of Japan and especially Kyoto might have eluded me. It was the postcard they sent me almost thirty years ago of two *maiko* (apprentice geisha) feeding orange carp in a mossy garden that made me want to visit Japan. I am grateful for their fascination with China, Hong Kong, and Japan and their desire to pass along the glories of these countries to their grandchildren.

I am profoundly indebted to my parents, Gordon and Katharine Abbott, who have always encouraged their children to follow their hearts. Thank you for your extraordinary love, support, and guidance over the years.

I am also grateful to my siblings, Christopher, Katrina, and

Alexandra, and extended family, Lexanne, Ben, Shaun, JJ, Nina, and Michael, who helped immeasurably by cheering me on from the sidelines as I worked on this project.

To my best friend, Margaret, thank you for always being there, before, during, and after Kyoto. Your weekly letters to Japan not only comforted and entertained me but also served as an invaluable resource.

When I left Kyoto for the first time back in 1987, I knew I wanted to share the beauty of this city and the art of tea kaiseki with others. I owe a world of gratitude to my agent, Angela Miller, for sitting down with me one cold January afternoon in her New York office and asking me what I really wanted to write about, and then encouraging me to do so. Thank you for your interest, commitment, and unflagging faith.

I am also immensely grateful to my editor, Jennifer Josephy, who expressed such enthusiasm for this project. Thank you for your insight, honesty, and thoughtful comments and suggestions all along the way.

Also, many thanks to her assistant, Laura Marshall, and so many others at Broadway Books. I am tremendously grateful for all your professionalism and creative input.

Allan Palmer was kind enough to spend time talking with me about the tea ceremony and tea kaiseki, as well as read through the manuscript. My sincere appreciation for your valuable role.

Also, numerous thanks to Glynne Walley, for sharing your extensive knowledge of Japanese history, as well as your thoughts on the manuscript.

I also appreciate the insight of Mr. Kaji Aso. Thank you for welcoming me into your tearoom and sharing your knowledge of tea.

My cousin, Susannah Gardiner, offered many thoughtful

suggestions for the manuscript. Thank you for all your heartfelt input.

Many thanks to my friend Alice Kelly, who offered immeasurable support from early on. Thank you for your generous involvement with the manuscript and many helpful comments.

Miki Sakakibara, with whom I shared dozens of cups of coffee and tea, thank you for your valuable insight about Japanese culture, including chopstick etiquette.

I am also indebted to all my friends in Kyoto for sharing with me the treasures of your city, the bounty of Kyoto's markets, the warmth of your friendship, and the spirit of Japan.

During the years I have worked on this book, my husband, John, has provided more love, compassion, and support than a person could ever hope for. Thank you for all you have shared with me. I am forever grateful for your profound understanding of human nature, unique insight, editorial wisdom, and most precious spirit.

Contents

Even in Kyoto
how I long for old Kyoto
when the cuckoo sings

Matsuo Basho, translated from
the Japanese by Sam Hamill

Prologue

Ever since I can remember, I have adored mixing up ingredients to experience new taste thrills. The first recipe I ever made was Betty Crocker's Polka-Dot Macaroni Bake, a dish of creamy elbows and cheese topped with salty hot dog slices. I was seven.

My passion for cooking grew as my mother taught me how to make her chewy cranberry bread, Dijon mustard vinaigrette, and Nantucket quahog chowder thickened with chopped clams, potatoes, and sweet onions. Then it reached new heights in college when I took a year off to study French cooking at Le Cordon Bleu in Paris, where I learned to master a mean spinach soufflé, make a perfect sauce Bordelaise, and craft authentic shiny chocolate-topped éclairs. When I was hired as the sous-chef at Le Potiron (The Pumpkin), a Parisian restaurant near Les Halles, I used my newfound skills to transform tough cuts of beef into tender stews, improvise with sweetbreads, and bake cakes from memory.

While all these cooking experiences greatly enhanced my life, they did not significantly alter it. At least, not in any profound way.

Then, at the age of twenty-five, I went to Kyoto, Japan, and started studying tea kaiseki, an ancient style of cuisine that accompanies the formal tea ceremony. And the more I learned about this multicourse meal that evolved in Kyoto's Zen monasteries, the more my approach to food began to change. Eventually, my outlook on the world began to change too. For it is tea kaiseki's link to Zen Buddhism that would turn out to have the greatest influence on my life, although it would take thirteen years before it became apparent just how.

Walking the Roji

I celebrated my arrival in Kyoto with a dinner of grilled eel, a sublime delicacy in Japan. In the water the fish resembles a ferocious jagged-toothed snake. But when sizzled over hot charcoal it looks like a fillet of sole that has spent the winter in Palm Beach. The skin turns crisp and smoky and the fatty white flesh, basted with a sweet soy syrup, becomes deeply tanned and as succulent as foie gras.

The restaurant was located in a cheery yellow mall beneath Kyoto Station, home to the southern bus terminal, north-south subway line, and Japan Railroad Tokaido Main, one of the four major bullet train routes. Being coatless and having underestimated how cold it gets in Kyoto in early November after the sun goes down, I had ducked into the mall in search of warmth and something to eat.

The restaurant lay at the end of a long corridor lined with

inexpensive clothing emporiums, elegant Japanese sweet shops, and trinket stores selling sandalwood fans, pottery tea bowls, and I Love Kyoto key chains. Like all the other eateries in the area, the eel restaurant displayed lifelike plastic models of the items on its menu in a brightly lit picture window. I chose a small wooden table for two in the back of the restaurant and sat down in the chair facing the kitchen. I was the only diner. The chef, sporting a clean, pressed, white cotton band around his forehead, came over to my table. He was apparently also the waiter.

"Are you kmrmshtka?" asked the chef.

"Hmmm?" My eyebrows shot up.

"What would you nsmsplka?"

I giggled nervously, then bit my lower lip. He gestured to the window and started walking. I followed him outside. "Unagiijxw-brp?" he asked. I began to tell him I wanted the tray holding the single, not double, fillet of grilled eel with rice, soup, and pickles, but he interrupted.

"No English," he said with a frown, shaking his head. I tapped my finger several times against the glass in front of the dinner I wanted, hoping he might make the connection.

"Ah, ah," he exclaimed, pointing at the glass, "Unagixpxwz." I squinted and leaned toward the window to read the plastic plaque marked with the meal's price in yen, then slowly wrote the price on my palm with my index finger and tapped the window again.

"Hai, hai." He beamed, nodding vigorously. "Kirin?" Now, that I understood.

"Yes," I said loudly, as if increasing the volume might lead to an increased understanding.

"Ladzkmttaka?" He opened his hands as if holding an invisible fire hydrant from top to bottom.

at! The professor's slides also featured food stalls,
pastel-colored pastries, and gem-like sashimi. I would
hing to eat Japanese food and did so for the first time
ka in Cambridge. That first bite of fat-streaked tuna
culinary epiphany. It was as though I had been wear-
on my tongue all those years and had suddenly taken
elvety fish had a rare beef-like core surrounded by a
ess from the marbled fat. The lightly vinegared rice
oy were like exclamation points at the end of a per-
. The wasabi added a final unexpected prickle of heat
my desire for more. That night I promised myself
I would eat sushi in Japan.

y arrived nearly two years after I graduated from col-
986 and I was barely making a living as an assistant
itive for a big Manhattan advertising agency. My co-
eeping with my boss. I had received one skimpy raise
d a half years since I had started working. And I had
on and off so many new accounts I couldn't re-
ther I was selling business-to-business services for
rgarine or promoting a heart-healthy spread for
elessness, AIDS, and cheap cocaine pulsed through
as like an infection. Stress poisoned the air. I was
reath.

become a monster," said my boyfriend, John, and he
unhappiness had sharpened itself to such a point I
g those I loved. So I began exploring my options.
is how in the spring of 1986 I found myself gluing
on hamburger buns, making fake ice cream from
rushing raw sausages to a mock skillet brown with
iquid and soy sauce to learn about food styling

"Yes!" I boomed, not having the foggiest idea of what he
had just asked.

The double-size beer arrived quickly, along with a glass. It
wasn't one of those huge Henry the VIII steins like we get back
home, but instead a teensy tumbler, similar to what budget hotels
in America use for juice glasses at their complimentary breakfast
buffets. I filled the glass and took a sip. The amber liquid tasted
bitter and refreshing.

After about ten minutes, dinner came to the table looking
identical to its plastic counterpart. Unfortunately, the eel's texture
was similar too. But the accompanying steamed rice, pressed into
the shape of a chrysanthemum, had a clean, delicate sweetness unlike any rice I had ever tasted. The tray also held a plastic bowl of
miso soup, clear in parts and cloudy in others. I stirred the mixture with the tip of my chopsticks, then picked up the bowl and
sipped the savory liquid enriched with diced tofu and emerald
wisps of *wakame* seaweed.

In a shallow dish sat a small block of bean curd splashed
with soy sauce and topped with pinkish curls of dried bonito that
looked like pencil shavings. I cut into the silky white cube and
tried to balance the craggy chunk on the slender pieces of wood.
It tumbled off. After trying again, success was rewarded with the
sweet taste of milky custard mingled with dark soy and smoky
fish flakes. There were pickles too, crisp neon-yellow half-moons
of sweet *daikon* radish and crunchy slices of eggplant. Although I
had not expected culinary brilliance from a mall restaurant, dinner was exceeding expectations. The ingredients were plain, but
exceptional in their purity and freshness.

As I moved around my tray—sipping, plucking, and
crunching—I thought of all I had seen that day. Exotic images
flashed to mind, including the painted orange gates of Yasaka

Shrine, shaped like giant croquet wickets. There were the street-lights, heralding safe crossings, which chirped "uh-oh" for north-south foot traffic and "wheesh-wheesh" for east-west. Ginkgo trees fluttered banana-yellow leaves shaped like tiny fans against the turquoise sky. Red and white vending machines, clustered near subway stations, glowed brightly with offerings of beer, batteries, and cans of hot sweet milk tea. In a tiny noodle shop near Tea Bowl Lane, where pottery shops flanked both sides of the street, I joined mothers, children, and old men to slurp thick starchy *udon* (white wheat) noodles from a bowl of savory fish broth. At Kiyomizu-dera (Clear Water Temple), a massive wooden structure looming over the city against a backdrop of vermilion maples, I stepped inside the main hall to see the female Buddha of Mercy and Compassion. Fabricated from gold, she stood on a pedestal waving her "thousand arms" in a dark room with slippery wooden floors and smoky air pungent with the musky sweet smell of incense. Afterward I drank cold clear water from an aluminum ladle at the Sound-of-Feathers Waterfall below the temple with a crowd of boisterous schoolchildren, then sampled a green tea butter cookie at a gift shop in the mall beneath Kyoto Station. Even the beer with dinner tasted new to me, cleaner, crisper, and less fizzy than what I was used to back home. It had been a day of pure exhilaration, an unexpected adrenaline rush in anticipation of the thrilling, unpredictable, hopeful promise of Kyoto—my new home.

><

I first became enamored with Japan through my grandmother, whom we fondly called Gunga. She and my grandfather used to travel to this chain of islands that looks like a chopped

chili pepper floating several h
Kyoto was my grandmother'
dens," she used to say. Kyoto
landscapes, groves of bambo
jagged rock islands.

Every Christmas my g
from their travels to "the Or
in a blue-and-white-speckled
Another year it was a red silk
ten, my mother, two sisters, a
coats. These were knee-lengt
that we would wear around
peach, my older sister's was
family, was white, and mine w
little robe and used to hang
When I opened my closet, th
me of this exotic place called

The discovery of my o
took several East Asian studie
Life in Japan," taught by a yo
her lectures she showed slide
Tokyo, which had become
Kyoto had been spared from
still had all its original temple
Japan, and in the professor's s
paper umbrellas stood outsic
tional old home where the p
spare elegance I had always as
colored *tatami* (straw mats) cc
screens separated the rooms.
to live.

And
restaurants
leave class
at Little O
sushi was a
ing a mitte
it off. The
creamy ricl
and earthy
fect senten
that kindl
that one d
The
lege. It wa
account ex
worker wa
in the two
been rota
member
Promise
AT&T. H
the city's
gasping fo
"Yo
was right.
was woun
Wh
sesame s
Crisco, a
dishwash

through a course at what is now New School University. I looked into catering, talked with owners of gourmet food stores, and began interviewing with various Japanese organizations to investigate jobs in Asian-American cultural relations. Then two important things happened.

That June I read John Wharton's book *Jobs in Japan,* an inspiring collection of real-life stories about how to secure a teaching position in a Japanese school. He made the idea of living in Japan sound doable, actually, incredibly easy. Around the same time, my grandmother died—the one who loved Kyoto. She had been suffering from emphysema, which made breathing "like sucking air through a squashed straw," she once whispered. I had flown up to Boston to visit her at the hospital when they took her off the respirator. Only my father got to see her laughing and eating orange sherbet in her johnny for the last time. When we went over to her house to pick out her burial clothes, my father gave me one of the most valuable pieces of advice I have ever received.

"The clock of life is wound just once," he said, turning to me. "If you want to go to Japan, now is the time." On November 4, 1986, I stepped off the bus in Kyoto.

"We are nanagwpkm shmplup," called the chef from the eel restaurant. "Do you chiwksha morplmraka?"

I held up my hand and fake scribbled on my palm, hoping the chef would know to bring the check. I drained my beer, then leaned back in my chair and sighed. All the hard edges had softened. I was no longer in flight. I had left my family, left my friends, left my boyfriend and my job in New York. There was nothing more to leave behind. In a way, I had walked the *roji*, the Zen term for "dewy path," which represents the transition from the outside burning world of dust and passions to the contemplative spiritual world of a Japanese teahouse.

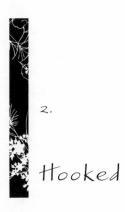

2.

Hooked

The focus of my trip to Kyoto was the study of tea kaiseki. I first learned about this esoteric cuisine from the reference librarian at the Japan Society in New York. One summer afternoon on my lunch break from the ad agency, I had stopped by the reference desk to ask about cooking opportunities in Kyoto. The Japanese woman behind the desk mentioned *chakaiseki* (tea kaiseki), a highly ritualized cuisine that accompanies the formal tea ceremony.

Tea first came to Japan in the sixth century by way of Japanese Buddhist monks, scholars, warriors, and merchants who traveled to China and brought back tea pressed into bricks. It was not until 1191, during the Song dynasty, that the Japanese Buddhist priest Eisai (also known as Yosai) carried home from China fine-quality tea seeds and the method for making *matcha* (powdered green tea). The tea seeds were cultivated on the grounds of several Kyoto temples and later in such areas as the Uji district just south of Kyoto.

Following the Chinese traditional method, Japanese Zen monks would steam, dry, then grind the tiny green tea leaves into a fine powder and whip it with a bamboo whisk in boiling water to create a thick medicinal drink to stimulate the senses during long periods of meditation.

Over time, many of the monks became tea masters and started whipping green tea for the imperial court. By the early fourteenth century tea drinking had become a social event and the powdered green tea, which was quite costly, became a standard item on the imperial court's list of imported luxuries. Lavish tea gatherings featuring rare tea-making utensils from China, such as tea caddies, scoops, and tea bowls, regularly took place in the pavilions of the aristocracy.

When guests attend a formal tea ceremony they usually receive a kaiseki meal to prepare their stomachs for the tea, which can be quite caustic. The meal resembles a French degustation in that there are a set series of tiny exquisite dishes that change with the seasons. After these delicacies, the tea master serves each guest a bowl of thick tea, followed by a bowl of thin tea. Because the bowl of thick tea is usually shared, it encourages the guests to bond with one another and their host in a somewhat spiritual manner, almost like taking communion.

This emphasis on spirituality dates back to when Kyoto served as the imperial capital from 794 to 1868. Buddhism, imported from China, became an alternative to Shinto, Japan's indigenous religion based on deities ruling over all things natural, such as mountains, rivers, rocks, and animals, with the sun goddess Amaterasu being the most powerful. (To honor and preserve the goodwill of these deities, the Japanese still hold festivals throughout the year at various shrines, often accompanied by offerings of sake and special foods.)

Numerous arts also flourished in Kyoto, such as *ikebana* (formal flower arranging), Kabuki theater, and *chanoyu*, the Japanese term for the formal tea ceremony. Chanoyu literally means "tea's hot water" and became one of the most influential art forms in the history of Japan. It affected architecture, painting, calligraphy, and food. Kyoto was where it all started.

"One could almost say Kyoto is steeped in tea," said the librarian, with a soft giggle.

The tea ceremony began to take on a spiritual dimension under several tea masters, including Sen no Rikyu, universally heralded as the most important tea master who ever lived. Having studied Zen for decades at various temples, Rikyu considered the tea ceremony a spiritual and artistic communion with nature that should embody harmony, respect, purity, and tranquility, the essence of Zen Buddhism. Rikyu saw making tea in a ritually prescribed manner as a form of meditation through which one could explore and polish oneself. In fact, it became one of the ways to reach enlightenment.

"Which meant," I said, "the teahouse became a kind of temple."

"Exactly," said the woman, smiling, clearly pleased I had made such a connection.

But Rikyu's idea of a temple was much more humble than the ornate pavilions of the imperial court. He wanted the teahouse to blend in with nature and become more of a backdrop for the tea ceremony, so he helped influence its redesign. Over time, the teahouse became a simple hut set in a garden with mud and plaster walls, a thatched roof, a bamboo lattice ceiling, tatami floors, and small paper-covered windows. It became a refuge in the city meant to echo a mountain retreat, where *samurai* from warring clans, lowly merchants, and even the emperor could come together on equal footing and focus on nothing more than the sensory pleasures of the tea ceremony, such as the gentle bubbling of the tea water on the brazier, the seasonal flower arrangement in the alcove, and the smell of the particular incense chosen to represent the time of year.

By the time the woman had finished talking, I was hooked. I would study tea kaiseki in Kyoto to learn about Japanese history, art, architecture, food, and Zen. I would teach English to pay my living expenses. And I would test my heart by living halfway around the world from the man with whom I contemplated spending my life. I headed back to the agency feeling for the first time in many months a palpable sense of hope.

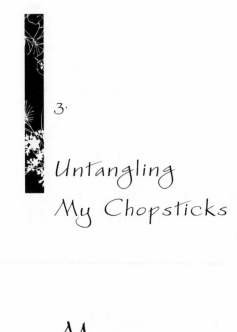

3.

Untangling
My Chopsticks

My first few weeks in Kyoto were a bit of a blur as I tried to find work, a school where I could study tea kaiseki, and a place to live. Thanks to the amorous connections of my old grammar school pal, Lauren, I had a place to stay when I first arrived. Her former boyfriend, Bob, had offered to put me up. "Call me when you get to Kyoto," he had said when I rang him from the States. "You can crash with me until you get your feet on the ground."

Bob's rented house was what Kyoto locals call "bedrooms of eels" because they have narrow façades that face the street and long bodies that stretch far back, concealing interconnecting rooms and an interior garden. According to Confucian principles, the farther back into the house you progress, the more intimate the space becomes and therefore your relationship with the owner.

Like most old homes, Bob's had dark slatted wood doors on the bottom level that rattled when cars drove by. There was an outhouse off the interior garden and tatami on the floors. The size of a traditional Japanese room is measured by the number of tatami it contains, since each straw mat is considered large enough to accommodate one person lying down. I slept upstairs in a three-tatami storage room that I reached by climbing up a rickety wooden ladder.

Shortly after my arrival, there were two things that struck me about Kyoto. One was that the city was far more modern than I had expected. Kyoto is the fifth largest city in Japan, with a population approaching 1.46 million. Once a massive lake bed, it sits nestled in a valley bowl surrounded by mountains to the north, east, and west of the city. Rising raggedly from the ground, these cedar-filled peaks originally formed an important fortification when Emperor Kammu declared Kyoto Japan's capital in 794. The mountains also give the city its own microclimate. In the colder months, freezing moist air whistles down from the north, saturating the city with a frosty wet chill. In the summer, the scorching heat lies trapped in the city bowl, filling every chink with a stagnant humidity that can buckle the folds of a delicate paper fan.

From the top of Mount Daimonji on a clear day, Kyoto looks like a miniature metropolis made of gray and white Legos. Emperor Kammu wanted to create an imperial capital as powerful and magnificent as the Tang dynasty's (618–907) Chinese city of Ch'ang-an (now Xian), so he laid out Kyoto in the same logical grid-like pattern. The Kyoto Tower and its observation deck, considered one of the city's greatest eyesores when constructed in 1964, shoots up through the skyline like a white church spire topped with a big red doughnut. The glittering Kamo River, a shallow rocky-bottomed expanse filled with fishermen in waders, tufts of olive-yellow marsh grass, and spindly-legged white cranes, flows north to south through the center of the city, thus creating a natural division between the eastern and western sections. Originally used for fabric dyeing and *sake* (rice wine) production, as well as transporting goods and people, the Kamo River now serves more as a place for recreation, with throngs of joggers, walkers, and bicyclists moving up and down the sandy dirt paths lining the stone reinforcements along the embankments.

Not surprisingly, many of Kyoto's traditional industries, such as fabric dyeing and woodcrafts, have given way to commercial enterprises. The result is that most Kyoto natives would now rather pay one dollar for a cheap comb made of plastic than ten dollars for one hand carved from sandalwood. Timeworn teahouses sit squeezed between storefronts flashing neon signs. Sacred shrines lie tucked away in bustling shopping arcades. Real estate costs a fortune. And Kyoto's wooden shops and homes are gradually disappearing because exorbitant inheritance taxes make it cheaper to tear down a traditional wooden dwelling and replace it with a modern one complete with central heating, air conditioning, and hot and cold running water.

Yet, despite the encroachment of technology and innovation, the other thing that I realized about Kyoto was that it was far more beautiful than I had imagined. The age-old restaurants, exquisite inns, imperial villas, and almost two thousand temples and shrines imbue the city with a spirit of elegance and grace. Traditional Japanese architecture uses organic materials in muted and recessive tones, which blend into their natural surroundings, almost as if growing there. You see the grain of the wood, the texture of stone, and the warmth of sunlight pouring through ivory paper screens. Fences are fabricated from bamboo. Roofs are often thatched with Japanese silver grass. Woven reed blinds hang from shop windows to provide coolness and shade.

The culture's reverence for nature accentuates Kyoto's innate beauty. Designs on fabric, pottery, lacquer, and folding screens depict swirling water, budding branches, and birds in flight. Delicate woodcuts and scrolls celebrate the moonlight, rain, and snow. Elegant restaurant dishes arrive with edible garnishes of seasonal flora.

The sense of serenity that permeates Kyoto also enhances its visual appeal. Kyoto was originally called Heian-kyo, or Capital of Peace and Tranquility. It is a well-deserved name that reinforces itself at the most unexpected moments: a late afternoon walk up a quiet winding back street with the auburn light of dusk slanting across the pavement; a chance turn into an empty temple courtyard where the only sign of life is a fistful of incense burning in an urn; or the sight of an older gentleman practicing dance steps alone in a small park.

As I got to know my new home, every day held something novel to pique my senses. Sometimes it was pleasurable, other times painful, like the evening I learned about the electric bath at the *sento* (public bath). After washing myself, I climbed into a tiny tub to soak. Suddenly, I was zapped with several ferocious currents meant to "stimulate tired muscles." I screamed and leapt out of the tub, sloshing water all over the place, then hurried home and climbed into my futon, still shaking.

Another afternoon I experienced the poetic beauty of Japan's maple leaves in the western district of Arashiyama, about an hour's bus ride from downtown Kyoto. At first glance, Arashiyama offered little more than miles of restaurants, ice cream stores, and cheap souvenir shops north and south of the

Togetsu-kyo (Reach-moon Bridge). Vendors stood on the sidewalks luring passersby like me into their stores with tasty samples of pickled vegetables, sweet bean pastries, and special tea "made only in Kyoto" from herbs and salted dried cherry blossoms.

But like so many things in Japan, behind the façade lay another view. So it was only after I had hiked into the woods far from the bridge that I found a fluttering world of persimmon, ocher, scarlet, and cabernet secreted away in a mossy garden of curving stone paths. When it began to rain, the colors deepened and the leaves, shaped like baby's hands, spiraled down onto the plush green carpet and sleek dark rocks. I stood there motionless, attending to this quiet transition from life to death, feeling the same aching sense of awe—like a great hand pressing against my throat and urging me to cry—that I encountered as a child every time I went to church with my grandmother. It was a powerful wordless beauty that swept me up toward something magnificent and greater than myself.

Everyday transactions became a fascinating study in courtesy and care, like the way the waitress at Le Petit Chou café arranged my coffee set—cup, saucer, spoon, cream holder, and napkin—on the table, as if creating a small mosaic. Or the way uniformed gas attendants pulled down the pumps dangling from the eaves of garages to dispense the gas, then lined up in rows to bow to the customers as they drove off.

There was such uniformity of behavior, like the way everyone knew to stay on the left side of the train station escalator, so others could run up the right side to catch their train. Or the way no one ate in public, which is considered rude.

There was also an ingenious approach to limited space through the use of folding and unfolding. Gardens unfolded themselves as you walked along. Fans folded open and then collapsed back into their compact shape. Meals unfolded through multiple courses. Even people folded themselves inward to create private worlds in public, staying silent on buses, covering their book jackets with plain paper, and closing their eyes on the subway.

I also noticed a fixation on wrapping, which the Japanese have elevated to an art form almost like origami. The careful way the Japanese seal items, whether fruit, slippers, sushi, or tea sweets, reflects their respect for the contents inside and their desire to shield private items from the public eye. Everyday purchases, such as books and plastic pouches of rice crackers, are covered with bright paper before being placed in a protective bag. Talismans at temples and shrines are tucked into small brocade drawstring sacks. And tea bowls are swathed in silk before being nestled in padded wooden boxes.

But this solicitousness toward wrapping is not just a matter of concealing and protecting. The way packages are enveloped conveys important information about the contents inside. This is essential because the Japanese rarely open gifts in public, yet a proper "thank you" is expected. As a result, stores mark their wrapping paper with regional designs and logos, while clerks use special knots, ties, and seals to offer further insight to the receiver, so he or she can thank the gift giver accordingly, using polite language and a low bow for a nice gift, or extremely polite language and a very deep bow for an extravagant one.

Everyone had an extraordinary penchant for cleanliness, driven by Shinto's emphasis on freshness and purity. Uniformed servers at Mr. Donut shops were constantly buffing the already pristine automatic glass doors. Train conductors habitually carried long metal kitchen-like tongs to pick up cigarette butts and gum wrappers at station stops. Gentlemen in ironed chinos regularly wiped down vending machines with moist cloths. One night

I had to step around an elderly man vacuuming the subway stairs in downtown Kyoto.

Even my first taxi ride proved to be a cathartic experience (cleaning out my wallet too, since the meter began at six dollars). The driver greeted me in a neatly pressed slate-blue suit that matched the taut fabric on his police-style cap. His black shoes had a patina like fine lacquerware and his gloves were chalk white. As I reached for the door, it automatically swung open to reveal soft seats covered with stretchy snow-white fabric that hugged them like fitted sheets. Lacy white covers capped each headrest. Smart brochures filled the plush fabric pouches behind the driver's seat, which reached down to a spotless carpeted floor.

There was also a peculiarly Japanese adaptation of things foreign. I first noticed this one rainy November evening when I stopped by Rub-a-Dub, a funky reggae watering hole located near the Pontocho, the city's former red-light district now known for its restaurants, bars, and geisha teahouses. After ordering one of the bar's famous daiquiris, I anticipated receiving an American-style rum-in-your-face daiquiri with an explosive citrus pucker. Instead, I was handed a delicate fruity drink that tasted more like a melted lime Popsicle. Over time I noticed other items had been similarly adapted. McDonald's offered hamburgers with sliced pineapple and ham to satisfy Japanese women's notorious sweet tooth. "Authentic" Italian restaurants topped their tomato-seafood linguini with thin strands of *nori* seaweed, instead of grated Parmesan. And slim triangles of "real" New York–style *chizu-keki* (cheesu-cakey) in dessert shops tasted like cream cheese–sweetened air.

Not surprisingly, Japan's culinary scene proved to be one of the best gateways to the culture. Simply tasting my first Asian pear was a revelation in ripeness. It was so swollen with sweet juices that when I bit into it I had to lean over the pavement to avoid drenching my shirt. Purchased from a fancy fruit stand where sixty-dollar cantaloupes rested in cushioned gift boxes next to thirty-dollar pineapples, the Asian pear, cultivated to perfection, cost only two dollars.

Casual eateries offered additional insight. Although Bob had a kitchen in his traditional home, it was quite cramped. What's more, only cold water ran into the stone sink and instead of a range, a portable two-burner electric stove sat on a smooth slate work area just big enough to hold a cutting board. I contemplated cooking, eager to throw myself into the markets. In the end, not wanting to inconvenience Bob and his two roommates, I decided to eat out.

As I tried various restaurants, certain preconceptions came crashing down. I realized not all Japanese food consisted of carefully carved vegetables, sliced fish, and clear soups served on black lacquerware in a highly restrained manner. Tasting *okonomiyaki* (literally, "cook what you like"), for example, revealed one way the Japanese let their chopsticks fly.

Often called "Japanese pizza," okonomiyaki more resembles a pancake filled with chopped vegetables and your choice of meat, chicken, or seafood. The dish evolved in Osaka after World War II, as a thrifty way to cobble together a meal from table scraps.

A college classmate living in Kyoto took me to my first okonomiyaki restaurant where, in a casual room swirling with conversation and aromatic smoke, we ordered chicken-shrimp okonomiyaki. A waitress oiled the small griddle in the center of our table, then set down a pitcher filled with a mixture of flour, egg, and grated Japanese mountain yam made all lumpy with chopped cabbage, carrots, scallions, bean sprouts, shrimp, and bits of chicken. When a drip of green tea skated across the surface of the hot metal, we poured out a huge gob of batter. It sputtered and heaved. With a metal spatula and chopsticks, we pushed and nagged the massive pancake until it became firm and golden on both sides. Our Japanese neighbors were doing the same. After cutting the doughy disc into wedges, we buried our portions under a mass of mayonnaise, juicy strands of red pickled ginger, green seaweed powder, smoky fish flakes, and a sweet Worcestershire-flavored sauce. The pancake was crispy on the outside, soft and savory inside—the epitome of Japanese comfort food.

Another day, one of Bob's roommates, Theresa, took me to a *donburi* restaurant, as ubiquitous in Japan as McDonald's are in America. Named after the bowl in which the dish is served, donburi consists of sticky white rice smothered with your choice of meat, vegetables, and other goodies. Theresa recommended the *oyako*, or "parent and child," donburi, a medley of soft nuggets of chicken and feathery cooked egg heaped over rice, along with chopped scallions and a rich sweet bouillon. Scrumptious, healthy, and prepared in a flash, it redefined the meaning of fast food.

The automatic sushi bars expanded upon the concept. After grabbing a free stool around an oval floor pit, you push a handle-less ceramic mug against a self-serve spigot until it brims with scalding green tea. While sushi chefs slap thin cuts of fish over logs of vinegared rice, you squirt soy into a small dish from a plastic squeeze bottle and load up on pickled pink ginger from a plastic tub on the counter. Then you grab whatever kind of sushi looks tasty as it glides by on a rubber conveyer belt. You pay by the number of plates stacked in front of you, which range from one to two dollars each.

><

My first fancy meal in Japan was at an elegant restaurant on a small side street around the corner from Bob's. High-end restaurants in Japan can be intimidating, since the staff rarely speaks English and most menu items and prices are written in characters.

Nevertheless, having made the decision to splurge one Saturday night not long after my arrival, I headed down the smooth stone walkway toward the entrance. The black rocks glistened, having been sprayed with water earlier that evening. Most restaurants in Kyoto do that to evoke a feeling of freshness, a time-honored Kyoto tradition stemming from the desire to purify the stones from the dust of the once-dirt streets.

A three-paneled cream cloth marked with gray squiggles hung over the top third of the pine-slatted door. This cloth, called a *noren*, indicates the name of the restaurant or the type of food it serves.

To the right of the entrance stood what looked like a bamboo music stand holding the menu, ten vertical rows of Chinese characters penned in black ink on expensive white paper. If you tipped your head slightly, you could see the delicate silvery-white bamboo leaf design that had been pressed onto the sheet.

Behind the menu was a window looking into the restaurant, only it was angled so as to reveal nothing more than a beautiful turquoise vase displayed in an alcove along the back wall. To discourage people like me from fogging up the window to decipher the kind of food the restaurant served, someone had cleverly erected an artistic bamboo blockade.

Still unsure of the restaurant's cuisine, I tentatively slid open the door and stepped in. Several Japanese patrons glanced over from their seats at a polished cypress counter. There were no tables. Two sushi chefs yelled out their greetings and looked up at me. I thought I saw one of them wince before lowering his head back down toward his work.

Suddenly, the room grew hushed and I realized people were staring at me. My very presence had punctuated the room's stillness, as if I had cannonballed into a private pool and splashed water all over the club members, who were quietly reading on lawn chairs.

Just as I was contemplating leaving, a young male waiter gestured for me to sit down at the counter. He handed me a washcloth and then a menu, his hands trembling slightly. I tried to offer him my most relaxed smile and then looked around.

On my right, two women were plucking at small tangles of what looked like daikon radish strands, tossed with creamy pillows of sea urchin, and peppery red sprouts. One had several gold cocktail rings on her slim fingers, which twinkled as she used her chopsticks. The two women hardly spoke, but delicately ate and sipped sake, like two shore birds pecking along the ocean's edge.

On my left, two men were drinking beer and waiting for dinner. One had loosened his tie and slung his tweed jacket over the back of the chair. His companion, who had rolled up his shirtsleeves, leaned forward and nodded a rosy-faced hello. I smiled back, then looked down at my menu, blankly staring at the flourish of indecipherable characters on the lavender sheet.

Soon the waiter came around with a porcelain mug of brewed green tea and put it down. He started fidgeting with his apron strings. "You speak Japanese?" he asked, his lip quivering.

"No, not really," I said, shaking my head. "Do you speak English?"

He blew out a stiff laugh. "Little."

At that moment, the door slid open and in walked an elderly couple. They bowed to the sushi chefs, who looked up and called out their greetings. "Moment," said the waiter, dashing off to fetch the couple's menus, visibly relieved to leave his post.

With nothing else to do, I sipped my tea and watched the sushi masters. With quick precise strokes, they transformed glistening blocks of fatty tuna and gray mullet into smooth neat rectangles. The morsels shone like jewels, the color, cut, and shape perfectly showcasing the seafood's freshness. The two men snatched handfuls of rice from a wide wooden bowl and shaped them into ovals as if preparing for a snowball fight. They say the most talented sushi masters can form their rice so that every grain points in the same direction.

The two men worked rapidly, wiping the starch from their hands on a damp cloth on the counter, before placing thick strips of fish over wasabi-smeared rice bullets. Their actions were clear, smooth, and Zen-like in their economy of movement. A woman's hands are supposedly too hot to make sushi, which is why sushi masters are always men, a convenient bit of folk wisdom for this male-dominated profession.

Overcome with hunger, I realized the only way I was going to get dinner was to ask for what I hoped lay in the fish case. How much could ten pieces of sushi cost? Twenty dollars? Thirty? I figured ten pieces was a reasonable amount to order.

The waiter returned with a small pad and stood silently with downcast eyes. "Sushi," I announced, hoping to set him at ease. I then proceeded to tick off my favorites—*chutoro* (fatty tuna belly), *hamachi* (yellowtail), *anago* (conger eel), and *uni* (sea urchin). I then added on *saba* (mackerel). Aside from being cheap, it has a luscious metallic tang, like the blood-dark portions of bluefish and swordfish. The waiter nodded, handed the order to the sushi chefs, then hurried off.

I slipped my chopsticks out of their paper wrapper and then broke the top portion apart. I had heard that Japanese men twitch with pleasure every time they snap the sticks open. New chopsticks are said to be like young virgins; the snap symbolizes their deflowering.

What I didn't know then, but would discover years later, was that there are approximately fifty different types of chopsticks in Japan, made of wood, bamboo, ivory, bone, and various metals, and that numerous dos and don'ts have arisen regarding their use at the table. One of the more notorious taboos is to rub those disposable wooden chopsticks together. This implies the chopsticks are cheap, and therefore so is the restaurant, which could insult your host and/or the chef.

Another no-no is to drag a bowl or serving plate toward you by hooking your chopsticks over the edge of the dish. It is also impolite to stab an item, perhaps a slippery mushroom cap, with the tip of your chopstick.

You should avoid holding your chopsticks midair and hovering over a variety of dishes while you try to decide which delicacy to pluck, as well as making a drippy mess when picking up a morsel of food covered with sauce or in a soup.

If you wish to help yourself to a communal dish after you have begun eating, you should always use the serving chopsticks. If there are none, you should turn your chopsticks around and use the clean tops to grasp the food. This sanitary practice is derived from the Shinto belief that one's spoiled spirit can be passed on to others through shared foods.

You should also refrain from passing anything from chopsticks to chopsticks during a meal. That's because when someone dies, relatives of the deceased pass the bones from chopsticks to chopsticks at the crematory before the ashes are transferred to the urn.

Instead of resting your chopsticks on the edge of your plate or soup bowl, you should place your chopsticks on the chopstick rest. If there is none, you should make your own from the paper wrapper.

Thankfully, I knew enough to do that while the sushi chef prepared my meal. He kept his head down the entire time, then after about ten minutes, placed a white stoneware rectangle holding ten pieces of sushi on the flat top portion of the glass fish case. Only after bowing, did he quickly look up, then utter something. I held my hands in a prayer position and bowed back. The waiter brought over a cruet of soy sauce.

I could feel the chef's eyes boring into me as I poured way too much soy into my saucer. The Japanese use a minuscule amount of soy to accent, not overwhelm, the delicate flavor of the fish. With my chopsticks I transferred a nubbin of wasabi, about the size of a raisin, into the salty brown sauce and swirled it around until it dissolved. Mistake number two. I looked up at the sushi chef.

He produced an expression that hovered somewhere between curiosity and doubt. Would this nice but verbally dumb Westerner ruin his fine work? Would she know what to do? And do it well? I glanced over at my dining companions, then suddenly got all tangled up in my chopsticks. On my right, the elderly woman with her gentleman companion was eating sushi with her fingers! And instead of dipping the rice portion into the soy, as I had always done, she grazed the fish end. Not only that, she bit the oval in half and discreetly chewed with her hand across her lips in a gesture of politeness.

The men on my left were doing the opposite. With their chopsticks, they were picking up pieces of sushi as big as Devil Dogs, dragging them through the soy, and cramming them into their gaping mouths. Their cheeks puffed up like trumpet players as they vigorously masticated their food.

Maybe chopsticks are for men and fingers for women? I wondered. That doesn't make sense. Then again, neither did many things in Japan until I took the time to figure them out. Years later I would discover that eating sushi with your fingers is an old Tokyo tradition. Chopsticks are for sashimi. Back when Tokyo was called Edo, sushi connoisseurs used to eat their fill of fish, then wipe their dirty fingers on the short split curtain hanging over the door of the sushi shop. The more gooey the curtain, the better the shop.

I would also learn that in former times, it was considered immodest for a Japanese woman to let anyone see the inside of her mouth, which explains why most Japanese women cover their mouths with their palm when they chew, smile, or laugh.

I used my chopsticks to eat the sushi, which was exquisitely fresh and flavorful. The sea urchin tasted so sweet and custardy it was like eating crème brûlée seasoned with essence of the ocean.

When I had finished dinner, the waiter brought over the check. I held out a credit card, but he shook his head. I fished out thirty dollars' worth of yen and placed the bills on the money tray. He carried them away.

When he returned with my change, the tray held a small paper-wrapped packet. "A *purezento* (present)," the waiter mumbled, bowing. I bowed back and thanked him. I looked up at the sushi chefs and bowed. They bowed back. I then backed out of the restaurant bowing once more and repeating my thanks.

Back in my room, I opened up the packet. It was *furikake,* a dry seasoning mix of nori flakes, sesame seeds, freeze-dried granules of fish stock, and pickled plum to sprinkle over steamed rice.

Gift giving is an important part of social etiquette in Japan. A visit to someone's home requires a gift. If you ask a favor, you offer a gift for asking. If the favor is granted, you issue a gift of thanks. First business meetings usually involve an exchange of gifts. The teller at the Sumitomo Bank had given me a gift when I opened my savings account. I had noticed a stack of goodies piled by his window, a handy cloth pouch filled with travel-size toiletries, pastel packets of guest soap, and bottles of cologne. After completing our transaction, the teller handed me a tiny packet of plastic bags. Apparently, the size of one's deposit determined the size of the teller's thank-you.

Travelers always bring back gifts from their voyages. And if by chance you forgot to buy one, train stations in almost every major Japanese city sell specialty food items from all over Japan. So, for example, if you lived in Osaka and traveled to Sapporo, but neglected to buy a gift in Sapporo, you could easily find a specialty food from Sapporo back at your home train station in Osaka.

Typically, once a gift is given the Japanese respond with a "return" gift. Its value is usually half that of the gift received, so the exchange doesn't needlessly continue back and forth.

I looked at the packet from the restaurant trying to decipher the contents, then crouched down and held it under the pull-cord of the Japanese paper floor lamp in my bedroom. Did something move? I lay down and picked up the light and held it directly over the packet. The seasoning was infested with tiny white worms!

I threw the gift into the rubbish bin, chuckling to myself as I returned to my room. Appearances could be so deceptive in

Japan. When I first arrived, I thought everyone had black hair. Then hundreds of variations began to appear, including blue-black, brown-black, and red-black. Japan was the place where "maybe" meant "no," bathtubs shocked you, and worms wriggled in the fancy restaurant's furikake. Even the simple act of eating had become an enormous adventure in this part of the world. Cooking would prove even more so.

Japanese Pizza (Okonomiyaki)

This "cook as you like" pancake bulges with crunchy vegetables and juicy chunks of shrimp and chicken. The assorted garnishes add moistness and vibrant punches of flavor. Japanese mountain yam, available in most Japanese markets, is an important addition to the batter. It is beige and slightly hairy on the outside and gooey inside. When finely grated and added to the batter, it helps the pancake develop a chewy golden exterior. Okonomiyaki sauce, flavored with Worcestershire, is also available in most Japanese markets. Worcestershire sauce came to Japan in the second half of the nineteenth century, although the flavor has been made more mild to suit the delicate Japanese palate.

> 1 cup all-purpose flour
> ½ teaspoon baking powder
> ¼ teaspoon coarse salt
> 1¼ cups dashi (page 48)
> 1 large egg
> 1 cup grated Japanese mountain yam
> 2 cups coarsely chopped green cabbage
> 1 cup fresh bean sprouts
> 1 medium carrot, peeled and shredded
> 1 bunch scallions (about 6), trimmed and thinly sliced

2 tablespoons vegetable oil

One 4-ounce boneless, skinless chicken breast, thinly sliced into
small pieces

10 medium shrimp, peeled, deveined, and sliced lengthwise in
half

FOR THE GARNISHES

Mayonnaise

Okonomiyaki sauce

Shredded red pickled ginger

Dried bonito flakes

Shredded nori

1. Whisk together the flour, baking powder, and salt in a large
bowl.

2. Whisk together the dashi and egg in a medium bowl. Whisk
in the grated yam. Add the wet mixture to the dry mixture and
whisk until the batter is smooth. Stir in the cabbage, bean
sprouts, carrot, and scallions.

3. Heat a griddle or large nonstick skillet to medium-high. Brush
a tablespoon of the oil over the surface. When the griddle or
skillet is hot, ladle half of the batter into the center. Spread the
batter with the back of a wooden spoon so that you form an
8-inch round pancake. Scatter half of the chicken and shrimp
over the surface of the pancake (this is why some people call
okonomiyaki Japanese pizza), and gently push them into the
batter. Reduce the heat to medium-low and cook the pancake
until the top edges appear cooked and the bottom has stiffened
and turned golden brown, about 4 minutes. Using a metal spatula,

turn the pancake and cook for 3 to 4 more minutes, pressing gently down on the disc, until the other side is golden. Repeat the process with the remaining oil, batter, chicken, and shrimp.

4. Transfer each pancake to a large serving plate. Cut it into wedges and let each person top with the garnishes by first spreading creamy mayonnaise over the wedge, then squirting on a generous helping of tangy okonomiyaki sauce, next, scattering on some crispy salty ginger shreds, sprinkling on some bonito flakes, and finally adding a generous pinch of nori.

Makes 2 pizzas, or 4 servings

Chicken and Egg Rice Bowl (Oyako Donburi)

Hot, soupy, salty, sweet, and satisfying—that just about sums up donburi, which is Japan's quintessential comfort food. For variety, consider adding fresh spinach leaves, bamboo shoots, and sliced water chestnuts to the broth. You can easily substitute scallops or shrimp for the chicken; simply adjust the cooking time accordingly.

4 cups hot cooked rice (page 32)
1 cup dashi (page 48)
¼ cup soy sauce
1½ tablespoons sugar
1 tablespoon mirin
4 large eggs

½ pound boneless, skinless chicken breasts, cut into ½-inch
nuggets

I bunch of scallions (about 6), trimmed and cut into I-inch
batons

I. Prepare the rice.

2. Pour the dashi into a medium heavy-bottom saucepan, along
with the soy sauce, sugar, and mirin. Bring the mixture to a boil,
reduce the heat to low, and simmer for 2 minutes.

3. Break the eggs into a bowl and stir with chopsticks until the
yolks and whites are mixed but not totally blended.

4. Add the chicken to the dashi mixture and then gently pour in
the egg. Sprinkle the scallions over the egg. When the egg starts
to become firm, after about 3 minutes of cooking, gently stir it
with your chopsticks. (The chicken and scallions will have
finished cooking in the hot liquid.)

5. Lay out four deep soup bowls. Spoon even portions of the
rice into each bowl and top with the soupy chicken and egg
mixture.

Makes 4 servings

Everyday Japanese White Rice

*Perfect Japanese short-grain rice is sweet, pearly, and sticky enough to
pick up with your chopsticks. Try to find the excellent Nishiki brand, which is
available in most Japanese markets. Also, please do not skip the rinsing and*

soaking process. The initial rinsing rids the rice of the powdered bran and polishing compound, while the soaking plumps the grains with water to render them tender and slightly tacky. Since the texture of the rice can change depending upon how old it is, the amount of water you use may affect the texture of the end result. New rice (less than one year old) will be moister than old rice and thus might require a tiny bit less water for cooking. While an electric rice cooker yields wonderful results, this stovetop method is just as good.

1½ cups short-grain rice

1. Place the rice in a fine mesh sieve and rinse under cold water, using your hand to gently stir the rice until the milky white liquid runs clear, about 2 minutes.

2. Transfer the rice to a deep heavy-bottom saucepan and add 2 cups cold water. Let the rice soak for at least an hour.

3. Bring the rice to a boil. Reduce the heat to very low and cook the rice, covered, for 10 minutes. Turn off the heat and let the rice rest, covered, for 10 more minutes, so it can settle and finish cooking.

4. Remove the lid and spoon out the rice with a wooden rice paddle (or spoon). If by chance some rice sticks to the bottom of the pot, don't despair! Simply spoon out all the soft grains, then scrape up the crispy bottom portion to eat as a snack sprinkled with coarse salt.

Makes 4 cups

4.

"Have a
Riddle Taste"

$\mathcal{N}$ot wanting to impose on Bob any longer, I moved to the Kyoto English Guesthouse in mid-November. This hostel of sorts lay in the northern region of Kita-ku, bordered by several small mountains that received their first dusting of snow on Thanksgiving Day. In exchange for 45,000 yen ($265) a month, I received an unheated five-tatami room complete with a *futon* (cotton floor mattress) that I wrestled to the floor each night from its waist-high sliding cupboard built into the wall. Since there were no sheets or quilts, I was thankful I had brought my sleeping bag.

Included in the rent was the use of a unisex bathroom with showers to share with the twenty or so other boarders consisting mostly of Americans, Canadians, and Australians in their twenties and early thirties. News spread quickly in such close confines and

I quickly learned who was genuinely glad to be in Kyoto and who was not.

The optimists had come to write novels, study arts like papermaking, or master the Japanese language. They relished being in the city and passed on helpful bits of advice. I learned about the health food store down the street stocked with nutty whole wheat bread, not available at the bakery around the corner, which sold only cottony white loaves and sweet buns. I heard about Nihongo Gakko, which offered the best Japanese language classes in Kyoto for the least amount of money. I found out about T's Rocket Restaurant, where tacked on the bulletin board inside the entrance were flyers advertising teaching jobs, secondhand bicycles for sale, and apartments to rent. Additionally, I discovered the restaurant made a fabulous spinach salad topped with corn, tomatoes, roasted pumpkin, and a creamy ginger-soy dressing; a tip I, in turn, passed along to others.

Those boarders who could not stand living in Japan openly admitted it. Having come to Kyoto to earn some quick teaching money, they could not have cared less about the culture. In fact, they would often sit around the den in the Guesthouse eating boiled eggs, imported Cheerios, and peanut butter sandwiches, carping about how expensive, cold, and cramped the city was and how weird and uptight the Japanese were.

What made up for any discomfort at the Guesthouse, however, was the spacious communal kitchen. Outfitted with several refrigerators, a mammoth stove, and plenty of pots and pans, it provided all the essentials necessary to cook in Japan. Finally, I could delve into the markets and start experimenting with all the unusual ingredients I had spotted thus far.

In the beginning, sight and taste guided my food purchases,

an easy and pleasurable exercise at the traditional food shops selling basic items like rice and miso. All I had to do was point, hold up my fingers for the number of kilos or grams I wanted, and pay. Admittedly, it took some experimenting to understand all the various grades and types of these ingredients. At the rice shop, for example, I tasted dozens of varieties, including the stubby glutinous grains often used for desserts and the partially polished ones that retained their germ, before settling on a favorite.

The miso store also entailed much sampling. Although all miso consists of crushed boiled soybeans, salt, and a fermenting agent called *koji*, the types differ based on whether rice, wheat, or barley is added to the mix. The flavor and color of each style can also change, depending upon the amounts of soybeans, type of koji (made from either beans or grains, inoculated with the mold *Aspergillus*), and salt that are added, as well as how long the miso ages. Brick-red miso, for example, comes in both sweet and salty varieties and is made with either barley or a mixture of barley and rice. Because it tastes somewhat coarse, it usually seasons hearty dishes, such as brothy seafood stews. Similar in flavor is the chocolate-brown miso. Mainly composed of soybeans, it has a bold earthy tang best enjoyed in robust dishes, such as potatoes simmered with miso.

Shiro miso, or "white miso," is a Kyoto specialty. Smooth, golden, and quite mellow, it is said to have evolved to suit the tastes of the effete aristocracy during the fourteenth and fifteenth centuries. It is used extensively in Kyoto cooking, including tea kaiseki, and often comes seasoned with herbs, citrus, and mustard. Because of its delicate nature, it tends to be used as a sauce, mainly to dress vegetables and grilled foods. A saltier version appears most often in American markets.

These traditional food shops, with their dark wooden interiors, slumping stone floors, and split curtains out front, mush-roomed all over Kyoto when a huge merchant class developed to serve the aristocracy. With few exceptions, the same families still own them, using the original wood-burning stoves, hand tools, and careful methods that their great-grandparents once did, car-rying on a legacy of extraordinary craftsmanship and quality.

One afternoon when I stepped into an age-old tofu shop, I saw a ninth-generation artisan, whose ancestors made tofu for the imperial court, charring rectangles of tofu on a small grill. So I bought one, all soft, warm, and tinged with smoke and made it the star of my *soba* (buckwheat noodle) soup that night, food fit for an emperor.

My knowledge of Japanese cuisine expanded enormously when several Guesthouse boarders tipped me off to the availabil-ity of free sampling in the massive food halls located in the base-ments of department stores, such as Daimaru and Takashimaya. In addition to selling vegetables, meat, fish, and other goods from farms and factories across Japan, the food halls showcased cooked dishes, sushi to go, and a plethora of imported products, includ-ing British shortbread, Häagen-Dazs ice cream, and Moët & Chandon champagne.

At first I felt self-conscious helping myself to all these nib-bles. After all, Westerners stand out in Japan, particularly hungry ones. But then I told myself it was all part of a grand plan to learn more about Japanese cuisine, and as long as I purchased something, these free tastes would help inform my decisions.

And they did, starting in the sweet section, where the main escalator dropped me off. Kyoto is known for its marvelous cin-namon cookies, snappy and dense and shaped like small roof tiles. They have sesame seeds in the dough and come plain or dribbled with the same kind of icing used to decorate hard gingerbread.

On each visit, I would grab a few, nod enthusiastically, and then head over to the section giving away sweet bean cakes.

Strangely enough, the Japanese base most of their traditional desserts on beans. Called *an,* this smooth chocolatey-looking paste is made from azuki beans boiled in sugar and water. I encountered it for the first time one afternoon when I helped myself to a traditional Kyoto sweet resembling a triangular ravioli stuffed with fudge. What a shock to find a center made from azuki beans, instead of cocoa beans!

Sometimes sweet makers choose chestnuts or white kidney beans to make the an, which they craft into dainty flowers, leaves, and fruits that look just like marzipan. Using special tools and food coloring, they fashion such masterpieces as prickly green-jacketed chestnuts with dark brown centers, winter white camellias with red stamens, and pale pink cherry blossoms with mint-colored leaves to commemorate the flower's arrival in April.

The bean fudge also fills and frosts other confections, including pounded glutinous rice taffy called *mochi* and bite-size cakes, made from flour, water, and eggs that are baked until golden. These moist confections go by the name of *namagashi* and are always served before the thick whipped green tea at the tea ceremony.

Before the thin whipped green tea, tea masters serve dry sweets called *higashi,* made from rice flour and sugar. In Kyoto, most sweet makers use a rare kind of purified sugar called *wasanbon.* Handcrafted in a two-hundred-year-old tradition on the southern island of Shikoku, the wasanbon goes through a twenty-day process to render it completely free of impurities. Confectioners then pour or press the sugar-rice flour mixture into molds to turn out pastel-colored sweets that instantly dissolve on the tongue.

Since green tea always accompanies these sweets, dozens of

nearby counters sold loose leaves ranging in price and quality. Black, green, and oolong tea all come from the same plant, an evergreen shrub related to the magnolia. I quickly learned that it is the way the leaves are grown and treated, however, which accounts for their individual characteristics and quality. To make black tea, the leaves undergo fermentation before they are heated and dried. For green tea, the fermentation process is skipped and the leaves are simply steamed and then dried. Oolong tea consists of leaves that are partially fermented before being heated and dried.

The fanciest grade of green tea in Japan goes by the name of *gyokuro*, meaning "jade dew." It consists of the newest leaves of a tea plantation's oldest tea bushes that bud in May and have been carefully protected from the sun under a double canopy of black nylon mesh. The leaves are then either steeped in boiled water or ground into a powder to make matcha (literally, "grind tea"), the thick tea served at a tea ceremony. (The powder used to make the thin tea served at a tea ceremony comes from grinding the older leaves of young tea plants, resulting in a more bitter-tasting tea.)

The middle grade of green tea is called *sencha*, or "brew tea," and is made from the unprotected young tea leaves that unfurl in May or June. The leaves are usually steeped in hot water to yield a fragrant grassy brew to enjoy on special occasions or in fancy restaurants.

For everyday tea, the Japanese buy *bancha*. Often containing tiny tea twigs, it consists of the large, coarse, unprotected leaves that remain on the tea bush until August. When these leaves are roasted, they become a popular tea called *hojicha*. When hojicha combines with popped roasted brown rice, a tea called *genmaicha* results.

After the tea and sweets section, I would usually stop by the area selling rice crackers. Considered a form of dessert, these crispy morsels are made of rice or wheat flour dough stretched thin and baked in metal molds. The dough often contains egg, seaweed, or spices and is usually brushed with soy before baking to render the crackers shiny and salty as they puff and harden. The least expensive ones, such as the short orangey rods wrapped with nori seaweed, generally appeared as samples. The fancier crackers, including the wafers imprinted with ferns, small horns crusted with pink icing, and white daisies with yellow soybean centers, lay in clear cellophane pouches in elegant gift boxes.

The section proffering pickles and salted vegetable mixes to accompany steamed white rice was always ripe for samples. Kyoto, being an inland city, has earned a reputation for the quality of its vegetables, particularly the round, watery, sweet eggplants and succulent bamboo shoots. Since every Japanese meal traditionally ends with pickles, this area was thick with prospective buyers.

"Oh, what is this?" I'd ask with my eyes, stabbing a juicy chunk of salted turnip on a toothpick. I would then scrunch up my face, pretending I didn't care for it, and try another pickle, equally as crunchy and delectable. When I felt I had pushed the limits of freeloading, I would stab one more pickle and nod as if to say "very good," then step away to visit another section.

If I was lucky, hot foods would appear, such as plump oily knobs of grilled mackerel or eel glazed with soy and mirin. Male clerks dressed in navy-and-white cotton kimono-like jackets worn over their Western-style shirts and trousers would pass sample trays like waiters at a cocktail party. "Have a riddle taste," they'd say, flourishing their dainties. Copying the women around me, I would pop the hot morsel in my mouth and utter "*oishii,*" which means "delicious." And it was. Of course, the Japanese women would purchase whatever was being promoted, since few Japanese would ever sample a product without buying it. I usually would slink off to another section to look for something more affordable, such as a bag of bean sprouts for my evening's stir-fry.

Informative as these sampling seminars were, my understanding of Japanese cuisine skyrocketed when I met a young Japanese woman named Tomiko. Shortly before moving to the Guesthouse, I had landed a job teaching conversational English to five- and six-year-olds every Friday afternoon at a school she ran from her Western-style home. Tomiko's husband, Yasu, was a carpenter and had built the two-level house complete with hardwood floors, central heating, and an indoor shower and bath. It was light, warm, and modern—the antithesis of a traditional Japanese dwelling.

One Friday after teaching, Tomiko and I were having tea in her family room when the conversation turned to food. It was apparent from our first get-together that Tomiko was not a woman to trifle with her stomach.

"I am a gourmand," she had confessed, patting her ample rice belly. Tomiko had grown up appreciating rare foods and fine cooking as the only child from an upper-class family in Osaka, a city known for its outstanding cuisine. She also loved to cook. When I told her I still did not recognize the majority of ingredients in modern markets, an expression close to pain crossed her face. I offered her another cookie. It seemed to help. For as she chewed, she came up with a plan: she would take me to her local "supermarket" the following week to explain the contents of the aisles.

The tour began in the refrigerated section of a modest six-aisle establishment. Instead of metal carts to accommodate jumbo cereal boxes, double-value packets of toilet paper, and super-size bottles of detergent, a tidy stack of green plastic baskets rested on the floor inside the glass doors that automatically split open when Tomiko stepped on the ribbed rubber mat.

Fruit and vegetables filled the right side of the store across from a section of chilled items, including tofu and fresh udon noodles, the only two items I recognized. Tomiko grabbed a basket, slipped it into the crook of her elbow, then picked up a plastic-wrapped square resembling a sage-colored sponge.

"Any idea?" she asked, cocking her head. I took the square, dented with her fingerprints, and studied it for several seconds. I admitted I didn't have the foggiest idea what it was.

Which is basically how the tour went. Tomiko would hold up foods. I would shake my head. Then she would explain what they were and how to cook with them.

The green sponge turned out to be *fu* (wheat gluten), a high-protein Buddhist staple food often flavored with herbs and spices. The pink-and-yellow cigarette lighters turned out to be yogurts. The lime-green yo-yos were rice taffy cakes bulging with sweet white bean paste.

As for the vermilion-colored mollusks, they were a kind of cockle called blood clams (or arc shell) and, according to Tomiko, "delicious as sushi." The jumbo green sprouts came from the daikon radish and were "tasty in salads." And the pebbly-skinned yellow fruit was *yuzu*, an aromatic citrus with a lemony pine flavor that was "wonderful in soup."

Toward the end of the tour, Tomiko stopped in the seaweed aisle and asked if I knew how to make *dashi*, the ubiquitous Japanese stock made from kelp and shaved bonito. Although I had made it several times back in New York, I asked her to explain.

"We have two types, primary and secondary dashi," said Tomiko. She set her basket on the floor and then went up on tip-toe to pull down a package of dried *konbu* (also spelled *kombu*), or kelp, from the top shelf. For both styles, she explained, a strip of dried konbu is added to a pot of cold water. Just when the liquid comes to a boil, the seaweed is removed to avoid turning the stock bitter. Then dried fish flakes are added to the broth. Tomiko leaned over to retrieve a bag from the lower shelf.

"These are *katsuobushi*," she said, displaying the flesh-colored curls. The clear plastic bag crinkled in her hands as she described how the flakes are made from bonito, a kind of skipjack tuna, which is cut into chunks, boned, boiled, dried, cured, smoked, and then aged until it becomes as hard as wood. The dried hunks, which resemble fat brown plantains, are then shaved with a special blade held in place in a small wooden box with a drawer to catch the pinkish petals. When the smoky-tasting flakes have come to a boil in the kelp broth, the heat gets turned off immediately, and the liquid rests for a couple of minutes before being strained. The resulting mixture is primary or first dashi, a transparent whiskey-colored stock tinged with a delicate fish flavor used to make elegant clear soups.

For secondary dashi, which forms the base for soups seasoned with miso or other strong ingredients, the original piece of kelp and bonito flakes from the first dashi go back into a pot of water to be simmered until the stock takes on the desired briny flavor. Tomiko grabbed a little brown jar filled with instant dashi granules off the shelf and held it up. "If you're feeling lazy, you can always use this," she said, sheepishly.

The tour concluded with our buying the ingredients for *shabu-shabu* to enjoy that night with Tomiko and her husband. Sitting around the wooden table in Tomiko's kitchen, we drank frosty Kirin beers and munched on *edamame*, fresh steamed soybeans, nutty and sweet, that we pulled from their salt-flecked pods with our teeth. Then Tomiko set down a platter resplendent with gossamer slices of raw beef, shiitake mushrooms, cauliflower florets, and loamy-tasting chrysanthemum leaves to dip with long forks into a wide ceramic bowl of bubbling primary dashi. I speared a piece of sirloin. "Wave the beef through the broth," instructed Tomiko, "then listen." Everyone fell silent.

As the hot dashi bubbled around the ribbon of meat, it really did sound as though it was whispering "shabu-shabu," hence the onomatopoeic name of the dish.

I dipped the beef in a sauce of toasted ground sesame and soy and as I chewed, the rich roasted cream mingled with the salty meat juices.

"Try this one," urged Tomiko, passing another sauce of soy and sesame oil sharpened with lemony yuzu, grated radish, and hot pepper flakes. I tested it on a puffy cube of warm tofu that Tomiko had retrieved from the dashi with a tiny golden wire basket. The pungent sauce invigorated the custardy bean curd.

When we had finished all the meat and vegetables, Tomiko boiled down the cooking juices until they became dark and concentrated. She then added chewy cords of udon noodles to the glaze and turned them with her chopsticks until they became slick and salty. More cold beer provided relaxing liquid refreshment and brewed coffee and chocolate cake capped off what had been an extremely informative afternoon and the most magnificent meal I had eaten thus far in Japan.

If this was home cooking, I could only imagine what lay ahead in the rarefied world of tea kaiseki.

Spinach-Squash Salad
with Creamy Ginger Dressing

Kabocha squash has a dense, sweet orange flesh, similar to acorn squash, which you can use as a substitute. To turn this salad into a whole meal, try topping it with small squares of pan-sautéed tofu, or chunks of broiled salmon. Instead of croutons, this salad calls for Japanese rice crackers, which add a welcome crunch.

One 2-pound kabocha squash, halved and seeded
8 cups spinach leaves, rinsed and patted dry
1 cup corn kernels
1 cup diced cucumber (about one third of a medium cucumber)
2 plum tomatoes, chopped
⅓ cup mayonnaise
3 tablespoons dashi (page 48), or chicken or vegetable broth
4 teaspoons soy sauce
1 tablespoon rice vinegar
1 teaspoon sugar
1 tablespoon grated fresh ginger
⅔ cup mixed Japanese rice crackers

1. Preheat the oven to 400° F. Place the squash, cut side down, in an ovenproof dish coated with nonstick spray. Roast for an hour, or until the squash is tender when pierced with a sharp knife. Let cool.

2. Cut the peel off the squash and slice the flesh into bite-size chunks. Mound the spinach in a salad bowl and top with the squash, corn, cucumber, and tomatoes.

3. Whisk together the mayonnaise, dashi, soy sauce, vinegar, sugar, and ginger until the sugar dissolves. Just before serving, spoon the dressing over the salad and toss to combine. Garnish with rice crackers.

Makes 4 to 6 servings

Japanese Beef and Vegetable Hotpot (Shabu-Shabu)

Similar to fondue or Mongolian hotpot, this cold weather favorite involves cooking vegetables and thinly sliced beef in a dashi base. As the ingredients cook, the noise they make sounds like "shabu-shabu," hence the dish's name. The two dipping sauces below are typical accompaniments and are commercially available in most Japanese markets (along with the thinly sliced beef, which is usually in the freezer section). If you do not have a traditional shabu-shabu pot, an electric fondue pot works just as well. A small strainer is handy for cooking the tofu. However, if you don't have one, simply add the tofu to the cooking liquid and after one minute retrieve it with a slotted spoon.

6 Chinese cabbage leaves

One 15-ounce can whole bamboo shoots

1 small head of cauliflower, cut into bite-size florets

12 shiitake mushroom caps

3 leeks, white and light green parts only, trimmed, rinsed, and cut into 1-inch pieces

¾ pound spinach, leaves rinsed and trimmed

1 pound firm tofu, drained and cut into 1-inch cubes

1½ pounds well-marbled beef sirloin, cut into very thin
    ribbons
8 cups dashi (page 48)
Two prepared dipping sauces (pages 49, 50)
½ pound fresh (or partially cooked) udon

1. Bring a large shallow saucepan of water to a boil for
pre-cooking the cabbage, bamboo, and cauliflower. Beginning
with the cabbage, add the leaves to the boiling water and cook
for 3 minutes, or until crisp-tender. Remove the leaves from the
water with kitchen tongs and pat dry. Roll each leaf into a
cylinder and cut in half to create two rolls. Set aside.

2. Drain and rinse the bamboo. Cut each piece lengthwise in
half and then cut each half into ½-inch-thick semicircles. Bring
the same large saucepan of water used to cook the cabbage back
to a boil. Add the bamboo and cook for 30 seconds. Remove
with a slotted spoon and rinse under cold water. Set aside.

3. Bring the same saucepan of water back to a boil. Add the
cauliflower florets. When the water returns to a boil, cover and
cook the cauliflower until crisp-tender, about 4 minutes. Drain
and cool on a clean tea towel.

4. Arrange the cabbage rolls, bamboo shoots, cauliflower,
mushroom caps, leeks, spinach, tofu, and beef on one or two
large platters.

5. Heat all of the dashi in a shabu-shabu pot, or half of it in
an electric fondue pot until bubbling. Add several leeks and
mushroom caps to the broth to begin softening. Using long
forks or chopsticks, pick up the meat and vegetables from the

central platter and swish them through the dashi to cook. (For the tofu, place a cube in a small strainer and place the strainer in the broth. After a minute, lift the strainer from the broth to eat the tofu.) Dip the cooked meat and vegetables in either one of the sauces before eating. (If using a fondue pot, add the remaining broth to the pot, as needed.)

6. When no more meat or vegetables remain, add the udon to the remaining cooking liquid (adding more if necessary to the fondue pot) and simmer until tender. Divide the noodles and broth among six soup bowls.

Makes 6 servings

Dashi

In Japan, dried kelp and large bonito flakes (not the small thin bonito curls used to garnish dishes) briefly simmer in water to create a delicate amber broth called "first" or "primary" dashi, which is the basis for most clear soups. To make "second" dashi, the kelp and bonito flakes are added to a new pot of water (like a used tea bag) to make a weaker stock for more boldly seasoned dishes, such as miso soup. Although instant dashi granules and bottles of concentrated dashi are terrific timesaving substitutes, their taste is less subtle and refined than dashi made from scratch.

FOR FIRST/PRIMARY DASHI

1½ ounces dried giant kelp (konbu)

1½ ounces (or approximately 7 cups) large bonito flakes

1. Place 6 cups cold water and the kelp in a large saucepan over high heat. When the mixture comes to a boil, immediately remove the kelp (if it boils it can turn the broth bitter) and reserve it for the second dashi.

2. Add ½ cup cold water (to cool down the stock) and then the bonito flakes. When the mixture has returned to a boil, immediately turn off the heat (the fish flakes can also turn the broth bitter if boiled). Let the broth rest for 2 minutes, then pour through a cheesecloth-lined sieve, making sure to avoid pressing down on the solids (which will turn the dashi cloudy). Save the fish flakes for second dashi.

Makes 5 cups

FOR SECOND/SECONDARY DASHI
Place the reserved kelp and bonito flakes in 8 cups cold water. Bring to a boil, reduce the heat to low, and simmer for 30 minutes. Strain the broth through a cheesecloth-lined sieve, pushing down on the solids before discarding them.

Makes 6 cups

Toasted Sesame Dipping Sauce

To grind seeds, nuts, and herbs into a fine paste, the Japanese use a suribachi, a ceramic bowl with an unglazed fine-combed interior, and a special wooden stick with a rounded end. A small food processor is a fine substitute (and much less work!).

½ cup toasted unhulled white sesame seeds

2 tablespoons sweet white miso (shiro miso)

2 tablespoons mirin

2 teaspoons soy sauce

2 teaspoons rice vinegar

1½ teaspoons sugar

½ cup dashi (page 48)

Place the sesame seeds in a suribachi and grind until very flaky. Alternatively, place in a food processor and process until pasty. Blend in the miso, mirin, soy sauce, vinegar, and sugar until smooth. Blend in the dashi. Transfer the sauce to six small decorative bowls.

Makes enough for 6 sauce bowls

Sour-Soy Dipping Sauce

Sansho is a tongue-tingling spice made from the ground seedpod of the Japanese prickly ash. We have no Western equivalent of this aromatic ingredient, which often pairs with fatty foods, such as beef, to cut the richness.

½ cup soy sauce

¼ cup yuzu (available bottled in Japanese markets), or fresh lemon juice

1 tablespoon grated daikon radish

1 teaspoon toasted sesame oil

Pinch hot pepper flakes

Pinch sansho

Combine the soy sauce, yuzu or lemon juice, grated radish, sesame oil, pepper flakes, and sansho in a small bowl. Transfer the sauce to six small decorative bowls.

Makes enough for 6 sauce bowls

5.

Passing
the Test

$\mathcal{S}$oon after arriving, I realized the Tourist Information Center (TIC) in downtown Kyoto was *the* place to find answers to any questions I might have about the city. Run by the Japan National Tourist Organization, the small office had scores of pamphlets and desk clerks to guide visitors to Kyoto's finest *ryokan* (traditional inns), the sake breweries in the southern district of Fushimi, and numerous other delights, including choice places to sample authentic Kyoto cuisine.

This last category, I discovered, consists of four distinct styles of cooking: Buddhist vegetarian food (called *shojin ryori*); tea kaiseki (an offshoot of shojin ryori); restaurant kaiseki (a variant of tea kaiseki); and *Kyo-ryori* (literally, "Kyoto cooking"), known for its delicately seasoned dishes made from local specialties, including tender wheat gluten, white miso, and *yuba,* the custardy skin that is skimmed off simmering soymilk.

I had stopped by TIC one dry bright November morning to locate the names of several schools where I might teach conversational English and study tea kaiseki. There were two women working behind the office's counter. One was helping a bearded gentleman with an Australian accent find his way to the nearby city of Nara. The other was an attractive woman in her forties. She was on the phone and her black bob was doing just that, bouncing up and down as she chatted into the receiver. I waited for her to hang up and then asked her if she had a list of schools where I might teach English.

"Just a minute, please," said the woman, then headed over to the back wall lined with thick blue binders. She pulled one down, clicked it open, and returned with a list of English conversation schools in Kyoto and Osaka.

"It's not easy to find work here," she said, pursing her lips. "Everyone wants to work in Kyoto. And you," she said, glancing at the door, "are quite late. The Japanese school year begins in April."

I felt deflated. "Wait until you get to Japan to find a job," cautioned a friend, who had recently returned from teaching in Tokyo. "Schools in Japan know you want security, so they charge you for that. You'll earn a fraction of what you could if you sign the contract in person." I took a different tack.

"How about a list of schools where I might study tea kaiseki?"

"Tea kaiseki?" she said, her brows lifting. "Maybe you want to eat kaiseki?"

I paused. "No, actually, I am interested in studying tea kaiseki."

"Hmmm, tea kaiseki," said the woman, tapping her fingers on her lips as if to play a little tune. "That is very difficult. Wait a minute, please." She disappeared into the back office. I could hear cabinets sliding open. People talking. She reappeared.

"You say you want to study tea kaiseki?" she asked again, as if I hadn't answered her correctly the first time.

"Yes, I was told it originated in Kyoto."

"I see." She looked at me for a moment before speaking. "Maybe you want to study the tea ceremony?" I knew why she was confused. Most foreigners come to Kyoto to study the tea ceremony, not tea kaiseki. They enroll in full-time programs to study tea, which includes classes on tea kaiseki. I asked her if that was necessary.

"Just a minute, please." She stepped into the back office again. I heard more talking. Someone dialed a phone. Several minutes passed and then the woman emerged.

"There is a school called Mushanokoji that offers just tea kaiseki classes. But you'll need an introduction and classes are very expensive." Her eyes narrowed. "They are also taught in Japanese. Do you speak Japanese?"

"*Sukoshi* (a little)," I said, squeezing my index finger and thumb together in the air. She was hardly impressed. Nor should she have been, really. I had only gotten to page ten in my *Japanese for Beginners* book and tape set I had bought three weeks before leaving for Japan.

I jotted down the name of the tea school and slid it into my knapsack, along with the list of language schools. The woman reached for the phone.

"Thank you for all your help," I said with a little bow. The woman's hand hovered over the receiver.

"Is there anything else?"

"No, thank you so much for all your time." She bobbed her head, then began to dial, while I helped myself to a map of Kyoto and left the office.

Back on the sidewalk I stood in the sun for several seconds gathering my thoughts. Then, swinging my knapsack over my shoulders, I headed uptown with a renewed sense of purpose. I had a list of English conversation schools. I had the name of a tea kaiseki school. Now all I needed was an introduction.

It was Florence Harada who helped provide me with the introduction. The wife of one of my father's college roommates, she was a wealthy urbane Japanese woman married to an American diplomat and living in Kyoto. In addition to speaking perfect English, she understood the American culture and the art of networking.

I met her for tea one fall afternoon toward the end of November in her modern ranch-style home, surrounded by *bonsai*, with huge picture windows that looked out over the city. I had just come from my first Japanese language lesson at Nihongo Gakko, where my professor, Mr. Hideo, had filled my head with basic vocabulary words, such as *taberu* (eat), *sensei* (teacher), and *kamera* (camera). I was learning there were three types of Japanese words: indigenous, Chinese-derived, and those borrowed from modern foreign languages. The indigenous and Chinese-derived ones were words like taberu and sensei, which had no Latin roots and therefore needed to be memorized. The borrowed ones, however, were often taken from English and thus easy to remember, like kamera.

Because I was hoping to ask Florence for an *onegai*, or "favor" (indigenous word with no Latin root), I had brought her a tin of

Danish butter *kukki,* or "cookie" (borrowed English word). I also figured the sugar-topped knots and swirls would make a nice hostess gift, which Florence, in a distinctly non-Japanese manner, promptly opened and set out for us to enjoy with our brewed green tea. After polishing off a few knots, I asked her where I might study tea kaiseki.

It turned out Florence had an English-speaking Japanese friend, Mrs. Hisa, who was taking tea kaiseki classes at Mushanokoji, the same tea school the woman in the tourist office had mentioned.

The famous tea master, Sen no Rikyu—the one who had helped transform the tea ceremony in the sixteenth century—had three grandsons, each of whom established a Kyoto tea school to carry on Rikyu's unique art of tea.

Grandson Sen no Sosa established Omote Senke (*senke* means "school"); Sen no Soshitsu established Ura Senke (written Urasenke, which has branches all over the world, including New York City); and Sen no Soshu founded Mushanokoji Senke. These three schools became and still are the leading tea schools in Kyoto, if not all of Japan.

Since the Heian period in the ninth century, art forms preserved their purity by being handed down through a highly skilled family, referred to simply as an *ie* (family). Over time, the term's definition changed slightly to mean the male head of a particular house (or school) of traditional arts. In turn, the term for that person became *iemoto.*

Florence told me she would call her friend to see if she would be willing to introduce me to Mushanokoji's iemoto at his earliest convenience. To my surprise and delight, later that evening Florence called back with the plan: Mrs. Hisa would meet me at

Mushanokoji on Friday at noon. She would show me the school, then present me to the iemoto, also called the Grand Tea Master.

For some schools of traditional arts, a person's lineage is often more highly regarded than the quality of his skills. But the Grand Tea Masters of the big three Kyoto tea schools are also heralded for their capabilities. They must train for decades to learn the art of the tea ceremony so perfectly it appears all but encoded in their genes.

Nowadays, men and women can study tea for a year or a lifetime, depending upon their level of commitment. As they progress up the tea ladder, they attain higher levels of expertise until they reach the topmost status of a tea master. But a male tea master, regardless of his expertise, will never become a Grand Tea Master, or iemoto, unless he is a descendant of Rikyu, or marries into the "house."

During their training, male and female tea students learn the seamless choreographed movements necessary to boil water, measure out powdered green tea, and whip the two together with a small bamboo whisk to create thick and thin tea. To an outsider, this process sounds as simple as making a glass of instant lemonade.

Which is what is so bewitching about Japan: things seem so easy until you try to understand them. An American acquaintance now living in Tokyo said that after his first week, he felt he could write a book about the country; a year later, only a magazine article; after fifteen years, only one sentence. Remove the mask, draw the curtain aside, learn the language, and you face a web of complicated mazes.

The art of making tea entails a litany of movements and emotions that turns the process into a sort of spiritual ballet that changes slightly for each of the seventy-five or so different tea ceremonies the student might encounter in his or her career. What's more, students must learn the history of the many different utensils they will use—at least ten per ceremony—for all the different tea ceremonies they will perform. A tea bowl appropriate for autumn, for example, will likely be heavier and more somber in color than a tea bowl for summer. And the bowl chosen for autumn will probably differ in color and shape, depending upon whether the tea ceremony takes place in the morning versus the afternoon. Advanced students even learn to coordinate various tea utensils in an appropriate combination based on the era in which they were produced. For example, if a tea practitioner wants to use a tea scoop identified with a famous sixteenth-century tea master, he or she should choose a tea bowl made by a potter within one generation of the same era.

Tea students also need to learn the proper social graces and way to dress in the teahouse. They must know, for example, how to wear a kimono and which one to choose for winter, summer, or a certain festival. Each age group and sex has specific guidelines. Young girls can wear bright colors, yet they should refrain from wearing busy patterns more appropriate for parties and festivals than tea gatherings. As women age, their kimono colors should become more subdued. Men traditionally wear only quiet dark colors.

The fabric of the kimono also matters. Hemp or lightweight silk is appropriate for summer tea gatherings, while heavyweight silk is usually worn in winter. The fabric on the *obi* (waist sash) should be elegant and understated, along with the type of knot that holds the obi in place. Elaborate knots are frowned upon because they draw attention away from the tea ceremony and to the person wearing them.

Tea students must additionally comprehend the hundreds of

details involved in facilitating a guest's journey from the outside world to the teahouse, such as the proper accoutrements to put in the garden's waiting pavilion and the appropriate stone to step on when greeting the guests.

Last, but not least, tea students' studies include learning the art of tea kaiseki. They must understand how to choose appropriate seasonal menus, often based on important Japanese historic events or holidays. They need to be able to prepare the recipes and to know what serving dishes and utensils should be used and in what order. They must also understand the proper etiquette involved in serving, eating, and clearing a tea kaiseki meal, as well as the intangible spirit that lies behind it.

Meeting the Grand Tea Master of Mushanokoji would entail much more than a quick handshake and cheerful *"herro."* It would be a delicate process involving a series of favors exchanged back and forth among the tea world, the real world, and those who traveled in between, like Mrs. Hisa.

Getting introduced to Mushanokoji's Grand Tea Master was akin to meeting the pope, a privileged encounter bestowed upon a chosen few. Only in my case, I wanted to leave our encounter with more than a blessing.

The Grand Tea Master, although not directly related to Rikyu, had married one of his descendants, a woman named Sen Sumiko. And it was Sen Sumiko who taught all the tea kaiseki classes at Mushanokoji. If my introduction to her husband proved successful, I would be permitted to enter her classroom.

Friday morning arrived along with the moment of truth: I would rendezvous with Mrs. Hisa by the front gate of Mushanokoji, whereupon we would go inside and meet the man who might grant me enrollment.

To calm my jangled nerves, I rose early and went for a long jog along the Kamo River. As often happens during such times, the world came into stark relief. As I ran up the embankment, details popped, such as the nickel-blue river, topaz marsh grass, and leafless trees that looked almost silk-screened onto a paper panorama of Kyoto.

Flushed with endorphins, I dashed back to the Guesthouse feeling much calmer about meeting with the Grand Tea Master. By 8:00, I was down in the den drinking coffee and breakfasting on persimmon toast. Persimmons had recently come into season and, when sweet and jelly-soft, made a luscious topping for crisp buttered whole wheat bread.

After scanning the newspaper, checking the weather and the exchange rate, I headed up to my room to get dressed. Now what to wear?

Mrs. Hisa had suggested a skirt, although she had not indicated what length. A short skirt would rise dangerously high above the knees when sitting on the tatami, a flagrant breach of tea etiquette. After much deliberation, out came the Labels For Less black wool suit with its matching purple-and-black-patterned blouse that tied in a bow at the neck, black stockings, and black "comfort" pumps. On went some eyeliner, a dab of lip-gloss, and some simple pearl studs. Voilà. It was the best I could do, short of renting a kimono.

It was only later that I found out the outfit was appropriate. Tea devotees consider loud clothes, jangling jewelry, makeup, and perfume flashy material distractions in the spiritual world of tea.

After taking the subway to a stop near the Imperial Palace—a dark wooden structure sitting in a vast white gravel park—I got out and walked down Karasuma Street, where I turned right at the Young Men's Christian Association, toward Mushakoji Street. *Mushakoji* means "Samurai's Path," likely because this small road served as a popular thoroughfare for these fierce warriors on their way to the Imperial Palace. Ironically, the samurai became enamored with the tea ceremony around the turn of the thirteenth century, a time when political power lay not with the emperor and aristocracy, but with the head of the military government, called the *shogun*, and his warrior clan of samurai. Intrigued with the discipline of the tea ceremony that mirrored their strict codes of conduct, these warriors began patronizing the spiritual world of the teahouse.

After almost ten minutes of walking, I came to Mushanokoji, an elegant caramel-colored stucco building built in the early 1600s when mud and timber were in style (and still are for traditional teahouses). Vertical brown beams decorated the façade and a small gray roof, like the top of a birdhouse, ran the length of the compound's wall. Several maple and pine trees rose up from an interior garden, creating a lush natural fence.

In front of a bamboo and wood entrance gate stood a small elderly woman with silver hair that softly curved around her temples. As I came up to her, she dipped her head as if to bow.

"You must be Virginia," she said, with a shy smile.

"Yes, I'm Victoria," I said, hoping she would subconsciously pick up the correction. "And you must be Mrs. Hisa."

"Oh, yes, oh, I am sorry, I meant Victoria," she said, somewhat flustered. She pushed open the gate. "Let's go in." I followed her down a narrow stone pathway flanked by gravel and low green bushes. At the end of the walkway stood a flat stone ledge, where we slipped off our shoes before stepping up to the tatami waiting room.

A young maid in a chartreuse kimono decorated with red and gold cranes came forward to greet us. Split-toed white socks muffled her steps as she led us down a series of smooth wooden corridors perfumed with the faint spicy sweetness of sandalwood. As we passed through various tearooms—seven in all—paper screens filtered in diffused ivory light. The chirping of sparrows could be heard from one of the tearooms, whose screen had been pulled open to reveal an enchanting moss garden.

As my grandmother discovered long ago, the Japanese excel in cultivating nature. Their gardens come in numerous styles, including paradise gardens, dry-landscape gardens, stroll gardens, and tea gardens. Although each type has its own goal, they all share the same principle: nature is manipulated to create a miniature symbolic landscape.

A paradise garden is meant to evoke the Buddhist paradise through the use of water dotted with stone "islands." Dry-landscape gardens, usually tucked away in Zen temples, use dry pebbles and stones to create minimalist views for quiet contemplation. Stroll gardens offer changing scenes with every step, a pool of carp here, a mossy trail there, and a small bridge to link them both, while a tea garden provides a serene path to take you from the external world to the spiritual one of the teahouse.

The tea garden at Mushanokoji had smooth black and gray stones of various sizes zigzagging around the moist carpet of green. This was the roji, and its angled path suggested that the road to enlightenment is rarely straight.

A large stone urn stood in the middle of a mossy patch, not far from the Amigasamon, a gate made from a simple latticework of bamboo poles topped with a roof that resembled an *amigasa*, the large woven bamboo rain hats monks often wear.

Farther on lay various waiting pavilions, where tea guests

would sit and enjoy a small cup of boiled water, either plain or lightly flavored with a seasonal accent, such as a salted spring cherry blossom, before entering the teahouse. Since the boiled water comes from the same source the tea master will use for the water at his tea ceremony, this thoughtful offering enables the guests to anticipate the quality of the whipped green tea.

According to Mrs. Hisa, every bush, fern, and blade of grass in Mushanokoji's garden was there for a reason, mainly to suggest the feeling of being on a remote mountain. Flowering plants rarely appear, since they might distract the mind from the tea ceremony to come. Also, a bloom in the tea garden could detract from the beauty of the floral arrangement in the alcove inside the tearoom.

After a tour of the tearooms, the maid ushered us around the corner of the complex to the cooking school, a faded pink stucco building with rippled glass windows and cracked cement steps.

Up until World War II, Mushanokoji had been a thriving enterprise that attracted hundreds of wealthy tea devotees. By the time the Japanese surrendered in 1945, the tea population had become so reduced the school faced financial disaster. To shore up its coffers, the Grand Tea Master at the time decided to build a cooking school on the premises with his daughter, Sen Sumiko, serving as the school's tea kaiseki expert: she could never be a Grand Tea Master because she was a woman.

Despite the confining nature of her kimono, the maid scurried up the stairs to the cooking school with Mrs. Hisa and me in tow. After turning right, she scuttled down a black linoleum hall, whereupon she turned left and led us into a small dark room furnished with little more than a few floor pillows and a low lacquer table. She bowed and left.

Before we could catch our breath, the Grand Tea Master entered the room. He appeared to be in his late seventies. A smooth stubble of gray hair covered most of his head, while a handsome black kimono hung in loose neat folds around his slight frame. He said nothing, then bowed to Mrs. Hisa and me. Not sure how low to bow, I bent over at the waist and stared at the yellow weave of the tatami, thinking how smooth they felt beneath my stockinged feet. After what I thought was an appropriate passage of time, I straightened up, feeling the blood drain from my face, and smiled.

Mrs. Hisa and the Grand Tea Master began speaking. He did most of the talking, while she nodded and occasionally looked over at me. In an effort to appear respectful, I focused on the Grand Tea Master's knobby blue-veined hands so studiously trained in the art of whisking tea, arranging flowers for the tearoom alcove, and writing calligraphy for the seasonal scrolls. Suddenly, the Grand Tea Master stopped talking. I looked up.

"Would you like a cup of tea?" asked Mrs. Hisa, turning to me. I nodded solemnly, assuming the correct answer was yes. She said something to the Grand Tea Master, who then bowed again and left the room.

At this point, Mrs. Hisa suggested we kneel on the floor pillows to make ourselves more comfortable, a relative term in Japan. The Japanese know how to kneel, having done it since they were children. The legs of most women, in fact, bow outward as a result. Like most Westerners, I found tucking my toes beneath my bottom for long periods of time to be a horrendously painful ordeal. Nevertheless, I told myself that if I wanted to be accepted into Mushanokoji to study tea kaiseki, then I should probably contort myself into this "proper" position.

Now that I was kneeling, the moment had arrived to sip the tea. "Here are the sweets," said Mrs. Hisa, eyeing the maid in the chartreuse kimono. The young woman set down two small black plates each holding a puffy red-orange maple leaf. Mrs. Hisa lifted up a pointed flat wooden stick from the edge of her plate. It looked like a toothpick fit for King Kong. Traditionally carved from the spicebush, the pick had a tan pointed end and mottled brown top. Mrs. Hisa sliced open her maple leaf, carved out a small wedge, and stabbed it. "Oishii," she murmured, closing her eyes and gently chewing. I cut my leaf into little wedges and pierced one. The sugary sweet had a dense velvety consistency.

"We eat the sweet first before drinking the tea," said Mrs. Hisa with her mouth full of bean paste. I had heard the tea would be bitter.

Eventually, the maid came in carrying two bowls of thin whipped green tea. She handed a black tea bowl to Mrs. Hisa and a cream-colored bowl embellished with red, orange, and gold maple leaves to me. Hundreds of tiny bubbles covered the surface of the emerald green liquid, giving it a pebbly texture that almost glowed in parts.

Just then the Grand Tea Master walked in. And before I knew it, he had settled down on a cushion next to me! He leaned forward and bowed, so close I could see a small mole near his right ear. My heart skipped a beat. I bowed back. Now what?

I looked over at Mrs. Hisa, who shifted the bowl from her right hand and placed it in the palm of her left. Then, steadying the bowl with her right hand, with her thumb facing her, she bowed to the Grand Tea Master. I did my best to copy her, swiveling around on my cushion to face the Grand Tea Master. I had lost all feeling in my left leg.

Mrs. Hisa then gently gripped the bowl, still resting it in her left palm, and turned the bowl about ninety degrees clockwise. When I did the same, several maple leaves came into view inside the tea bowl. Mrs. Hisa took a sip and said something, dropped her right hand to the floor, and then drank the remaining tea, making a loud sucking sound as she finished.

My first sip tasted like warm pureed grass. Not that I had ever drunk grass, but it was what I imagined grass would taste like if whirled in a blender with a jigger of hot water. I bowed and smiled at the Grand Tea Master then drank the remaining tea, noisily slurping the last bit like Mrs. Hisa, hoping it hadn't been a case of loose dentures.

After running my tongue over my teeth, I smiled. Mrs. Hisa took a deep breath and let out a satisfied sigh before thanking the Grand Tea Master. She then picked up her bowl and spoke. She must have been admiring the bowl, given the way she kept turning it her hands and looking back at the Grand Tea Master. I picked up my bowl, cocked my head, and said "*kirei* (beautiful)," one of the few adjectives I knew.

The bowl really was beautiful. It felt as weightless as an eggshell and had been glazed in a traditional Kyoto color, a soft golden ivory that reminded me of warm Cream of Wheat glistening with melted butter. The maple leaves looping around the bowl had been rendered with such a fine hand I could almost imagine them fluttering in the breeze.

Mrs. Hisa slowly and deliberately placed her bowl on the lacquer table in front of her. I did the same. Then she began conversing with the Grand Tea Master. She kept both hands clasped in her lap as she spoke, occasionally looking at me, and then back to the Grand Tea Master. He looked at me, paused, and said something to her. She shifted her gaze to me.

"According to the Grand Tea Master, there is an entrance fee of fifteen thousand yen (almost $95) for the cooking school," said Mrs. Hisa. "After that, each class costs nine thousand yen (about $56) each. He would like to know if you can afford that?"

Both legs had gone completely numb. I took a breath, puffing up my chest slightly, and assured Mrs. Hisa I had enough money; I had brought over a good supply of traveler's checks and had already deposited several hundred dollars from teaching into my Sumitomo bank account. She translated this back to the Grand Tea Master, who got up and left the room.

After a long period of silence, a maid in a red- and mustard-flowered kimono came in carrying several papers. She said something to Mrs. Hisa, who nodded and then turned to me with a serious look on her face.

"The Grand Tea Master"—she cleared her throat and began again—"the Grand Tea Master has decided to grant you entrance to study tea kaiseki at Mushanokoji." She coughed, as if to dislodge a grass ball, and then swallowed.

"You can bring the entrance fee next week"—she cleared her throat again—"along with your payment for the first class."

I silently yodeled with joy. The maid handed me the paperwork, which Mrs. Hisa helped translate. Once it was complete, the maid left the room to get it stamped. Several minutes later she returned with my copies in an envelope.

Mrs. Hisa rose from her cushion, smoothing the wrinkles from her dress with her palms. I tried to stand up, but my toes had turned to ginger ale. My knees buckled, just as the Grand Tea Master appeared. Forcing myself up on two tingling stumps, I asked Mrs. Hisa to please thank the Grand Tea Master very much for his hospitality and his willingness to let me attend his school to study tea kaiseki. She conveyed my sentiments, then turned to me. "He is honored you would like to attend."

After much bowing, we eased our way into the hall, where the maid in the chartreuse kimono stood waiting. She escorted us back to the stepping stone where we had left our shoes and waved us off.

As Mrs. Hisa and I made our way toward the subway, I told her how grateful I was for all her help. She was living proof of how vital personal introductions are in Japan. "Truly, I can't thank you enough for all you did," I said, slowing down to match my pace with hers. She modestly waved her hand as if to say it was nothing, then stopped and looked up at me with a crinkled smile.

"I was happy to do it. Florence is my good friend."

We reached the subway platform, and in the middle of my good-bye, Mrs. Hisa unsnapped her purse. "I almost forgot," she said, riffling through her belongings. "There is an American gentleman also studying tea kaiseki." Her train pulled in.

"I asked him the other day if he could translate the classes for you and he said he would." She retrieved a slip of paper and handed it to me. "Here," she said, stepping onto the train. "His name is Stephen. He is expecting your call."

6.

Japanese
Julia

The next night after supper, I came into the Guesthouse den to practice my Japanese characters while waiting for the only phone to become free. There are three kinds of characters in the Japanese language: *kanji, hiragana,* and *katakana.* Kanji are the Chinese characters that the Japanese adopted, while hiragana and katakana are each a series of roughly forty-six characters that the Japanese developed to represent the sounds of syllables. Hiragana is used for native Japanese words, such as ki-mo-no. Katakana is used for words of foreign origin, such as New York.

That particular night I was practicing kanji to a hauntingly beautiful cassette tape I had just bought for my Walkman called "The Silk Road" by the Japanese musician Kitaro. Inspired by nature, Kitaro wrote the music in such a way as to re-create the sound of flowing brooks, rustling wind, and even Buddhist drums. "Flow of Time" had come on and I had just finished my last kanji character for flower *(hana)*, when the phone became free. So I dialed Stephen.

"*Moshi-moshi* (hello)," answered a high-pitched male voice.

"Hello, is Stephen there?" I inquired.

"It's me."

"Oh, hi, it's Victoria." Silence. "Mrs. Hisa gave me your name. I was wondering—hello? Are you still there?"

"Uh-huh."

Clearly, Stephen was a man of few words, at least on the phone. So I got right to the point and asked him if he really was willing to translate the tea kaiseki classes from Japanese to English? Was he sure it wouldn't be too much trouble?

"Well, Musha (Mushanokoji) asked me if I'd teach some tea kaiseki classes in English," confessed Stephen, "and I said I would. Working with you will help me organize my thoughts."

Relieved to know he would also benefit from our arrangement, I told him to consider me his guinea pig. He snorted, then became serious. "You should buy some books." I asked him which ones and he proceeded to rattle off several titles: *Japanese Cooking: A Simple Art; Good Food from a Japanese Temple; Kaiseki: Zen Tastes in Japanese Cooking;* and *A Feast for the Eyes.*

"I know they're expensive, but they're essential," he said. "They explain many of the techniques and dishes we'll be covering in class." I said I would try to buy them as soon as possible.

"If you can't afford them right away, you can come over to my place and look through mine." I thanked him for his generous offer.

"Bring a notebook with you to class," he added. "After we

eat we can go over my notes." I thanked him again and then we agreed to meet "at Mush" on Saturday around 1:00.

Saturday arrived cold and bright, a typical December day in Kyoto and ideal for walking. I gave myself three hours to get to the tea school, not because I feared getting lost—I had found as long as I knew which side of the Kamo River I was on, I no longer needed a map—but because I wanted to slow down. Too often I found myself racing around the city focusing on my destination, instead of enjoying the journey.

Most tourists who flock to Kyoto miss the city's small back streets unencumbered with sidewalks and traffic. With limited time, they hit the top ten temples, shrines, museums, and gardens, ticking them off like errands on a to-do list.

But to truly feel the soul of the city, you need to tear yourself away from the bright lights and slip into the shadows where you'll find the shops, homes, and people that embody the traditions and values of Kyoto's elegant past.

Take the sagging wooden building I passed with nothing more than a cream-colored fan displayed in the shop's glass window, a sandalwood arc perched on a red cushion, spread open to charm the eye with a tiny green bird sitting on a leafy red maple branch. The view was simple at first and something you could easily miss as you hurried by. But behind those cream-colored folds lay something else, the romance of a time when a scented fan was a woman's most elegant accessory.

During the ninth century, Heian-period women would wear up to twelve layers of colorful overlapping kimonos. It was fans, not necklaces, earrings, or pendants, that accented the delicate lines of their attire. By the fourteenth century, when the kimono had dropped down to three layers and silver and brocade waist sashes had grown in popularity, again, it was the fan not jewelry that remained the accessory of choice.

This folding work of art was also utilitarian. In a country squeezed for space, its compact nature enabled women and men to store it in the breast pocket fold of their kimonos. When they were hot, they simply flipped it open to create a cooling breeze often scented with sandalwood from the fan's carved wooden supports. In knowing hands, the plaited curve could also be an erotic device, particularly when a woman coyly held it across her face.

At a tea ceremony, the fan is considered a guest's most important accoutrement. When guests enter the tearoom on their knees, they place their closed fans in front of them as a gesture of politeness. The closed fans also serve to draw a "line" of respect between the guests and their host, since one of the Chinese characters for the word fan means "line." When the tea master Rikyu forbade the samurai to bring swords into his tearoom, a fan became an appropriate substitute. As a result, guests never cool themselves inside the tearoom with their fans, since opening them would be akin to brandishing a sword. Instead, they keep their fans neatly closed on the tatami behind them, or for women discreetly tucked into the waist sashes of their kimonos, since that is where female samurai used to carry their swords.

Beyond the fan shop lay other signs of old Kyoto, such as the husband and wife in matching white aprons, hairnets, and black rubber boots, who had already finished making the day's supply of bean curd. At one time, every village and town in Japan had its own tofu maker. Although this no longer holds true, Kyoto remains the bastion for Japan's finest tofu. Creamy and rich, it tastes as different from commercially made tofu as Wonder Bread does from a freshly baked Parisian baguette.

The couple stood on the worn stone floor washing their wooden buckets and storage boxes, while the delicate tofu floated like puffy white sea creatures in a stainless steel tank.

Next door, a woman in a beige apron swept up leaves outside her pickle store. The bamboo-handled twig broom she used made a loud scratching sound as it grazed the pavement. In the Shinto tradition, she would purify the swept area with a bucketful of water.

Farther on, I came to a soba shop, which I had come to recognize by the enormous red-and-black lanterns hanging out front, along with an irresistible cloud of dashi that smelled like caramelized onions seasoned with clam juice and soy.

Adjacent to the soba shop stood a small convenience store. Next to it was a creaky wooden sweet shop, where an elderly woman sat on a stool, peering out from the dark like an owl. The glass case in front of her held rows of glossy glutinous rice dumplings filled with red and white bean fudge. Just as I had passed the store, an old woman, bent over like a shrimp in a teal kimono, shuffled in to buy some sweets.

Many women in Kyoto still don kimonos, but usually only for special occasions, such as a concert, a special luncheon, or a tea ceremony. They wear these silken robes pulled tightly around the neck and belted so as to hang just above the ankles, unlike the geisha, who let their kimonos swirl about their feet and dip open in the back to reveal whitened shoulders marked with a sensual prong of unpainted flesh.

Across from a new green-and-red Fuji film store sat a small restaurant in a decrepit old building offering dusty plastic models of tempura-topped rice bowls and fat rice-stuffed omelets belted with ketchup. The eatery appeared more distressing than appealing, at least on the surface.

The Japanese believe that beauty can reside in things that are rustic, withered, faded, simple, imperfect, or incomplete. This aesthetic concept applies to people, as well as things, and stems from the words *wabi* and *sabi*. The spirit of wabi tends to be inward and subjective and often refers to a path or way of life, while sabi generally pertains to material objects, art, literature, and external events. A monk living in self-imposed isolation in the woods, for example, embodies wabi because he coexists with nature in a state that is physically impoverished but rich in spirit. The restaurant with its dusty models had a sabi quality because, by being housed in a crumbling wooden building next to a modern business, it evoked the corroded elegance of another era, like an antique kimono in a closet of designer wear.

The cooking school at Mushanokoji embodied a sense of sabi. Unlike the meticulously maintained tearooms clustered around it, the school stood in shabby disarray. Yet, this worn-out classroom served as the humble stage upon which occurred the most revered form of Japanese cooking—tea kaiseki.

"Are you Stephen, by any chance?" I asked, turning to the only Western man in the hall outside the classroom. It was just before 1:00, and I was still out of breath, having sprinted for the past five minutes to avoid being late for our first tea kaiseki class.

"Yup," he said, modestly laughing. I introduced myself, thinking how different he looked from the reedy academic with horn-rimmed glasses I had imagined on the phone.

Stephen clearly wasn't subsisting on sushi. He had a well-upholstered frame and dark beady eyes set into a soft fleshy face, like two raisins pressed into a dinner roll. He had brushed his straight brown hair forward so that it created a sort of V in front that pointed directly to his long nose, flattened at the tip as if someone had filed it off. A navy-blue sweater covered his Buddha belly, which he had tucked comfortably into a pair of faded blue pants, belted so high I could see the cuffs of his white athletic socks worn under his Birkenstock sandals. His most characteristic feature was his smile; a perfect orange-section grin that had earned him the self-described nickname "the happy one."

At precisely 1:00, Stephen and I filed into the classroom, along with a cluster of middle-aged Japanese women and one Japanese gentleman, who turned out to be a restaurant chef. A worn baby-blue plastic curtain, looking more appropriate for a shower than a cooking school, hung across the back of the room. Pine cabinets, some with their doors hanging off their hinges, flanked both sides of the room, while dusty metal blinds blocked out the sunlight from the rippled glass windows. Stacks of cardboard boxes, sun-bleached papers, and miscellaneous crockery covered the remaining shelf space.

A long black counter with a built-in metal sink and large gas burner for cooking demonstrations ran across the front of the classroom. Behind it hung a forest-green chalkboard. In front of the chalkboard stood our teacher, Ms. Sen Sumiko.

"*Konnichiwa* (good afternoon)," she trilled in a voice uncannily similar to Julia Child's. Although much shorter than our American icon, she had the same I-love-to-eat look that she had eased into a black shirt and stretchy black turtleneck. She had pulled her raven hair into a loose bun and dabbed pink lipstick on her full lips, which pursed into a pretty pout.

As she continued to talk, her words sailed past me like curve balls. I labored to catch at least one familiar ingredient or cooking term, but they flew off into the distance, leaving me marooned at my desk with a blank notebook.

"Always wet your cutting board to soften the surface so it won't dull the knives," Stephen leaned over and whispered. He was sitting next to me and had been madly scribbling along with the other students. Japanese Julia babbled on. I uncapped my pen.

"A stomach four-fifths full knows no doctors," Stephen said. I wrote that down.

"The food served at a tea kaiseki should be just enough to satisfy hunger, but not so much as to spoil your appetite for the tea." Stephen tapped his pen on my notebook. "That's very important."

I jotted down what I could, then supplemented my notes with Stephen's explanations in a nearby coffee shop after class. Basically, what I learned was this: it was Kyoto's temples that inspired the development of tea kaiseki. Based on early Indian Buddhist practice, Japanese monks were allowed only two meals a day, breakfast and lunch. However, since the monks often engaged in physical labor, such as scrubbing floors and raking leaves, they became quite hungry toward what would normally be dinnertime. To trick themselves into feeling full during evening meditations, they often tucked hot stones into the front fold of their kimonos, the pocket-like area that forms when the left side folds over the right. These stones, which had been heated in piles of burning leaves and twigs and then wrapped in cloth, triggered the release of gastric juices when pressed against the stomach. This, in turn, brought about a sense of satiation. The monks called these stones *yakuseki* (literally, "medicine stone"), because *yaku* means "medicine" and *seki* means "stone."

Over time, the hot stones gave way to small dishes of simple vegetarian foods prepared in a minimalist manner, a bit of steamed rice, miso soup, and some vegetables. This modest repast became known as a yakuseki. The monks called it such because by considering this small meal "medicine," they were healing the "illness" of hunger and, thus, not opposing Buddha's teachings.

As the tea ceremony began to spread beyond the temples, the monks started conducting tea ceremonies at the imperial court to amuse the wealthy patrons who supported the temples. However, the aristocracy wanted more than a spartan temple meal to precede their whipped green tea (which at the time wasn't always the highlight of the gathering). They wanted something more akin to the formal banquets they frequently enjoyed, called *honzen ryori,* meaning "main-tray cooking." Modeled after Chinese court cuisine, honzen ryori consisted of up to seven trays of food holding up to three soups and eleven side dishes, plus rice, pickles, and several ornamental dishes. (This multicourse feast still appears today at Japanese weddings, funerals, and festivals.)

In an effort to please the aristocracy, the monks began serving a variation of honzen ryori cuisine before the whipped green tea. Featuring elaborate ingredients fashioned into numerous courses served on rare dishes with many rounds of sake, the meal was called a *kaiseki* because one of the many meanings of *kai* is "group" and *seki* can also mean "gathering place."

"Now we're going to cook," said Stephen, licking his lips. He often did that in a moment of anticipation before a good meal. His eyes also started blinking rapidly.

"You'll be my partner," he announced, heaving his bulk out of the tiny wooden chair. I followed him over to one of the six cooking stations situated throughout the room. The housewives had divided into pairs; Mrs. Hisa partnered with the Japanese chef and took the cooking station behind us.

Our preparation space consisted of a waist-high stainless steel counter, which dropped down to a thigh-high metal shelf holding three gas burners. Wooden cutting boards and knives sat in the center of the counter surrounded by our ingredients. Pots and pans rested above our heads on a stainless steel shelf attached to two metal poles welded onto the counter.

Looking at my watch, I calculated we had ten dishes to make in an hour and a half. But since all our recipes were in Japanese, I was going to have to rely on Stephen for everything, including what we were going to cook.

"We're making New Year's foods," said Stephen, strapping on an apron. "In tea, you have two New Years because you have the New Year's in November to celebrate the start of the new tea year and then you have the New Year's that comes after Christmas." He reached for a wooden-handled pot and passed it to me, along with a bamboo steamer.

"We're making the post-Christmas type of New Year's foods. So the menu has lots of red and white ingredients for happiness and congratulations. You know, pretty foods," he said, grinning. "Cheerful foods." I tied on my apron.

"Okay, wipe down this piece of konbu," he instructed, handing me a large piece of brown kelp speckled with white. "When you're done, measure out one cup of vinegar and half a cup of sugar. That's your marinade." I busied myself with the seaweed, while Stephen pulled out flexible opaque salmon bones. After skinning the fish, he sliced it down the center seam, creating two pieces, which he cut into quarter-inch-thick slices. Then, like magic, he transformed a knob of ginger into a miniature golden haystack.

I handed him the slippery piece of kelp, which he squared off and placed on a bamboo sushi roller. Next, he laid several slices of salmon across the shiny middle, sprinkled it with a few threads of ginger, and rolled it up like a nori roll. After sealing the cylinder in plastic wrap, he handed it to me.

"Cut this into bite-size pieces." The sweet and tangy kelp yielded like a cooked lasagna noodle under the sharp knife, creating exotic coral-and-sienna pinwheels.

Next, we made delicate egg crepes to wrap around thick oily slices of mackerel that we had soaked in a bracing mix of dashi, sugar, and soy. This was followed by a small "salad" of lightly salted white fish "noodles" tossed with salmon roe and lemony yuzu.

As we buzzed around our stations, the room filled with the sweet briny aroma of dashi. Pans clattered. Seafood sizzled. And Japanese Julia walked around the room passing out morsels of advice.

But Stephen hardly needed any. He had been living in Kyoto for the past twelve years and studying tea kaiseki for the past eight. He clearly knew what he was doing. In fact, he was doing most of the work.

After I steamed four giant clams over a skillet of sake, Stephen ripped out the meat and hacked it into chunks. With cupped hands, he scooped up the chewy bits and threw them in a bowl. Then he stirred in spicy red-and-white radish wedges and a warm dressing of wasabi, sugar, and sweet white miso that I had stirred in a small saucepan over a low flame until it became thick and shiny. Following his directions, I spooned the golden clams back into their shells. Stephen garnished them with a pink-and-white "congratulatory" flower of spongy wheat gluten. "Precious," he said, winking at me.

Next, we made sea urchin–egg balls, first blending creamy lobes of sea urchin with raw egg yolk and a little dashi. Stephen cooked the mixture until it formed a stiff paste and then pressed it through a sieve. I plopped a golden dollop in a clean damp cloth and flattened it into a disc. In the center I put three crescents of lily bulb tenderized in salt water.

"Try one," urged Stephen, handing me a wedge of lily bulb. It was mealy and sweet, kind of like a boiled cashew. Stephen brought together the four corners of the damp cloth and twisted it gently to create a bubble of eggy sea urchin paste stuffed with lily bulb. When unveiled, it looked like a Rainier cherry. I twisted out nineteen more balls, which we later arranged on fresh green leaves draped across black lacquer trays.

Next, we impaled several fat shrimp on two metal skewers, sending one rod through the head and the other through the tail. We grilled the grayish pink bodies until they became rosy on one side and then flipped them over until they turned opaque. Stephen painted golden egg yolk for prosperity over the juicy crustaceans and returned them to the grill until they smoldered and charred.

After the shrimp, we made "sandwiches" fashioned from crisp lotus root rounds and chewy plum leather. We sliced the lotus root into thin wheels and then blanched them before steeping them in a syrup of sugar, rice vinegar, salt, and water. The sandwiches tasted like sweet-pickled jicama topped with guava paste, odd on their own, but a fabulous tangy-sweet interlude in a multicourse tea kaiseki.

Toward the end of class, Stephen and I created apricot-and-radish-stuffed crabapples. We gently scooped out the fruit's flesh with tiny spoons, brushed the inside with lemon water to prevent browning, and then filled them with a sticky mix of chopped apricots that had soaked overnight in vinegar, sugar, soy, and the fiery juice of grated daikon radish squeezed through cheesecloth.

After that, we made miso-pickled lettuce spines wrapped with smoked salmon. We sliced off the curly green portion of several romaine lettuce leaves to reach the pale crisp rib, which we cut crosswise in half. After coating the watery spines with sweet white miso, we let them pickle for ten minutes. Then we wiped them clean and wrapped them with strips of smoked salmon, like rollmops. A nice cocktail hors d'oeuvre, I thought, looking at the pink-and-green bundles.

The climactic course was the *wanmori*, a bowl of choice ingredients surrounded by a first dashi, lightly seasoned and delicately garnished. *Wan* refers to the type of lacquer bowl in which the dish is served and *mori* is from the verb *moru*, meaning "to pile up." When choosing the menu for a tea kaiseki the chef first settles upon the wanmori, then plans the rest of the menu around it. This is because the wanmori is considered a culmination of the chef's talents, the quality of his broth combined with the freshness, flavor, color, aroma, texture, taste, and arrangement of the seasonal ingredients in the bowl.

Stephen and I made our wanmori with duck. With a razor-sharp knife, I carved off excess fat from the plump maroon breast, then cut the meat into bite-size pieces that I dredged in potato starch. While Stephen made dashi from choice fish flakes and kelp, I chiseled a brilliant orange carrot into chewing gum–shaped rectangles. Stephen blanched fresh spinach leaves, then squeezed them into bundles, trimming them down to size to match the carrots. After that he grilled pounded rice dumplings (mochi) over the burner's flame until they blistered like campfire marshmallows.

Shortly before 3:00, we slipped the duck into simmering dashi and cooked it until the center turned ruby pink. Then, after placing a nugget of duck in a black lacquer bowl, we arranged a bundle of spinach over the fowl, leaned a rectangle of carrot up against the spinach, tucked in the grilled mochi ball, and perched a tiny wedge of lemony yuzu zest over the greens. Steadying his hand, Stephen ladled a bit of amber dashi around our masterpiece. After making another bowl, we placed the covers snuggly in place to trap all the flavors. Finally, it was time to eat.

Or so I thought. I had anticipated slowly working our way through all ten courses, like guests at a tea ceremony. I glanced over at my classmates and saw one woman washing dishes.

"Here," said Stephen, handing me a set of chopsticks. He picked up his wanmori. "Savor the fragrance." He gently squeezed the lacquer rim of the bowl to loosen the cover. I did the same and a savory jet stream of duck, citron, and toasted mochi rushed up from the bowl. I sipped the limpid broth. It had a delicate gamy flavor underscored with soy, minerals, and cured fish. The duck tasted juicy and tender. The carrot had a treacly crunch, while the gooey mochi draped with soft spinach had a smoky sweetness.

Maybe I'll try one of those crepe-wrapped mackerel rolls, I mused, surveying our delicacies. All at once the metallic tear of foil ripped through the air. I looked up. The women had taken charge and were dividing up the goodies. *Wait a minute, guys, what are you doing?* I heard the suck of air being released from several plastic containers. Knives clattered in the sink and suddenly there was a rush of water. *This must be some kind of mean trick, no?* Pots clanged as they hit the sides of the metal sink. The cutting boards made a dull thump. *This was supposed to be dinner.* Aprons flew onto the counter and piled up in a heap. Clack! Clack! Clack! A stack of lacquer bowls joined them.

Then the storm was over. The dry counters gleamed. Slick cutting boards leaned against the metal poles and pots dripped from the racks overhead. I finished drying our wanmori bowls and minutes later joined Stephen in the hall.

"Are you sure you don't want any of this?" he asked, waving good-bye to several classmates. "This is a lot of food." His canvas tote bulged with foil-wrapped packages.

"That's okay," I replied. "I don't think this stuff would go over too well at the Guesthouse." I could just imagine: Oh, Eric, instead of your usual tuna salad on white, how about a lotus root sandwich filled with plum paste?

Stephen shrugged. "Well, David will be happy." He pulled down the sleeves of his coat, first the left one and then the right, and picked up his bag.

I followed him outside, securing the tiny leather belt on my knapsack. The sun had disappeared behind the gray winter clouds, casting a sad pall over the afternoon. All those exquisite dishes filled with greetings of happiness and goodwill now lay wilting in Stephen's tote.

And yet, as I replayed the class in my head, a tingly flush of elation rose up inside of me, as if I had just sipped an extraordinary champagne. I had flirted with tea kaiseki and now felt giddy. The food had been fascinating, succulent, beautiful, and exotic. Just one taste and I was thirsting for more.

Miso-Pickled Romaine Stems Wrapped with Smoked Salmon (Chisa no To no Sake Maki)

In Japanese markets you can find various grades of white miso (shiro miso). Spring for the pricier versions, which taste sweeter than the less expensive brands. In this recipe, you'll notice the difference.

12 large romaine lettuce leaves

¼ cup sweet white miso (shiro miso)

1 tablespoon mirin

12 slices smoked salmon, cut lengthwise in half

1. With a sharp knife, cut off the leafy green portion of each lettuce leaf (save for another use), so that you have twelve long stems. Cut each stem crosswise in half.

2. Whisk together the miso and mirin in a large bowl. Add the romaine stems and, using your fingers, gently toss to coat. Let the stems pickle for 10 minutes.

3. Remove the stems from the miso mixture and with a clean paper towel gently wipe off the miso. Wrap the salmon slices around each pickled stem, like rollmops, so that a portion of the lettuce stem sticks out from either side of the fish.

Makes 24 salmon-lettuce rolls

Duck Wanmori

A crystal clear dashi-based soup filled with artfully arranged ingredients is one of the hallmarks of elegant Japanese cooking. Ideally, the soup is served in a bowl with a lid to lock in the fragrance of the citrus zest. Since dried mochi is what is most commonly available outside of Japan, that is the form called for in this recipe.

4 dried mochi cakes (about 2 ounces each)

1 medium carrot, peeled and trimmed

I small bunch fresh spinach (about ½ pound)

4 cups dashi (page 48)

2 teaspoons soy sauce

¼ teaspoon coarse salt

One 4-ounce boneless duck breast, skinned

2 tablespoons potato starch

4 tiny diamond-shaped pieces of yuzu or lemon zest (each one
about the size of a peanut)

I. Using a pair of kitchen tongs, hold each mochi cake over a medium flame until lightly charred all over. Bring a large pot of water to a boil. Add the charred mochi, turn off the heat, and let them soften (this will take about 5 minutes).

2. Slice the carrot crosswise in half. Using only the top half, slice the carrot into four 2-inch-long thin rectangles. (Set aside the remaining carrot for another use.) Blanch the carrot slices in a small pot of lightly salted water until crisp-tender, about a minute. Drain and set aside.

3. Bring a small amount of lightly salted water to a boil in a medium shallow saucepan. Add the spinach, cover, and cook over low heat until the leaves have collapsed and just wilted, I to 2 minutes. Drain, form the spinach into a fat bundle, and lightly roll in a clean tea towel to remove the excess water. Cut the spinach bundle into four 2-inch-long rounds.

4. Place 3 cups of the dashi in a medium saucepan. Add the soy sauce and salt and bring to a simmer. Keep warm over very low heat.

5. Bring the remaining I cup dashi to a boil in a small saucepan. Cut the duck meat along the bias into four pieces. Dredge each

one in the potato starch, tapping off any excess. Add the duck to the dashi and cook over very low heat until just pink, about 5 minutes.

6. For each wanmori, place a morsel of duck in the center of a bowl. Add a mochi cake and a bundle of spinach. Lean a carrot rectangle up against the spinach, then garnish it with a tiny diamond of yuzu zest. Ladle the seasoned dashi around the ingredients and cover the bowl with a lid.

Makes 4 servings

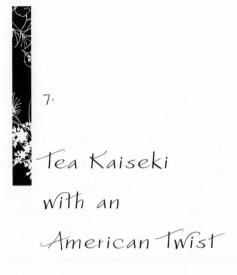

7.

*Tea Kaiseki
with an
American Twist*

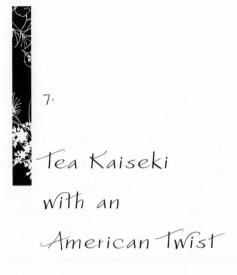 unexpected stroke of luck came my way when Stephen called about a week after our first tea kaiseki class. He and his partner David were planning to host an afternoon kaiseki and tea ceremony at their home to celebrate the coming of winter and New Year's. If I was free, I was welcome to come by and see the whole thing from start to finish. "You can help me cook. David does the tea," added Stephen.

In contrast to Stephen, David resembled a Zen monk. He had a buzz-cut helmet of gray hair and often dressed in gorgeous kimonos. He was a teacher at one of the three big Kyoto tea schools and his patient gentle demeanor suited him well to the quiet and deliberate world of tea, as did his sharp mind and knowledge of Asian history.

I told Stephen I would love to help him. What better way to

spend a Saturday? I could study Japanese at home in the morning and then swing by his place right after lunch. "What time should I show up?" I inquired.

"As early as you can," he replied. "We have lots to do. I'll be up at six."

The next morning my alarm went off at 5:30. As if embarking on some kind of culinary Outward Bound, I got dressed in the dark and headed downstairs with my knapsack, purple fleece jacket, red woolen scarf, and mittens. After a strong cup of coffee, I quietly locked the Guesthouse door behind me. It was 6:15.

Since Stephen and David lived around the corner from Mushanokoji, the most direct way to their house was to head west on Kitayama Street and then down Karasuma Street toward the Imperial Palace. But that morning I decided to take an alternate route to witness the frosty gray light of morning rise over the Kamo River. The cold damp air smelled like burning leaves as I made my way past the frost-crusted hedges along the embankment. Mist hovered over the water, shrouding the marsh grass and bridges in a diaphanous veil of platinum white. Just when I thought I was the only one awake, a loud flapping of wings broke the silence and a white crane lifted off the water. The sun had yet to break through by the time I reached Stephen and David's home. Much too early.

By taking the river route, I had arrived just before 7:00. So I circled the block. But by 7:15, I was back where I had started. Should I knock or should I leave? "I'll be up at six," echoed Stephen's voice in my head. Maybe he and David are awake, I thought. Maybe Stephen needs me. Maybe he's up to his elbows in dashi. Maybe he's wondering where I am.

I knocked on the gate. Silence. I knocked again. Still nothing. "Stephen?" I meekly called. "Are you there?" I craned my head around, but saw no one. Then I knocked a little louder. Silence. "Helloooooo," I called. I rapped the door and waited. And waited.

"Stephen!" I shouted.

"Coming," whined a voice. I heard a rustle along the garden path, and suddenly Stephen stood before me. He was wrapped in an extra-large white-and-navy casual kimono, looking like a big baby who had just been roused from his nap. He unlocked the gate and slid it open. "I hope I'm not too early," I said, looking at his tousled hair.

"Not at all. We're just having breakfast."

I came to the entrance of their home and swallowed hard. David was sitting on the floor like a rag doll with his bare feet stuck out from his cotton kimono. Two male guests, also in casual kimonos, were pouring themselves coffee in the kitchen. Futons, quilts, and pillows lay tossed about the tatami.

"You know," I said brightly, "I can easily come back. In fact," I said, heading back down the stone path, "why don't I just get some coffee and return in an hour."

"No, no, no," said Stephen, beckoning me back. "We need to start cooking. That means you two as well," he said, gesturing to his male houseguests. They rolled their eyes in mock disgust.

"You get a cup of coffee and I'll put on some clothes," said Stephen, handing me a chipped green mug.

While Stephen dressed, I made small talk with Brad and Kyle, who, as it turned out, were studying tea at one of the big three tea schools. Neither one was sure how long he wanted to stay in Japan, so each had enrolled in the school's one-year program, which was taught in English. David was their teacher.

"I want to practice making sweets," said Brad, stirring milk into his coffee. Stephen enjoyed making sweets for David's tea ceremonies and would often invite David's students to help.

Nowadays, it is fairly unusual for a tea master to serve homemade sweets, not only because of the time and skill involved, but also because Kyoto is so famous for its tea confections. Numerous old wooden shops, which have been in business for hundreds of years, have well-deserved reputations for the quality of their jellies, bean pastes, and sugary tablets.

Aside from the gorgeous colors and shapes of their confections, these Kyoto artisans are known for the poetic names they give to each sweet, particularly the moist ones served before the thick tea. Often based on notable historic events, characters, or even quotations in Japanese literature, the sweets become a kind of riddle that fits into the underlying theme of the tea ceremony. At the confectioner Shioyoshi-ken, for example, there is a special sweet named after Princess Kogo, a famous imperial concubine, who became so heartbroken when the emperor outgrew his love for her that she fled to a nunnery in the western region of Arashiyama. In the center of the sugary sweet lies a teardrop of salty fermented soybean—a reminder of the bittersweet nature of love.

The more ambiguous these thematic hints (and they are not just limited to the sweets at a tea ceremony), the more thrilling the discovery for the tea guests, if, indeed, they ever solve the riddle.

Stephen came into the kitchen sporting a jolly watermelon-pink shirt and pants the color of grape jelly. He beckoned me over to a sitting area near the sink. "Did you bring a notebook?"

I nodded.

"Good, pull it out." He collapsed on a stool, letting his legs splay open. I sat down Indian-style on the stone floor with my notepad on my knee.

"First of all, you need to understand the courses of a tea kaiseki and the ones we're going to serve today," he said, rubbing his nose. "The stuff we made in class last week, those are part of *osechi ryori* (honorable seasonal cooking), or New Year's foods. They might show up in different parts of a New Year's tea kaiseki, but they're not all that you'd get."

I scrawled what I could as Stephen went on to explain the various dishes we were going to make that day and how they followed the format of a traditional tea kaiseki. Despite his best intentions, he often veered off on tangents related to such things as his love of trees or his difficulty with finding comfortable shoes in Japan. But as he jackrabbited around the subject of tea kaiseki, I was able to piece together his remarks and ultimately understand the order and number of dishes served at a traditional tea kaiseki meal.

In reaction to the lavish honzen ryori–style kaiseki that the aristocracy favored in the sixteenth century, a movement arose to create a more frugal style similar to the "medicine" meals the monks ate in the temples before their whipped green tea. Sen no Rikyu is credited for this new perspective, known as the wabi-style of tea.

Drawing heavily on Zen Buddhism, Rikyu felt every tea kaiseki should be a humble expression of the heart, instead of a showy multiplicity of courses made with rare and expensive ingredients served on numerous gold-legged trays. At its essence, the tea kaiseki would be fit for a Buddhist monk, who through the drinking of the sacred whipped green tea might reach nirvana. According to Rikyu: "Chanoyu (the formal practice of preparing and consuming whipped powdered green tea) of the small room [teahouse] is above all a matter of practicing and realizing the way in accord with the Buddha's teaching. To delight in the splendor of a dwelling or the taste of a sumptuous meal belongs to a worldly life. There is enough shelter when the roof does not leak, and enough food when it keeps one from starving. This is the Buddha's teaching and the fundamental intent of Chanoyu."

In Rikyu's opinion, "enough food" translated into approximately one soup and three side dishes. In addition to the miso soup, there would be a marinated raw fish or vegetable dish, called the *mukozuke*, the climactic dish, or wanmori, and a grilled item, known as the *yakimono* (literally, "grilled thing"). This became the ideal format for a tea kaiseki.

After Rikyu's death, tea kaiseki developed along two paths: the wabi style he promoted and, once again, a more lavish form. The latter style surfaced around 1615, shortly after the Tokugawa Shogunate established control over the nation. It became more standardized during the Genroku era (1688–1704), when the merchant class rose to economic power and wanted to put on more elaborate kaiseki to show off their wares and new social status.

But there was a major problem: both styles of tea kaiseki used the same Chinese characters and people were getting confused. So around the 1750s several tea masters came up with the clever idea of using different sets of Chinese characters to distinguish between the two different styles of tea kaiseki.

For the frugal temple-style tea kaiseki that Rikyu's followers practiced, they chose the characters for "bosom-pocket stone." That is because one of the many meanings for kai is "bosom-pocket" and seki is "stone," and this spartan form of tea kaiseki served the same purpose as the heated "medicine stones" (yakuseki) that the monks once tucked into the front fold of their kimonos to ward off hunger. By creating a Zen Buddhist link between the two terms, this style of tea kaiseki became infused with religious overtones and thus is the standard version used today.

To describe the lavish party-style tea kaiseki, the original characters for "group-gathering place" were used. During the latter part of the Tokugawa/Edo era (1600–1868), when teahouses and traditional inns began serving food and sake, this fancy version left the tea realm for public restaurants. The tea component was basically dropped, and the courses were switched around and altered, leaving what now is known as restaurant kaiseki.

Since Stephen and David were hosting a standard Rikyu-style tea kaiseki, the first tray held the traditional offerings of miso soup, a bowl of white rice (considered so integral to the meal it wasn't counted as a "dish"), and the marinated raw fish dish. Counting the lids of the rice and soup bowls, plus the dish for the marinated fish, there were five serving pieces on the tray, a number that corresponded to the five nesting bowls monks eat their food from in Zen temples.

Originally, raw fish was not served in ancient Kyoto because of its inland location. Locals could not eat sashimi in the morning because the fishing boats from Osaka had not returned to port. By evening, the Kyoto people (being sticklers for freshness) felt the fish had been out of the water too long to be eaten raw. As a result, many fishermen salted much of their catch on the beaches and then had it sent to Kyoto by runners along what came to be known as the Mackerel Highway. It wasn't until the Meiji Period (1868–1912) that Kyoto began serving raw fish that wasn't salted or pickled.

Our next course would be the wanmori, similar to the simmered piled-up dish we had made in class. Only instead of putting duck in our wanmori, we would use turkey. Like all wanmori, it would require the host's greatest effort.

Following the wanmori we would serve the yakimono. Stephen had spotted some huge shiitake mushroom caps at the market that we would baste with mirin, sake, and soy and then grill over the burner.

After the grilled dish, we would continue to offer a few more items because even Rikyu broke his own rules, particularly when he was entertaining the emperor or members of the aristocracy. One such item we would offer is the *hashiarai*, meaning "chopstick wash." Consisting of a small amount of hot water served plain or seasoned with sour plum and salt (salt and plum being the Chinese characters for "seasoning"), it "rinses" the smoky charred flavors from the grilled course in order to ready the chopsticks and palate for the next one. It was a frugal temple-like move that enabled the guests to recycle their chopsticks, instead of switching to a new pair. This was a departure from the established court etiquette, whereby each guest would receive a new pair of chopsticks with every honzen ryori meal tray.

After the chopstick wash, guests would encounter the *hassun*, named after the square cedar tray upon which the foods are served. *Hatchi* means "eight" and *sun* is a unit of length just longer than an inch; when the two words combine, they're pronounced "hassun." The tray measures eight sun units on all four sides.

Every hassun at a tea kaiseki holds something from the ocean and the mountains; therefore our offerings would consist of cuttlefish and jumbo sugar-cooked black soybeans threaded onto green bamboo picks.

After that, we would end the meal like the monks do in temples with rice, pickles, and tea. Only instead of boiled rice, we would serve the traditional tea kaiseki rice dish of *yuto*, named after the black lacquer hot water pitcher in which the dish arrives.

In former times, when monks cooked their temple food over

fire, inevitably, a layer of scorched rice would cover the bottom of the rice pot. So in the Zen tradition of letting nothing go to waste, the monks would scrape up the cap of rice, break it into shards, and serve it almost as a soup in warm salt-seasoned water. As for the tea, that would be David's special offering.

"Let's get going," said Stephen, handing me an apron. I checked my watch; it read 9:30. The guests had been invited for noon. I set my notebook aside, pulled off my sweater, and pushed my turtleneck sleeves past my elbows. Under Stephen's guidance, I began to make lotus root balls.

Tea kaiseki dishes are highly creative, both visually and sym-bolically, yet use everyday temple fare, such as miso, tofu, and veg-etables, like lotus root. Not only that, in keeping with the monastic concept of plainness, tea kaiseki dishes are prepared in a basic manner, usually boiled, grilled, and simmered. They are also seasoned with an extremely delicate hand, to avoid compet-ing with the flavor of the tea to come. That means no onions, gar-lic, or strong spices. What elevates the food to a near divine status, however, is the thought and care involved in turning these ingre-dients into something special, combined with the setting in which they are served.

After peeling the potato-like tubers, I grated them into a slushy mound, which I pushed through a horsehair colander with my palm. After mixing in some dissolved lumps of kudzu—a rocky snow-white starch that resembles cocaine—I rolled the lotus root dough into marble-size spheres, then dropped them into sim-mering water. When they floated to the surface, like gnocchi, I re-trieved them with a small wire net and placed them in a bowl.

These tiny snowballs (hinting of winter and the coming of the New Year) would go into the miso soup on the first tray. But unlike a traditional tea kaiseki miso soup (a combination of red and white miso), Stephen's would be made exclusively with sweet white miso, and lots of it, to create a creamy blend as rich and thick as bisque. The lotus root balls would be a soft spongy fillip to break up the monotony of the smooth soup. I slid one into my mouth. It was light and mildly sweet like a potato dumpling. Several weeks earlier I would have said it tasted bland.

I confess when I first arrived in Kyoto, sushi aside, much of what I ate I felt lacked seasoning. Back in New York I would cook Asian food with masses of garlic, ginger, and toasted sesame oil. With John egging me on, I'd whack sticks of lemongrass, smash shallots, and grind up pungent spices all in the name of getting us high on flavor. And when those ingredients wore off, we'd hit the stinky shrimp paste, asafetida, and habaneros, bombarding our palates with more, more, more, until our scalps tingled from my overwrought creations.

Then I came to Kyoto, the city of refined and delicate Japanese cooking. And like a junkie, I initially craved my stimulants. But then, ever so slowly, I started tasting—really tasting—the ingredients. It was like entering a dark room on a sunny day. At first you can't see anything, but over time you begin to detect shapes, which slowly turn into discernible objects with real colors.

During those first few weeks, particularly when I encountered soups, ingredients would whisper at me from the bowl. Eventually, I would respond and recognize their subtle character, such as the light soy sauce favored by cooks in Kyoto for its gentle color and soft flavor. Or a dashi made with just kelp, instead of bonito flakes and kelp.

The mark of a highly sophisticated palate in Japan is a person's ability to distinguish slight differences between, say, ten different types of tofu, or sea bream, or soba. This knack for discerning such minute variations likely stems from the pastime *monoawase*, a sort of guessing game that the Japanese developed to compare various objects.

In the early part of the fourteenth century, tea contests became a kind of monoawase. The aristocracy would amuse themselves by tasting dozens of cups of whipped green tea in order to guess where the tea leaves had been grown and which of the many waters used to make the samples was superior. (Kyoto was known for the quality of its water.)

"Have you seen my *tabi?*" asked David, poking his head into the kitchen. These are the formal white socks worn with kimono that separate at the big toe to accommodate the thong of a sandal.

"No. Try the bedroom." Stephen didn't look up, but kept grating a gluey Japanese mountain yam into a bowl. It looked unnervingly like something fit for a Kleenex, but he assured me it would taste fabulous once the recipe was finished. After blending the yam with rice flour and sugar to form a dough, Stephen would form it into small flat rounds. In the center of these, he would place a smidgen of chopped dried dates, apricots, and Chinese papaya that had been macerated in plum wine, sort of like an Asian mincemeat. After crimping the dough into balls, he would steam them until light and cakey.

"Did you get the flowers for the *tokonoma?*" yelled David from the other room. The tokonoma is the decorative alcove in a teahouse. David and Stephen had a genuine teahouse on their property.

"I did not," whined Stephen. "David, I can't do everything. You're going to have to go out and get them. Now leave me alone." Stephen looked up at me and faked tearing his hair out.

"What can I do next?" I quickly offered.

"Place the beans on the skewers for the hassun," said Stephen, handing me a bowl of shiny stout black beans. "The skewers are on that shelf." He pointed to a cellophane packet of green bamboo toothpicks with their tops tied into pretty little loops.

"How many should I make?" I asked, popping a bean in my mouth. The skin was leathery, but then gave way to a creamy sugar-drenched interior. Served on the cedar tray with the chewy cuttlefish boiled in salt and sake, this dish would be a nice mix of sweet and salty. Kind of like peanut M&M's, I thought, eating another one.

"Make nine skewers," answered Stephen. "You'll need four for the guests, one for David, and then one for you, me, Brad, and Kyle to eat later."

"They're pretty, eh?" He ate a bean. "Try one," he said, pointing to the bowl. I took another.

"The secret is nails," he said. "Just wrap a few in cheesecloth and add them to the pot as they cook. Keeps the beans nice and black."

I stabbed a bean with the skewer. "How many beans to a pick?"

"Just three."

I continued making the tiny bean kebobs that looked more appropriate for a dollhouse of vegetarians than a roomful of tea guests. "Are you sure three is enough?"

"Yes," replied Stephen. "You want the guests to leave the teahouse just a little bit hungry, so they'll remember the meal and want to return for more."

While he and I worked in the kitchen, David and his helpers readied the tearoom. I couldn't imagine what they were doing. How much had to be done? Stephen assured me "lots," starting with the garden.

First, the roji had to be checked to make sure there were no twigs or shrubbery along the path that could catch on the hems and sides of the guests' kimonos. Then the stepping stones needed to be scrubbed. The moss around them had to be cleaned and "fluffed" with a broom. Gutters and drains needed to be freed of debris, including spiders, which if found, in the Buddhist tradition of considering all living things sacred, would need to be "relocated." The stone washbasin had to be washed and filled with fresh water because that is where the guests would purify their mouths and hands before entering the tearoom. "And then," said Stephen, laughing, "David has to prepare the tearoom."

Because it was the cold season, the fire pit in the tearoom would be used. In tea, the year divides into two parts: November through April, when the tea master uses a sunken hearth to boil the water for tea, and May through October, when he uses a portable charcoal brazier.

To prepare for his guests, David had to attend to dozens of details, including finding just the right-size pieces of charcoal to put in the sunken hearth. The size of the charcoal would determine the time it would take to create the hearth's proper temperature to boil water for the tea, which had to be calculated precisely to coincide with the end of our tea kaiseki meal.

By 10:30, Stephen and I had completed most of the cooking. Brad had briefly popped in to help Stephen prepare the sweets, then left to get dressed, while I had finished simmering the cuttlefish for the hassun. After Stephen put on the rice, he slipped the cedar tray in a sink of cold water to soak. The water would fill the wood's pores, thus preventing any strong flavors from seeping in. Wetting the rose-colored wood would also give the tray a look of freshness and offer the illusion that the beans had been just-picked and the cuttlefish recently caught.

David shuffled toward Stephen in a regal midnight-blue kimono and bowed. Tea kimonos differ from formal and dance kimonos in that the sleeves are shorter, to ease the practice of preparing tea. The front panel is also wider in order to stay snug during the constant getting down on one's knees. "Guests will be here in less than an hour," he announced, then shuffled out.

I felt a rise of panic. "Don't worry, dear," said Stephen, with a laugh. "We're doing fine. Just first-time jitters."

At 11:45, I heard voices in the garden. Tea guests traditionally arrive fifteen minutes early, whereupon they enter the main gate and head to the waiting pavilion. There, they remove their coats, set down umbrellas or packages, and enjoy the hot welcome drink. Stephen had prepared tiny cups of boiled water, drawn from the same source David would use for the tea, and flavored it with ginger juice. Brad put the cups on a tray and delivered them to the guests.

Kyle, now clad in a dashing wilderness-green silk kimono and spanking split-toed socks, stayed on our side of the *fusuma*, ready to serve the tea kaiseki. A fusuma is a thick paper-covered sliding panel used to separate rooms; in our case the kitchen from the tearoom.

After the guests had finished their hot drink in the waiting pavilion, David entered the tea garden to rinse his hands and mouth with water from a wooden bucket that he would then pour into a stone basin. Ideally, the water is drawn from a sacred spring or well at dawn, since dawn water is called "flower of the well" and is what traditionally was used to make religious offerings, as well as medicine. When David had finished purifying his mind and spirit, he would open the middle gate and greet his guests. By doing so, he would figuratively clear the path for the guests' journey to possible enlightenment.

Soon, the voices in the garden grew noticeably louder and

more distinct as the guests made their way from the middle gate to the tearoom. In traditional tea fashion, they would walk slowly to create distance between themselves. This would give them the appropriate personal space to transition from their material self to their spiritual persona, since walking the roji symbolically strips one naked. This baring of the soul enables the guests to share themselves with each other in the tearoom and stay open to transformation.

Several minutes later, I heard the guests admiring the scroll in the alcove. From what I could tell, there were two women and two men. The ideal number of guests at a tea ceremony (with or without a kaiseki meal) is four, so when the tea master joins them the group becomes five. That is because most tearooms are quite small (often four and one half tatami) and serving more than four guests would be cramped and cumbersome.

In addition to having a "first guest," or guest of honor, every formal tea ceremony with a kaiseki meal has a "last guest." The "first guest" is the one person the tea master has chosen to honor, for whatever reason (to commemorate a special birthday or personal accomplishment). The "last guest" is usually a friend or relative of the tea master, who is extremely knowledgeable about tea etiquette and can almost act as a "helper." The other two guests tend to be friends of the guest of honor.

At exactly 12:15, Stephen began the tea kaiseki. He didn't move fast but laid out four square black lacquer trays carefully and precisely on a small ledge in the kitchen—inches away from the sliding panel into the tearoom. He ladled out the creamy miso soup, whereupon I dropped in two lotus root balls and, as directed, helped Brad place the bowls in the bottom right corner of each tray. In the bottom left corner of the trays we placed a black bowl holding a small scoop of steamed rice. Toward the top of the tray, thus creating a triangle, Stephen set down the mukozuke (literally, "beyond attach"), because this marinated fish or vegetable dish is supposed to sit beyond the rice and miso soup but stay attached to them by virtue of being situated at the apex of the triangle. The fish of choice was a mouthful of *maguro* (nonfatty tuna) cubes tossed with diced avocado, dashi, wasabi, soy, and mirin.

Normally, tuna doesn't show up at a tea kaiseki because the brilliant ruby flesh is considered too gaudy. White fish is preferred for its pure understated elegance. Avocado also rarely appears because it is considered quite modern. But Stephen was giving his tea kaiseki an American twist.

He added another personal touch to his tea kaiseki by placing a "welcome dish" on this first tray. Apparently, first-time tea kaiseki guests are given such an offering, which in this case was a small saucer of slippery caramel-colored mushrooms tossed with yuzu citrus juice and grated daikon.

The last item on the tray was a pair of cedar chopsticks that had been soaked in water and wiped dry. Stephen rested them on the tray's edge so that they lay parallel to the bottom, sticking out just a tad on the right-hand side. These chopsticks are called *Rikyu-bashi* and are exclusively used for tea kaiseki. They're a combination of the words *Rikyu*, from Sen no Rikyu, who first started using them, and the Japanese word for chopsticks, which is *hashi*. (The "h" changes to a "b" when the words combine.)

Kyle came over to where Stephen was bent over his work.

"Ready?" he whispered. Stephen stood up and nodded and Kyle gracefully picked up the first tray and delivered it to the guest of honor. He returned and, one by one, brought out the remaining trays. Coos of approval drifted back to the kitchen.

While the guests ate, we started preparing the heart of the

kaiseki meal. But before it went out, Stephen handed Kyle a pot of hot sake. Kyle would deliver it to David, who in turn would serve it to the guests as an accompaniment to their tuna and avocado. I wondered if the sake would make the guests tipsy and ruin their appreciation for the tea.

"No, it will relax them," replied Stephen. "Nothing worse than a room full of uptight tea guests. Hiromi, who teaches tea with David, is out there and she could sure use a little loosening up." He cackled and handed me a stack of wanmori bowls.

Slightly larger than the plain black bowls used for the miso soup, the wanmori bowls were especially beautiful because of the graceful gold flowers painted around the base and lid. I lined them up on the kitchen ledge, and in the center of each Stephen laid a velvety slab of just-cooked turkey meat. Over the meat, I placed a square of soft wheat gluten. Stephen tucked in a slice of just-cooked carrot and perched a tight rectangular stack of blanched chrysanthemum leaves up against the turkey. I balanced a piece of yuzu zest—cut like a split pine needle—over the greens, while Stephen filled the bowl one third of the way up with a rich turkey broth. Brad placed the lids over the bowls and then handed one to Kyle, who carried it out on a tray to the guest of honor. We arranged the remaining soups on a large tray, which Kyle retrieved from the kitchen ledge.

Next, we began grilling the mushrooms for the yakimono. After the giant shiitake caps turned limp and soggy from their continuous soy-mirin basting, Stephen transferred them to a cutting board. "Remember, they're using chopsticks," he said, scoring the caps into bite-size chunks. "You don't want them to wrestle with the food and have it plop on their kimonos. Everything should be bite-size at a tea kaiseki. You want to avoid messy drippy sauces." This holds true for Japanese cuisine in general. Few dishes involve sauces because they cannot be eaten with chopsticks. Traditional Japanese cuisine tends to be so healthy because it uses no butter or cream. The Buddhist taboo against eating meat and dairy products until the Meiji Restoration (1868–1912) further contributed to the culture's aversion to greasy tastes.

For a pleasing contrast, Stephen piled the round brown caps on a cream-colored square dish. Japanese cooks, particularly tea kaiseki and restaurant kaiseki masters, treat food arrangement as a fine art. To create exciting patterns for diners, chefs carefully choose opposing shapes, such as a square vessel for round foods or a round container for block-shaped food. No two serving dishes of the same shape or style should ever be used in succession to avoid repetition.

If a square dish is placed on a square tray, the dish can be turned so that the angled corners face the flat sides of the tray, thus breaking the dull monotony of horizontal and linear lines. To juxtapose lengths, foods are cut into long and short shapes. To contrast size, chefs place both big and small foods on the same plate.

So many details, I thought, watching Stephen stack the mushrooms with his chopsticks. In addition to food arrangement, seasonality plays an integral part in the Japanese kitchen.

Eating a meal in Japan is said to be a communion with nature. This particularly holds true for both tea and restaurant kaiseki, where foods at their peak of freshness reflect the seasonal spirit of that month. The seasonal spirit for November, for example, is "Beginning Anew," because according to the old Japanese lunar calendar, November marks the start of the new tea year. The spring tea leaves that had been placed in sealed jars to mature are ready to grind into tea. The foods used for a tea kaiseki should carry out this seasonal theme and be available locally, not flown in from some exotic locale.

For December, the spirit is "Freshness and Cold." Thus, the colors of the guests' kimonos should be dark and subdued for winter, while the incense that permeates the tearoom after the meal should be rich and spicy. The scroll David chose to hang in the alcove during the tea kaiseki no doubt depicted winter, through either words or an ink drawing. As for the flowers that would replace the scroll for the tea ceremony, David likely would incorporate a branch of pine to create a subtle link with the pine needle–shaped piece of yuzu zest we had placed in the climactic dish. Both hinted at the winter season and coming of New Year's, one of David's underlying themes for the tea kaiseki. Some of the guests might never make the pine needle connection, but it was there to delight those who did.

Kyle discreetly slid open the tearoom panel to check on the guests' progress. "They're ready for the yakimono," he whispered.

"We're ready for them," Stephen said, handing Kyle the pile of smoky succulent mushroom caps. Each guest would take one from the communal dish.

Very often during a tea kaiseki, the tea master decides to serve several more dishes beyond the core meal. If guests request more sake, for example, the host has ready a dish to accompany it. Usually called the *shiizakana*, meaning "insisting fish," it is almost always seafood because that is considered sake's tastiest companion. In keeping with the Zen temple tenet of letting nothing go to waste, any ingredients left over from preparing a tea kaiseki would often be fashioned into a dish called the *azukebachi* (literally, "entrusted bowl"), so named because it is left in the tearoom with the guests, so they can serve themselves.

Because there were chrysanthemum leaves left over from our turkey wanmori, Stephen decided to serve them as an azukebachi. So we microwaved the bitter greens until tender, chopped them into bite-size pieces, and then dressed them with a syrup of boiled-down sake and soy sauce and crushed pine nuts.

Since it is tea kaiseki protocol for guests to request more sake, we had ready a very small portion of the "insisting fish" dish, creamy lobes of sea urchin livened with a puckery blend of lemon juice, soy sauce, and grated horseradish and garnished with a top-knot of shredded nori. I wondered how the guests would leave Stephen's teahouse "just a little bit hungry" given all this food.

"You must remember," emphasized Stephen, "each course consists of literally one or two bites."

Before my black bean skewers and salted cuttlefish went out on the cedar tray, each guest received a chopstick wash. Stephen ladled some kelp broth into a lacquer container shaped like a tall lidded custard cup. He added some hot water to dilute it and a drop of Kyoto-style soy, lighter in color than regular soy but saltier in taste and tinged with sweet sake, which is added during the aging process. Following his instructions, I tied together three stems of *mitsuba* (Japanese wild chervil) and dropped them into the broth.

"That," said Stephen, pointing to the knot, "means, 'Come back again.' " For those who knew the language of Japanese food, this small gesture would please them. For those who didn't, it was simply a pretty crunch of green.

Next came the cedar tray holding cuttlefish and black bean skewers. Sake always accompanies this course because it mimics a Shinto ritual called a *naorai*. At a naorai, the cedar tray is filled with food and offered to the deities, along with the rice wine. The followers then consume the food and drink in order to share in the divinity. The idea for using the cedar tray at a tea kaiseki has been attributed to Rikyu, who decided to place some tidbits on the Shinto tray to elevate his tea guests to the status of gods.

Since sake is considered the essence of rice, it is, therefore, the nectar of the gods. To add deeper meaning to the ritual, David would drink sake with each one of his guests, zigzagging his way down the line in a special choreographed manner. This is the only time during a tea kaiseki when the host shares anything with his guests.

While the guests enjoyed the cedar tray of goodies and sipped their rice wine with David, Brad began assembling various kinds of pickles. Called *konomono* (literally, "a thing for incense"), they got their name back in the tenth century when incense-sniffing contests were a popular game among the nobility. When the contestants felt their sense of smell was becoming dull, they would eat an astringent pickle to clear their nasal passages. At a tea kaiseki, the pickles serve a similar purpose; they cleanse the palate for the tea to come.

For the pickle course, Stephen had salted and pressed some chopped red, white, and green cabbage. Brad formed it into a small heap (about the size of a boiled egg) and placed it on a jade-colored stoneware communal dish. But instead of just dumping the cabbage in the center of the dish, he arranged it slightly off center, along with a few other pickled vegetables to create a pleasing visual. Irregularity of space adds rhythm and excitement.

The last course would consist of the scorched remains of the cooked rice that we were supposed to mix with lightly salted water. But here we encountered one of the many problems that threaten to destroy the integrity of a traditional tea kaiseki in today's world: technology. Stephen had made the rice in his electric rice cooker, which left no brittle cap of rice at the bottom of the cooking pot to mix with lightly salted water. So we had two options: one, get out a skillet and do some fast dry-frying to render the rice "scorched"; or simply fill the special black lacquer rice container with the dense remains of the rice cooker. Stephen chose the latter and out went the rice. The tea kaiseki was over.

As is customary, David would begin the formal tea ceremony by serving a moist sweet, after which the guests would leave the tearoom to rinse their mouths with water drawn from the stone basin in the garden. Several minutes later, they would return to the tearoom for the ceremonial tea. If there had been no tea kaiseki, the guests would have arrived, eaten their sweets, and waited for the tea master to prepare their tea.

Since the guests had eaten a tea kaiseki meal, however, we set about arranging the sweets, which, as Stephen predicted, were gorgeous. The grated yam balls had transmuted into ivory truffle-like puffs, which we placed on camellia leaves and arranged in various tiers of a stacking black lacquer serving box.

While the guests savored the sweets, we began washing dishes. We washed more dishes while David whipped and served the thick green tea. We continued washing dishes while the guests ate a dry sweet and sipped a bowl of thin green tea. By the time the last guest had tiptoed out of the garden and back toward home, we were wiping dry the last of the wanmori bowls and lids.

It was almost 6:30 when David stepped into the kitchen to help himself to some of the leftovers. Tea masters rarely, if ever, eat with their guests at a tea kaiseki because they want to concentrate fully on serving their guests. To a Westerner, this sounds odd. Imagine inviting four people over for a special dinner and spending the entire evening in the kitchen. (Granted, some cooks feel that way at the end of an ambitious dinner party.)

Most tea masters do not indulge because they see themselves as a master of ceremonies, or high priest presiding over the happiness and comfort of their guests. The exception, of course, is when the tea master shares the zigzag sake ritual during the hassun. (To avoid getting drunk, David had wolfed down a peanut butter sandwich shortly before the guests arrived.)

So between mouthfuls of leftover grilled mushrooms, rice, and chrysanthemum greens, David rightfully praised Stephen for the extraordinary tea kaiseki he had just put on. It had been an amazing display of culinary workmanship. Kyle and Brad also picked at some of the food, while I finished wiping the counters and cleaning the sink. Shortly before 7:00, I hooked the dishrag over the handle of the fridge and went to retrieve my coat.

"Are you sure you don't want to come with us to the sento?" asked Stephen, now slumped against the kitchen wall. "It's really amazing inside."

I certainly needed a bath, but gave a weary shake of my head. Maybe next time. I wound the red scarf around my neck and thanked Stephen and David for letting me help. It had been an incredible day, a day that had surpassed my greatest hopes. History, art, nature, food, and religion had all combined into a complicated aesthetic that defied comparison to anything I had ever experienced, even at Mushanokoji. David had practiced an ancient Chinese ritual that Kyoto's Zen monks had synthesized with the Japanese culture. He had placed a scroll and then a flower arrangement in an area of the tearoom modeled after the same type of alcove found in Buddhist temples. The flowers, arranged in a loose natural manner (compared to the highly stylized arrangements of ikebana) would be tossed out after the tea ceremony to represent the ephemerality of life. David had chosen specific tea utensils and serving pieces appropriate to the winter weather and formality of the occasion. The meal—a sumptuous sequence of nuanced flavors, textures, and visual artistry—glorified the bounty of nature. Sprinkled throughout the whole event were layers of symbolism that reinforced tradition, enshrined various aspects of the Japanese culture, and celebrated the very nature of temporal existence. I could not have imagined a more wonderful meal conceived, cooked, and enjoyed on so many levels than the one we had created that day. So instead of heading off to the public bath to wash it all off, I wanted to savor it again on the moonlit walk home.

8.

English
Fun World

$\mathcal{F}$ riends had warned me Japan would be expensive, and living in Kyoto had proved to be so. In addition to needing money to cover the cost of rent, food, and Japanese language classes, I had several unexpected purchases, including a small electric heater for my room at the Guesthouse, which I bought after catching a vicious cold that held me hostage to my futon for several days. I also needed money for tea kaiseki classes.

The natural solution was to teach. Hundreds of Japanese schools and vocational colleges needed "native English speakers" to improve the accents and language skills of their students. Businesses wanted teachers to work on their employees' diction and understanding of the American business culture. Housewives were eager to study English for the social cachet, as well as for those "emergency" moments when they might be asked to dine with one of their husband's Western business clients.

Through word of mouth and interviewing I managed to secure several teaching positions. This was astounding when I thought about it, considering the importance of education in Japan and the fact I had never taught. But since I had the requisite "professional attitude," "university degree," and "enthusiastic and reliable" demeanor, that is how I found myself teaching English to high school students at The New School in downtown Kyoto; businessmen at the Henkel Hakusai chemical company in Osaka; two housewives at a coffee shop every Tuesday morning; and five- and six-year-olds at Tomiko's school, English Fun World. Without a doubt, those children were my most challenging students, as evidenced by my first day.

"Ooooooo-eee—" squealed five-year-old Saki, bouncing around the English Fun World classroom like a human pogo stick. Her pigtails snapped back and forth as she chased and tagged several boys and girls, who had just arrived for their first conversational English class. Several small bowed legs, many patched with Hello Kitty Band-Aids, darted around the two wooden benches—one behind the other—facing a plastic wipe board.

"Sensei, sensei," wailed one little boy, hoping to be rescued from Saki's grip on his Snoopy backpack.

"Shhhhhh," I said, putting my index finger to my lips. I glanced at the clock hanging on the pink-and-white-flowered wall. It read 3:00. Class would last for one hour.

"Okay, okay, everybody, let's sit down," I said, motioning the children over to the wooden benches. Several small heads spun around, curious to see who was uttering these strange sounds. Japanese jabber flew around the room, while I gently guided eight squirming bodies to seats. A straggler walked in, deposited his Ninja Turtle backpack on the floor, and squeezed onto the bench. When the commotion had finally died down, I drew myself up to my full height and introduced myself.

"I am teacher Victoria," I announced. Fits of giggling ensued. I had gone to some trouble to look professorial in my black wool business skirt, black-and-earth-toned sweater, and black stockings. But I felt like a clown. My feet were swimming in the powder pink terry scuffs that Tomiko had insisted I wear "to avoid scratching up the parquet," she had said, handing them to me at the door.

I wrote my name on the wipe board with magic marker in big blue letters. "VIC-TOR-IA." I said it again slowly, tapping my chest.

"Bi-cu-to-ria," repeated Saki. She threw her head back in laughter, exposing a small strip of pink gum where her two front teeth were missing. Several tiny bodies hunched over and started shaking. After I had shushed most of the chatter, I pointed out that "Victoria" is spelled with a *V* not a *B*. I placed my front teeth over my bottom lip and made the *V* sound several times. This was an important distinction to make because the Japanese not only have no *V* in their language, they have no *L* sound either.

The room echoed with *V*s. But in seconds the aping game was over. I pointed to myself, said my name, and then pointed to Saki. She placed her index finger on her velvety nose and in a jittery I-am-about-to-pee-in-my-pants voice, cackled something in Japanese. The whole room broke up. She turned around to the row behind her, obviously pleased with her comic flair. I gave her a closed mouth smile then tried to redeem myself by convincing the rest of the children to say their names. I was met with perplexed looks and sputters of laughter.

I pointed to myself and again said my name. Silence. My eyes flicked to the clock. It stared back: 3:12. I looked down at the children. They gazed up at me. And then I realized I had nothing to say. The teacher before me had not explained the curriculum. Tomiko had not filled me in.

"Let's play Simon Says," I finally announced, gesturing for them to stand up. I told them to touch their fingers to their heads. Blank stares. I repeated the command, saying the word "head" and patting mine several times with my hand. They patted their heads and laughed. I opened my eyes wide, craned my neck toward them and said, "H-E-A-D. Simon says, 'touch your head.' " More laughs and head pats. The clock read 3:15.

"Okay, Simon says, 'touch your knees.' " I touched my knees and repeated the noun several times. Someone got the hiccups. The room broke up. Then I tried the word "head" again, not sure whether they were getting it. Getting anything for that matter. Laughter had become the language of the hour.

"Simon says touch your fingers. Touch your toes." I had forgotten that one wasn't supposed to touch the body part unless Simon commanded. Hey, at that point, it didn't matter. I figured we were learning body parts. We were passing time. 3:17. More hiccups.

At that moment, Tomiko stole into the room, carrying a folding metal chair. Several kids ran toward her. She spoke rapidly in Japanese, then shooed them back to their places. "I'm just here to observe," she said, glancing over at me and setting up her chair. "Continue."

I cleared my throat. The room became so quiet I could actually hear the clock tick. Tomiko looked over at me expectantly, as if to say, "I hope I've made a good investment." Frankly, I wasn't sure.

Tomiko, at the age of thirty-nine, had just established English Fun World, while at the same time teaching English as a second language at a school in downtown Kyoto. She understood Japan's need to enter the international market and knew the art of speaking English would be a critical skill for future generations. So she had turned a spare bedroom on the second floor of her home into a classroom.

Looking at Tomiko perched on her chair, I thought about how different she was from most Japanese women her age. Not only did she run her own business but she also had no children. She had gotten married late in life, perhaps because she did not fit the mold of a traditional Japanese woman. Instead of appearing modest and weak, she exuded a sense of confidence and strength. Instead of being slim and petite, she was quite tall and thick around the waist. A touch of makeup smoothed her ruddy complexion and nicely softened her strong features and pixie haircut. A slight underbite gave her an endearing grin, which she flashed often. She had a terrific sense of humor.

Saki jumped up and said something to Tomiko. Several other kids got up and started clowning around. "Okay, okay," I said, clapping my hands, "let's sit down, PLEASE!" Several of the children mimicked me and started clapping.

Tomiko shushed Saki and sent her back to her seat, along with the other kids. Saki nudged her seatmate. What an imp, I thought.

Suddenly, I had a brainstorm: birthday party games! That's it, I would amuse them with birthday party games. I ran through my childhood years trying to remember the different games I had played at friends' houses and my own: Stepping stones, similar to musical chairs, only instead of chairs you used colored squares of construction paper. Forget it, no paper. Under the broom? No. Pin the tail on the donkey? No. Red light green light. How did that go?

Saki got up and whispered something again to Tomiko, who must have scolded her because she came back and plopped herself down on the bench with a frown. Ha, serves her right, I thought, meanly.

I took a deep breath. Lullabies? Limericks? 3:28. Come on, brain, help me out. Then, suddenly, I was back at the North Shore Nursery School in Manchester, Massachusetts, singing along with my teacher Mrs. McDiarmid.

"Eeeeeeensy weensy spider crawled—" Several tiny hands flew to their mouths to cover the laughter. 3:31. A little boy farted. Everyone broke up. I changed songs, telling myself I wasn't getting paid enough to do this.

"All-rightee, Old Macdonald had a farm, e-i-e-i-o. And on that farm there was a cow—mooooooo," I bellowed. Saki doubled over. So did most of the other kids, who were still laughing over the fart. Balled fists punched into tummies as they wheezed and guffawed. I mooed again. More laughter. I smiled, not so much at the kids, though they were kind of cute and funny all scrunched over, but more at the absurdity of it all. What was I doing here? A psychology major in pink slippers mooing in a bedroom in Kyoto to a bunch of preschoolers. The same time a year before I had flown down solo to Trinidad and Tobago to meet with the head of the Tourist Board, since I had just been put in charge of the advertising account. I thought about how far I had fallen. Or had I? Maybe, given the paradoxical nature of Japan, I was on my way up!

With renewed enthusiasm, I started the song again. "Okay,

Old Macdonald had a farm, e-i-e-i-o. And on that farm there was a pig." I glanced over at Tomiko. Her eyes registered a mixture of amusement and hope. Even though I had put myself in the ungainly position of mimicking a sow, I still represented America, the place Tomiko had become enamored with on her first trip to California so many years ago. I was the country that said it was okay for her to feel different and live her life against the tide. So I continued oinking frantically to show her that she had fallen in love with something worthy.

Then Saki opened her mouth. And out of that little gap-toothed space came the shaky words, "O Macu-Donu ha-du ferm, e-ri-e-ri-ro." Why she chose to sing then, I'll never know. Perhaps giving in to my quiet desperation was simply another game. Or maybe she figured compliance would sponge away the dirty crumbs of her disruptive behavior before her mother came to pick her up.

Whatever it was, she clapped her tiny hands when she had finished. At 4:00, Tomiko stood up and announced the class was over.

I don't know how much the children understood that day, but in the end it didn't really matter. "They are here to learn the sounds of English," Tomiko assured me over tea several days later in her sitting room. "You can't expect them to learn grammar. That's not your job. Your job is to correct their pronunciation and help them feel comfortable speaking English." She bit into a biscuit and went on to explain that most Japanese read and write English exceptionally well but freeze when they have to speak it.

"They are afraid of making mistakes," she said, wiping cookie specks from her lap. "They are afraid of feeling ashamed."

The longer I stayed in Japan, the more familiar I became with the concepts of respect, obedience, and abiding by a community. Although I had been brought up in a society that prized individuality and independence, I came to understand the ways of a culture that encouraged people to let themselves be judged by those they loved and respected.

Tomiko had clearly found a haven of safety in our friendship, which worked because I offered her a mixture of the inside and outside. I could share in her native interests, such as a love of Japanese food, cooking, and art, yet as a foreigner, I would perpetually float outside her inner Japanese planet. This distance enabled her to share with me the Western side of herself that had no outlet in Japan.

But because Tomiko looked, thought, and acted differently from most Japanese women, she lived in a world of her own. And this made us both outsiders and ultimately good friends.

9.

Sliding Open the Shoji

They nicknamed me "the Bullet." It was a term of endearment I owed all to the tomato-red bicycle that Tomiko and Yasu lent me when I moved in with them the second week of December. They had invited me to live with them several weeks earlier over a dinner composed of *obanzai* (Kyoto home-style dishes), such as caramelized beef and potato supper pot and slow-braised radish wheels. The couple knew I had been looking for an apartment and offered the use of an empty classroom in their house. I had jumped at the chance to live with a Japanese family and experience their lives firsthand.

Their Western-style wood and stone home was located east of the Guesthouse in the same northern region of Kita-ku, so close to the mountains that from my bed at night I could smell cedar wafting through the open window. Cabbage patches, family restaurants, and modest homes dotted the neighborhood, often filled with the melodious croaking of local frogs.

Almost every morning, I would zoom off on the shiny red bicycle with my knapsack and books wedged into the front basket. After a day of teaching and studying Japanese, I would hop back on the bike, squeeze in an errand or two, and pedal madly uptown. After veering left at the neighborhood rice paddy, I would glide into Tomiko and Yasu's driveway, flushed, out of breath, and eager to catch up on their day over dinner. We were more or less like family.

Which was tremendously comforting. As everyone knows, living in a foreign country can be lonely. Japan magnifies this feeling because its natural geographic seclusion, combined with two centuries of self-imposed isolation, from 1638 to 1853, has made the culture more tight-knit and impenetrable to outsiders than almost any other country in the world. In fact, the Japanese word for foreigner is *gaijin*, meaning "outsider."

The culture also makes a strict delineation between interior and exterior. A carefully made-up face is what you show the outside world. Your true emotions stay locked behind the façade. What you do at home is your business. How you act in public is determined by the cultural code.

These rules of conduct evolved in feudal times when the various strata of Japanese society were given carefully prescribed ways to interact with one another. From the courtiers down to the samurai, craftsmen, merchants, and farmers, each class was forbidden to speak, eat, dress, and walk in any other way than what had been delegated to it.

A related hierarchy exists in the business world, where education and job achievement have become more important than class. This explains the vital practice of exchanging business cards.

At a glance you can determine a person's place in the corporate strata, then adjust your word choice and body language accordingly, using extremely polite language and a very low bow for a company president and casual language and a moderate bow for an entry-level worker. Many women even alter their voice pitch, using a higher tone for formal settings.

Outside of the business world, the "way" to behave emphasizes Confucian values of self-denial, obedience to authority, and silence over individual expression. Through observation, I rapidly learned how to conduct myself in public. When purchasing a drink from a vending machine, for example, I trained myself to stand next to the machine to finish the can's contents, then place it in the nearby recycle bin, instead of sipping the can on the go, which the Japanese consider rude. When wiping my hands with the moist washcloth in a Japanese restaurant, instead of leaving it crumpled in the basket, I remembered to neatly roll it back up just as I had found it, only with the soiled part hidden inside. And whenever I ordered something off a restaurant menu, such as a chocolate sundae at the Kyoto branch of the American-based Swensen's Ice Cream Company shop, I learned to scrape off the plastic whipped topping at the table, instead of making a fuss when ordering.

But Japan's cultural code can be elusive. Even among the Japanese, questions arise as to what is "appropriate." This was evident one afternoon when Tomiko took me to a female friend's art opening. After we had viewed the artist's ceramics, she served us each a cup of brewed green tea and a small sweet bean cake wrapped in tissue-thin rice paper. As I drank my tea, I noticed Tomiko tuck the cake in her purse, so I followed suit. Later when I asked Tomiko why she had taken the sweet, she explained that in Osaka, where she grew up, she would have left it behind. But in

Kyoto, she had learned to take the sweet with her to avoid insulting the host, who considered it a little gift.

Aside from having all these special manners and customs, Kyoto natives are known for being quite closed, which only adds to one's sense of estrangement. Even Tomiko described them as having an air of superiority; something I could understand having come from the small New England town of Manchester, north of Boston, Kyoto's Sister City. Nonetheless, despite their snooty attitude, even to other Japanese, Kyoto natives are respected. As a friend from Tokyo explained, "We're proud of them because they are carrying on all the old traditions."

Being an American woman in Kyoto closed the screen even tighter, particularly since women in Japan have highly traditional roles in this conservative society. What's more, every Westerner I passed on the street refused to make eye contact. It was as though by acknowledging me, I would ruin their Japanese experience. "Pretend you don't see me, so I can pretend I didn't see you," their body language seemed to say, as they quickly strode by.

But Tomiko and Yasu were different. They had reached out, slid open the shoji, and welcomed me into their home.

Before I moved, I had worried about the logistics of living with this Japanese couple. Who would use the shower first in the morning? Should I buy my own coffee for breakfast? How would we deal with dinner?

Because I was American, I was the only one who wanted to shower in the morning. I would rise around 7:00, go for a run, then shower when I returned. Tomiko and Yasu, like most Japanese, drew a bath in the evening to soak away the cares of the day before retiring to bed.

Yasu, a small, wiry man with thick black hair and steel-rimmed glasses, had often left for work by the time I came down for breakfast around 8:30. On those occasions when we did share breakfast, Yasu would kneel on a cushion in his blue jeans, work shirt, and bleached cotton athletic socks at the low redwood table on the rug in the family room fiddling with his walkie-talkie and eating the thick fingers of white toast that Tomiko prepared for him. He would then drive to his carpentry site, while Tomiko often crept upstairs for another snooze.

To my surprise, both Tomiko and Yasu drank coffee for breakfast. Tomiko would spoon out instant Nescafé and Cremora from family-size jars that sat on a white rolling cart parked by the stove. She then added boiling water to the mugs from an electric Thermos that also sat on the cart, next to the fruit bowl and telephone. I also drank the Nescafé because it was much less expensive than brewed coffee and more in harmony with "the group."

Yet, I often wondered what their fondness for coffee said about the future of Japan's traditional foodways. I had heard most schoolchildren now ate cold cereal or toast for breakfast, since housewives no longer wanted to get up early to make the traditional Japanese breakfast of rice, miso soup, cooked vegetables, and grilled fish. I couldn't blame them. But what other habits, rituals, and traditions were disappearing?

I began to feel a little guilty about all this as I ate my morning bowl of muesli with sliced bananas. Perhaps if I had made tea and miso soup, Tomiko would have joined me in a traditional Japanese breakfast, instead of eating cereal like me, or toast like Yasu. But in the end, we all preferred the taste of coffee (albeit instant), which, to be honest, would clash with the fermented salty smack of miso soup.

Supper required the most thoughtful planning. Who would decide the menu? Would I go to market, or Tomiko? Would she cook, or would we switch off? How much money should I contribute toward our food? Most important, would my evening teaching schedule interrupt their dinner routine?

Tomiko made it clear from the start that she would plan, shop for, and cook all meals. In a way, this was a relief. Or so I thought at first. To help, I insisted on setting the table and washing the dishes. It was the least I could do. As for money, we agreed I would pay her $150 a month to cover groceries and incidental expenses.

Since Yasu had grown up subsisting on vegetables as the son of a farmer, he refused to eat them as an adult. I noticed this same sentiment prevailed among many postwar Japanese. Since they finally could afford not to eat vegetables, they relished not doing so. Therefore, with Yasu happily rejecting most plant foods, Tomiko's dinners usually featured meat, particularly beef. She had grown up eating lots of red meat, as a result of her grandfather's influence. He had lived in a German-occupied area of China during World War II and, thus, developed a fondness for sausage, beef, bread, and cheese. Naturally, he passed these predilections onto his son, Tomiko's father, who, in turn, passed them onto Tomiko.

In contrast, if I never saw another steak, I would moo with contentment. So at Tomiko's I usually took a polite helping of whatever meat dish came to the table and then loaded up on rice and pickles. Occasionally, there would be a vegetable.

But it was never in the form of salad. Most Japanese cook or pickle their vegetables. The closest you'll come to a bowl of raw greens in Japan (with the exception of foreign restaurants) is the nest of shredded cabbage that garnishes *tonkatsu*, the deep-fried pork cutlets coated with fluffy breadcrumbs. Some say the Japanese avoid raw vegetables out of habit from the days when farmers used night soil as fertilizer. Others say raw vegetables lead to indigestion. Regardless of the reason, I often pined for leafy greens and the vegetable mixtures I saw piled high in Kyoto's markets.

Yet, vegetables were not just absent at Tomiko and Yasu's. Contrary to popular belief, Japanese restaurants rarely feature vegetables. Step into a sushi shop, for example, and you'll see what I mean. With the exception of a cucumber or two on the appetizer menu, it is seafood and rice from there on out.

Eel restaurants offer the same veggie conundrum. Order an eel dinner and you're likely to get clear soup containing the rubbery heart, a bowl of white rice, perhaps a slice of rolled omelet, and several fillets of eel. That's it. Nothing green. No vegetables, except for the requisite sliced pickles.

Likewise, rice bowls and noodles dishes rarely feature vegetables. The same holds true with restaurants featuring tempura, unless you order vegetable tempura, in which case your healthy vegetables are deep-fried. Oftentimes, the only green I encountered in a Kyoto-style restaurant was the jagged piece of plastic "grass" that separated the different foods.

The exception to this strange phenomenon is the foods served at extremely elegant restaurants, such as those featuring restaurant kaiseki (as opposed to tea kaiseki). Haute cuisine in Kyoto highlights peak seasonal ingredients, particularly vegetables. Elaborately prepared in Thumbelina-size portions, to avoid sending you home stuffed, they arrive on rare and beautiful tableware in a quiet contemplative atmosphere.

For a small fortune, you can sit in a private tatami room

overlooking a moss garden and savor this colorful sequence of seasonal specialties, a single *matsutake* mushroom in autumn, the sweet tip of a fresh bamboo shoot in May, and a tablespoon of slippery lemony-tasting water shield in summer. Of course, these plant-based treasures, this kind of feast, lay far beyond the grasp of my humble chopsticks.

But I could hardly complain. A few greens missing from my rice bowl at Tomiko and Yasu's was nothing compared to the privilege of having such a special place to park my bicycle at night.

Beef and Potato Supper Pot

This simple, comforting, home-style dish evolved after the Meiji Restoration, when beef entered the Japanese diet. You can easily use pork or chicken instead of the beef. Enjoy it on a snowy winter night with a side of greens.

I tablespoon vegetable oil

3 medium potatoes (about 1¾ pounds), peeled and cut into bite-size chunks

2 medium onions, peeled and coarsely chopped

⅓ pound lean beef, sliced into thin bite-size strips

1⅔ cups dashi (page 48)

3 tablespoons sugar

3 tablespoons sake

3 tablespoons soy sauce

I tablespoon mirin

Heat the oil in a large shallow saucepan over medium heat. Add the potatoes, onions, and beef and sauté for 5 minutes. Stir in the dashi, sugar, sake, soy sauce, and mirin. Reduce the heat to low and cook the mixture, partially covered, for 25 to 30 minutes, or until the potatoes are falling apart and melting into the syrupy sauce.

Makes 4 to 6 servings

Drippy-Sweet Daikon Wheels

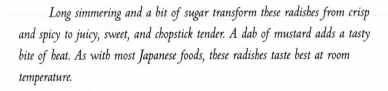

Long simmering and a bit of sugar transform these radishes from crisp and spicy to juicy, sweet, and chopstick tender. A dab of mustard adds a tasty bite of heat. As with most Japanese foods, these radishes taste best at room temperature.

> One 2-pound daikon radish
> 2½ cups dashi (page 48)
> 1 tablespoon soy sauce
> 2 teaspoons mirin
> 1 teaspoon sugar
> ½ teaspoon coarse salt
> Hot mustard (such as Chinese) for garnish

1. Trim and peel the radish and then cut into 1-inch-thick wheels. Place in a large shallow saucepan and cover with cold water. Bring the radishes to a boil, reduce the heat to low, and simmer, partially covered, for 40 minutes. Drain.

2. Pour the dashi over the cooked radishes in the same large shallow saucepan. Add the soy sauce, mirin, sugar, and salt and bring the mixture to a boil. Reduce the heat to low and simmer the radishes, partially covered, for 30 minutes. Let the radishes cool in the cooking liquid.

3. To serve, place several daikon wheels in a deep bowl with some of the cooking juices. Top each wheel with a little dab of hot mustard.

Makes 6 servings

10.

Christmas in Kyoto

One evening after a particularly gratifying supper of silken cabbage leaves padded with savory ground pork and braised in dashi until spoon tender, Tomiko made a proposition: "I think it would be fun to roast a chicken for Christmas dinner. What do you think?"

Christmas had been on my mind ever since I started hearing "Silent Night" and "Santa Claus Is Coming to Town" piping through the streets of downtown Kyoto around the first week of December. I told Tomiko I would love to roast a chicken. In fact, I would help plan, cook, and pay for the meal.

Strange as it sounds, the Japanese exhibit a real enthusiasm for Christmas. Although less than 2 percent of the population is Christian, families view the holiday as an opportunity to lavish gifts upon their children, while young couples see it as a chance to exchange heartfelt sentiments in the form of jewelry, stuffed animals, and dinners out. The carols, decorations, and silver and gold wrapping all play into the glittering romance of this secularized winter festival.

Shops, eager to fuel this fantasy, create elaborate displays, such as the Takashimaya department store, whose alpine scene looked like a Lilliputian version of the Sapporo Olympics. Through sophisticated mechanics, tiny skiers rode a red gondola to the summit of a snowy peak and then schussed down the plastic powder toward a pond of figure skaters lifting off for their next flying Axel.

Christmas cakes or *Ku-ris-ma-su ke-ki* (say it fast) are another manifestation of the holiday. These round white sponge cakes, heavily frosted with sweet whipped cream and ornamented with fresh whole strawberries and plastic Santa statues, appear in bakeries and stores all over Japan. While many young couples go out to dinner on Christmas Eve, families usually stay home and share a weirdly popular supper of fried chicken or pizza, followed by their cherished Christmas cake. Generally, the father of the family picks up the cake on his way home from work. He stands in line with all the other men to purchase his virgin-white prize, which drops drastically in value by Christmas Day, so stores can deplete their inventory by December 26.

This cake-buying frenzy has led to an interesting albeit sexist expression by which young Japanese girls are referred to as "Christmas cakes" after their twenty-fifth birthdays. For like the unsold cakes, their "value" diminishes considerably as the days tick by.

By mid-December I had become as sought after as a freshly baked Christmas cake. A flood of calls had poured in from schools and businesses eager to add some American spice to their annual holiday gathering. In need of money and curious to see how they would interpret this Christian holiday, I accepted every invitation that came my way.

Which explains why my last two weeks in December were peppered with such adventures as singing Christmas carols with businessmen, playing Bingo with kids, and eating crispy pellets of what one high school student proudly announced was "fried kitten." (Soon corrected with utter embarrassment to "fried chicken.")

In between all these parties, I set about buying holiday gifts for family and friends. My tea kaiseki and Japanese language classes had gone on hiatus for the winter break, along with most of the classes I taught. Thus, I had plenty of time to shop.

For local flavor, the choice was either old Kyoto or Tokyo modern. Most of Kyoto's traditional arts come from the gorgeous dark wooden shops owned by merchant families who have been crafting the same articles for generations. At the teensy Nijusan-ya shop in central Kyoto, for example, you can still buy the same style of hand-carved boxwood combs that have been sold since 1852, along with flowered black lacquer hair ornaments for geisha. Or, at Kagoshin near the Gion, you can find striking woven bamboo baskets and vases for Japanese flower arranging hanging from the sagging beams of this century-old store. Near the east gate of Nishi Hongan-ji temple you can visit the four-hundred-year-old incense shop, Kungyoku-do, to purchase slim wands of incense perfumed with flowers, herbs, spices, and sandalwood. And if shop hopping is not your style, you can visit the Kyoto Handicraft Center near the Heian Shrine in eastern Kyoto, as my grandmother did so many years ago, to buy lacquerware, red silk change purses, and flowered kimono-like happi coats.

With all that in mind, I loaded my bicycle basket with both modern and traditional treasures that weighed next to nothing, since postage to the United States was astronomical. In return, three Christmas packages came to Tomiko's, one from my childhood friend Margaret, one from my parents, and one from John.

Margaret's gift I opened on Christmas Eve day because that was when it arrived (the other two came later). It was a confetti-filled envelope packed with red and green M&M's, a candy cane, and some Trident gum, since I had written her that sugar-free gum was difficult to find in Kyoto. She had also tucked in a sparkly key ring "for your new home" and a picture frame, along with several photos of mutual pals.

I missed my family and friends, particularly John. How could I not? And there were some things I occasionally longed for, such as a big-screen movie in English with a huge tub of buttered popcorn and some Ben & Jerry's Chocolate Fudge Brownie ice cream. But I knew most of what I craved lay waiting back home, including my parents, several friends, and John, who were all planning to visit in the spring. Ultimately Kyoto was so profoundly stimulating, there was rarely time to dwell on what life lacked.

Christmas morning was just another workday for Yasu, who was out the door by the time I rose for breakfast.

As a little treat, I had splurged on some real ground coffee that I shared with Tomiko, along with some fresh fruit that we turned into fruit salad. It could hardly compare to the old-fashioned New England feasts my mother would prepare—spicy fried scrapple all lacy around the edges, rosy homemade applesauce sweetened with cinnamon heart candies, and thick wedges of sour cream coffeecake crusted with brown sugar and pecans—but the coffee and fruit were modest reminders of home.

Later that morning, Tomiko suggested we visit the huge flea market held on the twenty-fifth of every month at the Kitano Temmangu Shrine in northeast Kyoto. We could stop by for a few hours, then finish up our final food shopping for our Christmas dinner.

Kyoto is famous for its flea markets held at various temples and shrines on specific dates. Since the fairs had always fallen on days when I taught, I had never been to one. So after cleaning up, we climbed into Tomiko's white Honda and sped off to the shrine located just beyond the Nishijin textile district. After parking the car on a side street, we walked under the vermilion gate and crunched into the gravel courtyard.

At Kitano Temmangu Shrine, easily one hundred vendors sat crouched by their wares, laid out on plastic mats, newspapers, wooden benches, and hanging racks. There were old pieces of pottery—some chipped, some protected in padded baskets, and much of it simply heaped together—consisting of bowls, dipping saucers, and serving plates in various colors and sizes. Calligraphy tools—ink holders and brushes—lay near faded cardboard boxes holding rolled-up scrolls. For serious collectors, there were prints depicting sensual Edo period courtesans, tranquil landscapes, or quaint scenes, like women in kimonos bent under paper parasols clopping over snow-covered wooden bridges.

Stacked wooden lunch carriers, stools, and square wooden sake cups, all made miraculously airtight through interlocking joints, not glue or nails, lay in dusty disarray on one man's mat. On another's sat stacks of cloudy black lacquerware. Some of the cheaper bowls and trays were made of plastic or pressed wood chips. The best lacquerware had a carved wooden base.

Sealing wooden dishes with the sap of the lacquer tree is a technique imported from China. Depending upon the quality of the piece, the final surface can have anywhere from twenty to ninety coats of lacquer. Most Japanese arts that originated in China, including calligraphy, the tea ceremony, and papermaking, have been altered to suit Japan's unique aesthetic. In the case of lacquerware, the Japanese touch involves decorating the pieces with gold. Artists either adorn the surface with gold-painted designs (often based on nature, such as flowers, clouds, and waves) or abstract patterns made with gold powder or confetti-like specks.

For foreigners, probably the most popular flea market items are the used kimonos, which cost next to nothing, since most Japanese disdain anything secondhand. Heaped in piles like dirty laundry, these silk and cotton robes embody the idealized spirit of ancient Japan. Hoping to secure a piece of this romanticized past, I rifled through mountains of robes, lifting up each one for Tomiko's inspection. She fingered the fabric, checked the seams, and tugged on the lining. Then after a bout of tough negotiations with the kimono salesman, Tomiko took my one-thousand-yen note ($6) and handed me two prizes: a soft lilac kimono shot with abstract rods of crimson, cream, yellow, and gold and a pale cranberry silk kimono scattered with ivory and lime flowers.

By 3:00, we were back at the house unloading groceries from the back of the car, having made a detour to a special poultry shop to find a chicken that wasn't skinned, boned, and cut into tiny nuggets for teriyaki. After squeezing everything into the refrigerator, we set about preparing various parts of the menu.

Tomiko shucked fresh oysters, while I made stuffing from a recipe my friend Margaret and I had invented the year we both lived in Paris when I attended Le Cordon Bleu. To my surprise and delight, I had stumbled upon the Kyoto branch of Fauchon, where I had bought a real French baguette to tear up and toss with chopped fresh herbs, butter-sautéed onions, celery, and chestnuts, plus some beaten egg and chicken broth.

In honor of the occasion, Tomiko and I set the low redwood table in her sitting room Western-style with her best indigo-and-white cotton place mats, matching napkins, wineglasses, and silverware. Earlier that week, Tomiko had even erected a green plastic Christmas tree in the family room and festooned it with ornaments, red and gold garlands, and a gold metal star.

Shortly before 5:00, Tomiko and I headed upstairs to change. Toro, the cat, lay in a ball in his usual spot, asleep on the cream leather couch.

Around 6:00, Toro was joined by a couple and their toddler, who had been invited to share Christmas dinner. The wife was a slim Japanese woman who spoke excellent English; her husband was a British-born English professor. The pair had met in Kyoto and had a sweet son named Christian, whom they brought along for the evening in a pale blue sweat suit that could double as pajamas in case he got sleepy.

No sooner had I introduced myself to the couple than I heard Tomiko utter, "Oh, no," under her breath.

"What?" I asked, hurrying into the kitchen.

"We don't have a roasting pan." Tomiko was squatting in her dressy olive wool sheath rummaging through cookware under the kitchen sink.

"How about the tray from your toaster oven?" I figured we could cover it with foil and origami some sides.

"Too small."

"How about a rack?"

"I don't have one." Tomiko eased herself up and went over

to the refrigerator. She removed a very small platter holding a huge chicken and asked me to open the oven. I scurried over to the stove and pulled open the small white enameled door.

"I was afraid of this," she said, grimacing. There was a loud pop, as Yasu opened a bottle of sparkling wine.

"Do you need help?" The Japanese woman had come into the kitchen. Her husband, clutching a glass of bubbly, soon joined her. Then Yasu, who rarely set foot in this part of the house, padded over.

"Everything okay?" he asked, tapping out a cigarette from his silver canister. He lit the cigarette and tipped his head back to exhale a thick pillow of smoke.

"The chicken doesn't fit," said Tomiko, lugging the platter over to the kitchen table. She set it down and looked at Yasu with her hands on her hips. The British man chewed the inside of his cheek. His wife looked worried. Christian, alone on the couch, started to whimper. Suddenly, I had an idea: "Do you have a soup pot?"

Tomiko bent down again to look under the sink. "Here." She handed me a black-and-white-speckled pot. I placed it on the kitchen table, put in the chicken, and added some water.

"We can steam-cook it on the stove," I announced. Smiles broke out as I tented the pot with foil and set the gas to medium.

While the bird languished in its sauna, we attacked the oysters. Tomiko had dressed them with a blend of soy sauce, rice vinegar, grated radish, sugar, and red chili, a sort of Asian mignonette. The sauce added just the right savory sparkle to the slippery sweet mollusks. As we sucked and slurped, and sipped the sparkling wine, Christian amused himself with a small orange truck that he occasionally drove over Toro's head.

By 7:30 the kitchen had filled with an intoxicating scent of eau de poulet. Encouraged by its progress, I headed into the kitchen to prepare the lemon butter for the steamed broccoli. Tomiko stepped over to her tiny white microwave sitting on a tile shelf above the sink and squeezed a potato. They were still hard, so she punched in more time.

Around 8:00, I decided to check the chicken again. Lifting up the foil, I fluttered away the hot steam with my hand. I wiggled a leg. It resisted, so I cut into the joint area with a paring knife. Bloody juice trickled out, so I added more water, replaced the foil, and began fixing the salad.

The day before I had bought fresh spinach and enoki mushrooms to make a modified spinach salad, since Tomiko had never eaten one. But given the richness of the meal, we decided to leave out the boiled eggs and bacon. Despite these changes, the idea of eating raw spinach and raw mushrooms was novel in itself, as was blending rice vinegar with imported Maille mustard, crushed garlic, and olive oil.

With nothing left to prepare, I came back into the sitting room, where everyone except Christian was depleting a bottle of Merlot. Toro had managed to ease himself almost completely onto the boy's lap. Yasu poured me a glass of wine, Tomiko snapped pictures, and the chicken merrily continued steaming.

Around 8:45, Tomiko noticed the picture window had begun to fog over. I headed over to the stove and lifted away the foil. I blew away the steam, then plunged the knife into the bird's thigh. The juice was clear; the chicken was done.

Despite its boiled yellow pallor, the bird was incredibly succulent. Yasu carved thin slices of meat and neatly laid them on a platter. He surrounded the chicken with spoonfuls of moist stuffing. Tomiko heaped the baked potatoes into a bowl and set them on the table. Dinner was looking awfully white. But then out came the lemon-butter-drenched broccoli spears and spinach salad glistening with dressing. Murmurs of approval filled the room as we all relished the feast. Even Toro got to gnaw on a wing.

Since Yasu had never tasted chocolate sauce, I had made a decadent sludge based on a recipe from my childhood. Gritty with sugar and almost black, it turns chewy when spooned over ice cream. For more sensitive palates, I had made a strawberry Grand Marnier sauce. Of course, everyone sampled both over vanilla Häagen-Dazs purchased from the Daimaru department store's food hall.

Tomiko served brewed coffee, and then we were done. The wine was gone. The chicken had been devoured. And Christian was crying. We said good-bye, did the dishes, then trudged up to bed.

Although it was close to 3:00 in the morning, I opened my Christmas box from my parents. Inside were lots of lovely things, including a navy-blue cashmere cardigan with matching velvet piping that had belonged to my grandmother. I held it up, then tentatively brought the fine downy wool to my nose. It still smelled like her.

Earlier that day, Yasu had given me a print made by one of his friends who decorated lacquerware. On a soft lime-green background, the artist had stamped intermittent rows of silver rectangles, then flecked the entire surface with silver and gold confetti-like specks. It was beautiful and something I would cherish forever.

In turn, I had given Tomiko and Yasu silly (but expensive) sake cups with rabbits inside, since it would soon be the year of the rabbit. The gift seemed meager compared to the couple's ongoing hospitality and generosity.

I was surprised to find that being away from home made the spiritual aspect of Christmas come alive, the part I so often forgot about in the frenzy of buying presents, trimming the tree, and going to parties back home. What made me dwell on it in Japan was that everyone simply celebrated the glittering image of Christmas. So the spirit had to come from within.

And it did. That night, surrounded by gifts from my family, the scent of my grandmother, and the friendship of a couple who had welcomed me into their lives, I was filled with a deep sense of gratitude and love. Although that Christmas could not have been farther from the ones I knew so well and grew up celebrating, it was the truest Christmas I had ever experienced. Lying there in the dark I felt tremendously blessed. And just a tad sick to my stomach. Could it have been the oysters?

Christmas Cake (Ku-ris-ma-su Ke-ki)

This treasured holiday sponge cake resembles our American shortcake in that it combines white cake with fresh strawberries and whipped cream. Since most Japanese homes do not have enough room for an oven, families rely on bakeries for this light sweet treat. If you wish, you can decorate the cake as they do in Japan with a small plastic Christmas tree, a Santa Claus figure, and a Merry Christmas plaque.

5 large eggs

1 cup granulated sugar

2 teaspoons pure vanilla extract

¼ teaspoon cream of tartar

1 cup cake flour

2 cups whipping cream

2 tablespoons confectioners' sugar

⅔ cup naturally sweetened strawberry jam

10 fresh whole strawberries, hulls sliced off

1. Preheat the oven to 325° F. Coat two 8-inch round cake pans with nonstick spray.

2. Separate the eggs, placing the whites in a large bowl and the yolks in a medium bowl. Using an electric mixer, gradually beat in ⅔ cup of the granulated sugar with the yolks, until the mixture turns thick and yellow, about 5 minutes. Beat in the vanilla.

3. Using clean dry beaters, whip the egg whites in a bowl with the cream of tartar until soft peaks form. Add the remaining ⅓ cup granulated sugar and continue beating until stiff peaks form.

4. Sprinkle half of the flour over the egg yolk mixture. Using a rubber spatula, gently fold in the flour. Fold in half of the whites, followed by the rest of the flour. Fold in the remaining egg whites and gently scoop the batter into the prepared pans. Bake 25 to 30 minutes, or until a wooden skewer inserted into the center of a cake comes out clean. Let the cakes cool in the pans, before turning out on a rack.

5. Whip the cream until soft peaks form. Sift the confectioners' sugar over the whipped cream and continue whipping until firm peaks form.

6. Using a serrated knife, cut each cake crosswise in half. Spread the strawberry jam between each layer, creating two layer cakes. Spread a thin layer of the whipped cream over the top of one of the layer cakes and place the other cake on top to create a single

cake consisting of four layers. Frost the top and sides of the cake with the whipped cream, smoothing it with a spatula. Place the whole strawberries, cut side down, in a circle around the top edge of the cake.

Makes 1 four-layer cake, about 10 servings

Oysters Kyoto-Style

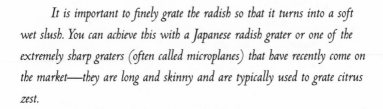

It is important to finely grate the radish so that it turns into a soft wet slush. You can achieve this with a Japanese radish grater or one of the extremely sharp graters (often called microplanes) that have recently come on the market—they are long and skinny and are typically used to grate citrus zest.

3 tablespoons rice vinegar
2 tablespoons soy sauce
1 tablespoon finely grated daikon radish
½ teaspoon chili paste
¼ teaspoon sugar
3 dozen oysters

1. Combine the vinegar, soy sauce, radish, chili paste, and sugar in a small bowl. Stir until the sugar dissolves.

2. Shuck the oysters and arrange on a bed of cracked ice. Spoon a little of the sauce over each oyster.

Makes 3 dozen oysters

Julia's Chocolate Sauce

This recipe is adapted from Essex County Cooks, *a collection of family-tested recipes from the friends, parents, and faculty of two Massachusetts-based elementary schools. While it was never clear who "Julia" was, her legacy lives on in this deep, dark, bittersweet chocolate sauce that makes a fabulous topping for ice cream, sponge cake, or cut-up fresh fruit.*

Four 2-ounce squares unsweetened chocolate

2 cups sugar

⅔ cup light cream

2 teaspoons lightly salted butter

2 teaspoons pure vanilla extract

Combine the chocolate, sugar, and cream in a double boiler. Cook until the chocolate has melted and whisk vigorously to combine the ingredients. Whisk in the butter and vanilla and serve.

Makes 3 cups

11.

Making Mochi

It was probably the chicken. Tomiko, Yasu, and I were hit with a bug that made us all feel nauseated and fluish. "Even Toro won't eat his food," said Tomiko the next morning when she stopped by my bedroom to deliver John's Christmas gift. She was still in her bathrobe when she handed me the package, a padded brown envelope holding a beautiful gold bracelet etched with leafy garlands.

Merry Christmas Sweetbread,

The only thing I wish for is your happiness, if not while next to me then far away. Wear this bracelet and think of me thinking of you . . .

*and although Christmas is not quite as special without you, it warms
me to think of you thinking of me.*

> *I love and miss you.*
> *Johnnycakes*

Later that day we talked on the phone, which made everything seem just a bit more cheery. By the end of the week, everyone felt normal. What's more, we had regained our appetites. And that was important: Oshogatsu was coming.

The celebration of Oshogatsu is Japan's greatest holiday. Beginning on the eve of December 31 and ending on January 3, it is a time of great joy and renewal. Families prepare for the holiday, loosely referred to as New Year's, by thoroughly cleaning their homes and decorating them with auspicious items. They also pay off all debts—physically and socially—and prepare an elaborate feast.

In the business world, "year forgetting parties" take place before December 31, in order to clean the slate before the New Year begins. Alcohol, a necessary social lubricant, encourages workers to muster up the courage to complain to their bosses about problems they felt too inhibited to bring up during the year. The issues are discussed, resolved, and all is forgiven and forgotten. That way, when people return to their jobs on January 4, the stains from the past year have been scrubbed away, physically and spiritually.

Preparations for the home, such as decorating and cleaning, also begin several days before Oshogatsu. Most Japanese bless their homes with the same talismans, usually placed in a sacred area of the home, such as the alcove or front entrance.

Because Tomiko and Yasu's Western-style home had no alcove, they arranged their Oshogatsu display in the front entrance or vestibule. This is the same area in traditional Japanese homes where people stand when they stop by to pick up or deliver something. Since visitors often do not go into the house, it is important the vestibule look attractive.

Yasu had paved their front entrance with smooth gray stones and placed a granite step opposite the front door leading up to the hardwood floor at the bottom of the staircase. A wooden cabinet running along the right side of the vestibule held shoes, boots, and other items. On top of this cabinet Tomiko had placed her *o-sonae* (honorable offering).

At first glance, the arrangement looked like a stack of white Frisbees topped with one of Yasu's neckties and some fruit that hadn't yet made it into the kitchen. Later that day, however, Tomiko set the record straight. "These are pounded rice cakes," she said, pointing to the Frisbees. "They are called the *kagami mochi*, or 'mirror rice cake.'" A sacred mirror, in addition to a sword and jewels, make up the three Imperial Regalia of Japan. In Shinto mythology, the sun goddess Amaterasu is the progenitor of the imperial line. When she hid in a cave after a confrontation with her brother, myriad deities lured her out of the cave with a mirror, in which she spied her own reflection.

Tomiko lifted up the limp green necktie. "This is konbu," she said. "It's the same kind of seaweed we use to make dashi." Since the Japanese greatly enjoy wordplay, konbu graces the mochi cakes because it sounds somewhat like *yorokobu,* meaning "joy."

"And this is *urajiro*," explained Tomiko, pointing to the two ferns that stuck out from either side of the pounded rice cakes like eagle wings. They were held in place with a skewer of dried persimmons, a fruit that represents health and success in life.

"And here we have a *daidai*." Tomiko pointed to an orange sitting atop the entire stack like a button on a beanie. This citrus symbolizes longevity because the Chinese word for daidai sounds similar to the word for "generation [to] generation" and in feudal times samurai families hoped to serve their lord from generation to generation.

To personalize the honorable offering, Tomiko had arranged several of Yasu's carpentry tools on the white cloth. A small bonsai arrangement sat nearby, complete with lumpy moss (suggestive of mountains) surrounded by snow-white pebbles. A tiny pine tree stood in the moss to symbolize long life because of the tree's hardiness, along with a baby bamboo plant denoting constancy and virtue. A pink-flowering plum had also been added to the arrangement to convey wishes for expanding good fortune throughout the year because of its many branches. With all the decorations in place, the time had come to clean.

The restorative home treatments began on December 30, when Tomiko's widowed mother arrived from Osaka to celebrate Oshogatsu. No sooner had the slim petite woman stepped off the fast-train than she was yanking on rubber gloves to beautify the house.

At first, I thought we would simply vacuum, dust, and tidy up the downstairs. "Where shall I start?" I asked, turning to Tomiko. She said something in Japanese to her mother, who pointed to the kitchen. Before I knew it I was holding a bucket of soapy water and a white terry rag.

"Start with the floors," said Tomiko. "Then do the walls. After that, come see me." I nodded, suddenly realizing I was about to receive a crash course on the Shinto concept of purification.

I had never washed a wall before. I can't say I really ever thought of them getting dirty. But in minutes the rag had turned gray. Tomiko's vacuum hummed in the other room, while sounds of flushing emanated from the bathroom as her mother freshened the toilet bowl.

As I gave the walls a dermabrasion, Toro, the cat, stretched from his warm spot on the leather couch then curled up in a ball. "Do you need another rag?" asked Tomiko, stopping in to check on my progress.

I said I'd love another one, so she hurried off and came back with a fresh stack. Renewed, I began washing the windows. Then the metal blinds. The sills. Toro looked up and yawned. I attacked the top of the television, crawled along the floor to wipe the molding, stood on tippytoe to wipe dust off the top of the china cabinet. I scoured the counters. Scrubbed the floors. Polished the stove. And buffed the coffee cart until it twinkled. Panting, I looked over at Toro, who lay fast asleep.

Since Tomiko and her mother showed no sign of slowing, I helped Tomiko beat the rugs, dust the ceilings, wet-mop the hall and stairs, and brighten doorknobs. We swept the vestibule and then washed and rinsed it. Even the washing machine was going full bore. It was a true group effort and by late afternoon the house sparkled. It had been swabbed, sterilized, and bleached into purity. It was a home worthy of being entered by the sun goddess herself to check for any dust with a sacred white glove.

After packing away all the cleaning equipment, we tossed the rags in the laundry for yet another load. Then we collapsed in the family room to convalesce over a cup of tea. We needed it. In a matter of hours, we would be making mochi with the neighboring Omura family.

With cooking off limits during Oshogatsu, mochi became a popular substitute for boiled rice. Shortly before New Year's, families would pound steamed glutinous rice in a stone mortar with a wooden mallet to create a smooth dough to form into cookie-like puffs to eat over the three-day period of rest.

The Japanese believe that pounding rice brings out its sacred power, and that mochi contains the grain's spiritual essence. For the deceased, mochi cakes are placed on altars to serve as sustenance for their journey up to heaven. Over Oshogatsu, families adorn altars at temples and shrines with mochi as offerings to Buddha or the Shinto gods, including the New Year's deity, Toshigami-sama. In the olden days, farmers used to drop mochi down their wells as an offering to the Shinto god of water. Ten days later, they would scatter more mochi in their yards. If the crows pecked it up, legend had it the year would bring a good harvest.

The idea of making mochi with the Omura family had materialized shortly before Christmas. Mr. Omura, like Yasu, was a carpenter. Because they frequently worked on jobs together, they had developed a close friendship. Often, at the end of the day, I would see Mr. Omura arranging lumber in the back of his truck in Tomiko and Yasu's driveway before he headed home to his family. Usually, he and I would just wave at each other as I dipsydoodled my bicycle around the back of the house to lock it for the night. But two weeks into December, Mr. Omura and I had chatted and the conversation had turned to pounded rice cakes. When I said I had never tasted anything but commercially made mochi, Mr. Omura insisted that he educate my palate.

"*Konbanwa* (good evening), herro," said Mr. Omura, sliding open the wood- and glass-paneled door to his home. His bushy black mustache curved over a crooked-tooth smile as he ushered us in. "Please, I take your coats," he said, helping Tomiko off with her padded denim jacket. I had just unzipped my fleece when several shrill screams blasted out of the kitchen, followed by two laughing boys, no more than six, chewing on what looked like kitchen twine. Skirting Mr. Omura's extended family, they raced around the vestibule screeching and pushing each other's backs. Several mothers tried to calm the youngsters, while the rest of the clan looked on with amusement, including the toothless grandmother—Mr. Omura's mother—who appeared somewhat weary sitting in a plump heap on a tatami-lined raised platform in the back half of the room.

Unlike the tiny shoe-filled vestibules in most traditional homes, the one at the Omuras' could have garaged two cars. Dark wood cupboards ran along the bottom part of the cement-paved room. The top portion consisted of putty-colored walls holding high wooden shelves laden with coils of rope, plastic bags, cardboard boxes, saws, and other tools.

Mr. Omura, clutching two small wooden boxes, came over to where Tomiko and I stood. "Some sake?" he asked, extending his offerings. As I took the box, I noticed his hands were red and callused. Pounding mochi would be a cinch for him, I thought, compared to what he did all day. Aside from constructing modern buildings, he and Yasu built traditional Japanese homes, as well as teahouses. But since cement, glass, and aluminum were winning favor over timber, mud, and straw, Yasu and Mr. Omura had become a dying breed of craftsmen.

When everyone had been served the cool clear rice wine, we

all raised our wooden cups to bestow a benediction on the coming New Year. The sake tasted light, sweet, and slightly woody.

These square cups are called *masu* and were originally used to measure dry goods, such as rice. Each cup holds the equivalent of one meal's worth of rice and families would go to their local rice shop to measure out the number of cups they needed. One thousand masu of rice are called a *koku*, which is how the samurai were paid. (One koku, roughly five bushels, represents approximately a year's worth of rice for one person based on three rice-based meals per day.)

Originally masu were made of cedar. Around the turn of the century, when sake was fermented in cedar tanks, they became a popular vessel for holding sake. Nowadays, sake producers use stainless steel or ceramic-lined tanks, so connoisseurs prefer lacquered boxes or cups of pine, like the ones we were using, to preserve the spirit's natural flavor.

To accompany the sake, I tried a piece of the kitchen twine, which turned out to be dried squid. Wonderfully salty and leathery, it was like jerky of the sea. Yasu tapped out a cigarette, and handed it to Mr. Omura. Soon the room filled with smoke, laughter, children's yelps, and Japanese chatter.

"The rice is ready!" squealed the boys, scampering into the room ahead of their uncle. An older man trotted in, red-faced and gasping under the weight of an enormous square wooden box filled with steaming rice. The grandmother pushed herself up from the tatami and shuffled toward the rest of the family rapidly gathering around a waist-high stone bowl in the center of the room. This was the mochi-making bowl, rough gray granite on the outside and smooth within. It sat in a wooden stand consisting of four angled posts, connected at the bottom, so as to form a cradled support.

With a fast flip and a loud "Oof!" Mr. Omura's brother reversed the wooden box to release a glistening square of rice. It fell into the bowl with a wet smack and Mr. Omura quickly peeled off the woven bamboo mat clinging to its surface. The brother trotted back to the kitchen with the empty box and mat, while Mr. Omura fetched the large wooden mallet. Worn smooth like a favorite salad bowl, it would whack the sacred power out of the rice.

Mr. Omura handed the mallet to his brother, who was dressed to pound in tan sweat pants with a white-and-navy-striped kerchief tied around his head. He grabbed the mallet and began to punish the shiny white mass. Thwack! Thwack! Thwack!

Mr. Omura plunged his hands into the bowl, turned over the rice, then yanked out his hands just in time. Thwack! Thwack! Thwack! Steam rose from the bowl. Plunge, flip. Thwack! Thwack! Thwack! The two men grunted and snorted as they flipped and thwacked.

"Who's next?" hollered the brother, readjusting his damp kerchief and stepping back from the bowl. Several nieces and nephews giggled and shoved one another forward. Yasu ground out his cigarette and came over to help a little girl in a pink sweater and blue pleated skirt. She could hardly lift the mallet, but when she did it dropped into the bowl with a dull thump. Yasu picked off the grains of rice clinging to the rounded end of the mallet, then helped several other children take their turn.

Prodded by Tomiko and Mr. Omura, I finally stepped up to the bowl to take a whack. I pushed up the sleeves of my sweater and picked up the mallet. It was bottom heavy and twisted in my hands. I tightened my grip and gave the rice a thwack. It felt like frozen pizza dough. Mr. Omura flipped the starchy ball over and I pummeled it again.

"Oh, the American is so strong, look at her pound!" someone yelled. Yasu whistled and others hooted. A soft burn rippled across my shoulders. I clenched my teeth and continued to bang. Flip. Bang! Flip. Bang! More cheers. Hot stabs of pain pulsed throughout my deltoids. Flip. Bang! Flip. Bang!

Just when I thought my sweater might ignite, the rice began to relax. "I think it's done," said Mr. Omura, giving the dough a sharp poke. He scooped up the warm white blob and carried it over to his mother, now back on the tatami raised platform. She scattered fine rice flour over a plastic board and then kneaded the warm white ball like bread dough. A tan flowered apron saved her gray jersey dress from becoming powdery white. Tomiko and several other women climbed up onto the tatami and offered to help. The old woman slowly karate chopped the ball in quarters and gave away the pieces. I got one, as well as Tomiko, and we followed the grandmother's lead as she tore off small blobs and rolled them into rounds the size of Oreos.

While we formed mochi cakes, the men pounded another batch of rice. When it was soft, they divided the rice dough into four pieces. They kept one in the bowl and added cooked bulgur, pummeling the dough until it turned nubby like tweed. They sprinkled the second blob with dried shrimp and banged it until it turned coral. Nori seaweed powder colored the third hunk forest green, while the fourth piece of mochi became yellow and pebbly with cooked corn kernels.

For variation, the grandmother rolled several plain mochi in a tan talc of sweetened toasted soybean powder. She also stuffed several dumplings with crimson azuki bean fudge. Then she smeared a thick gob of azuki paste across a mochi puff, pushed in a candied chestnut, and pinched the dumpling shut.

"For the American!" cried Mr. Omura, swiping his mother's creation. I looked up and he handed it to me. It was tender and warm. All eyes turned to watch the American. "Oishii!" I uttered with a full mouth. And it was delicious. The soft stretchy rice dough had a mild savory chew that mingled with the candy-like sweetness of the bean paste and buttery chestnut. The camaraderie and spirit in that room was boundless, as others joined in for a taste. Yet, the moment was bittersweet.

Sadly, making mochi is a dying tradition. In the old days, families across Japan used to gather together to pound the rice and form it into dumplings. It was an annual ritual that reinforced people's place in the group, strengthened family bonds, and celebrated the sacred meaning of Oshogatsu. Now professional rice pounders go door to door with rice steaming boxes, mortars, and pestles to produce the rice cakes for busy families. Some don't even do that anymore, instead relying on confectionery shops to make and deliver the fresh rice taffy. Still others buy manufactured dried mochi so stiff and plastic it clicks together like dominos. When hydrated in boiling water, the dried mochi turns gooey and tasteless, like a day-old wad of chewing gum.

A more recent phenomenon in the gadget-crazy country of Japan is the electric mochi-making machine for the home. As compact as a bread machine, this automatic device is rapidly becoming a countertop fixture for many Japanese families.

Other artisanal products, such as tofu, soba, and miso, face the same perilous future. With machines producing all these foodstuffs, they no longer contain the individual expression of the maker, and thus are robbed of their significance and spirit. I realized I would probably never taste homemade mochi like this again. Even worse, nor would many of the Omura children.

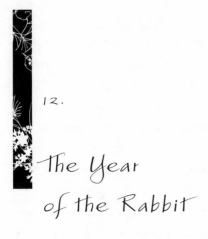

12.

The Year
of the Rabbit

New Year's Eve day began with a trip to Nishiki market.
My first pilgrimage to this temple of food took place several days
after I had arrived in Kyoto. Whenever I visit a foreign city, my
initial stop is rarely a famous monument or museum. It is a food
market.

I have always believed you can learn as much about a culture
by the ingredients they put in their mouths, as by the buildings
they erect. The abundance and freshness of the foodstuffs, for example, indicate the strength of a country's economy, as well as its
transportation system. The actual items on display offer insight
into people's diet, health, and lifestyle. An open market is like a
living museum of history. And that morning at Nishiki there was
a special exhibit: ingredients for the New Year's feast.

A fine mist hung in the air as Tomiko, her mother, and I approached the green-, red-, and canary-yellow-striped awning of the market. Surrounded by clanging *pachinko* parlors and two-hundred-year-old inns, Nishiki lies one block north of Shijo Street in the heart of Kyoto. The four-hundred-meter-long corridor of food stalls is called Brocade Street, after the colorful Nishijin textile district, where most of Kyoto's kimono makers reside. Although this was probably my sixth visit to the market, I could feel my heart quicken in anticipation of the more than one hundred fifty stalls that lay waiting.

Initially, Nishiki was a place to sell fish, sake, and produce. But after the warring samurai destroyed it in the Onin War (1467–77), the market was rebuilt in the early 1500s to its present expanded form. In the early morning, chefs from Kyoto's elite inns and kaiseki restaurants can be seen picking up delicacies for their evening menus. Mushanokoji tea school purchases foods for its tea kaiseki classes at the market. And that day, it seemed, the whole of Kyoto had wedged itself in that narrow colorful corridor to procure the bounty that lay pickled, iced, dried, smoked, pressed, piled, and carefully arranged for Oshogatsu.

Before I knew it, I had gotten caught up in the rush of mothers, babies in strollers, clusters of housewives, teenagers, old men, and kids. A grandmother in a kimono gored me in the ribs with her elbow. Someone butted me from behind. Several housewives jostled past me. This was a new sensation in a country where physical contact is reserved for the bedroom. I immediately sought refuge in a pickle shop, Tomiko's first stop. Wooden barrels lined with heavy sheets of clear plastic held dozens of pickled vegetables, including limp whole Chinese cabbages, skinny green cucumbers buried in rice-bran mash, and sweet white radishes seasoned with hot peppers and kelp. The store was jammed with people. Small white ceramic platters held samples to be picked up with tiny metal tongs.

Folded moist washcloths lay nearby to clean your fingers. "This is crazy," yelled Tomiko over her shoulder. "We'll find another pickle shop farther on." We plunged back into the crowd.

Like a leaf on a river, I was carried past a sushi stand selling *maki* rolls, fat rice logs covered with nori and bulging with sweet pickled gourd, carrot, braised shiitake mushroom caps, sweet omelet, and cooked spinach. I coasted past a dry cleaner on my left, a *yakitori* shop on my right, then a tea and herbal medicine shop, and a store selling bowls of sweet white beans and eel livers in a glossy brown sauce.

Suddenly, Tomiko swerved into a flower shop to pick up pine boughs, clusters of ruby nandina berries, and dusty-green ferns to use as decorative garnishes. After grabbing the greenery, she and her mother ducked into another store selling dried beans. They had the market list. They were in charge. I tagged behind.

The smell of roasting tea billowed into the air, mingling with the salty tang of miso, perfume, wet wool, and grilling fish. Bicycles and motorbikes leaned up against the sides of stalls, next to stacks of Styrofoam fish boxes. Men in rubber boots splashed about the puddled floors unloading fish onto white enamel trays.

I lost Tomiko and her mother at the eel stall. It was the place to buy prepared fillets of *unagi*, as meltingly tender as a stick of soft butter. A spotlight shone down on the delicate fillets, gleaming under a varnish of sweet soy glaze. Every eel shop and restaurant makes its own special glaze, which eel purists often forgo. All eel lovers, however, sprinkle on sansho, the tingly tongue-numbing green powder from the ground dried seedpods of the prickly ash tree that lifts the dish from sumptuous to sensational.

At that particular eel shop, the fillets, priced according to their fatty succulence, were still warm and drenched with sauce.

The next few shops were a sashimi lover's paradise. Spiky

forest-green sea urchins swollen with creamy yellow eggs sat in green plastic baskets beside huge steak-like sides of tuna, caught only hours ago from the icy waters off Japan. Gigantic octopuses with suction cups like the bottom of rubber bathtub mats rested on ice near sapphire-silver mackerel imbricated on round white platters.

I pivoted around on tiptoe trying to spot Tomiko or her mother bobbing about in the sea of black-haired women. They had disappeared. Fortunately, a Fuji film salesman outside the market had given me a Mylar balloon, which was still looped around my fingers. "Hold on to it," Tomiko had advised. "That way you'll be easy to spot."

So I kept moving with the crowd, soaring past a shop selling smoky pink bonito fish flakes and another one peddling wrinkly dried mushroom caps. I shot by a shop proffering wheat gluten, red and white for New Year's and shaped into knots and flowers, followed by a liquor store with ziggurats of sake, whiskey, and wine in the window. I flew past a stall crammed with split-toed white socks and restaurant tunics, a shop dedicated to fresh and dried yuba, the high-protein skin skimmed off boiling soymilk, and a pork store selling raw and cooked cutlets dredged in *panko*, the fluffy white breadcrumbs that look like snowflakes. Then I heard a familiar voice.

"Victoria, over here," called Tomiko, waving from a kelp shop. She and her mother were fingering huge olive-brown sheets that looked like skateboards. There were also cellophane packages of the dried algae cut into crisp snacking squares the size of Scrabble pieces. When I apologized for getting separated, Tomiko flicked her hand, in a gesture of "don't worry," then purchased a sheet of kelp. We would use it to make dashi for our New Year's Eve noodle soup, as well as other dishes.

We hurried on to several more stalls, buying eggs, soba noodles, long-whiskered shrimp, wheat gluten, cooked duck, and a chunk of tenderloin. I hooked a bag over my arm to make room for a new one filled with a bag of loose green tea, a bottle of sake, and some field yams, small brown shingle-skinned tubers that when peeled and cooked turn sticky and sweet. In went some broccoli, fresh shiitake mushrooms, and Japanese red carrots, rarely found outside Japan, and a box of strawberries wrapped like a Christmas gift in glossy white paper. Tomiko carried three bags, and her mother carried two. I staggered out with four. Then, after heaving the groceries into the trunk of the Honda, we drove home to cook.

With no time to spare, Tomiko and her mother spread our purchases around the kitchen to begin preparing the Oshogatsu meal called osechi ryori. I had thought the term referred to a single feast, like Thanksgiving, that we would cook New Year's Day and enjoy that night. I was mistaken. Osechi ryori consists of thirty-four or so small dishes that are cooked in advance of New Year's night and then eaten cold or at room temperature over the three-day Oshogatsu holiday period. To keep the foods from spoiling during a time when refrigerators did not exist, cooks would "preserve" them in a potent mixture of dashi, soy, and sugar before packing them into a three-tiered stack of lacquer boxes.

The practice of preparing this special feast to last in cold storage for several days evolved as a way to give everyone, including the family cook, a three-day period of rest. Shops closed, so foods were not available over the holiday. Families snuffed out the cooking fire in the floor pit of traditional homes on December 31 (it would be lit again after the New Year).

The word osechi is an abbreviation of *osechiku*, a term originally used to describe the special foods that were prepared to celebrate the *go sekku*, or five seasonal festivals. In a tradition brought over from China, seasonal offerings (such as newly harvested rice, vegetables, or fish) were made to the appropriate gods on the *sechi-bi* (ritual day). Most of the five sekku have lost their religious significance (many have become festivals for children) and the term osechi has become associated exclusively with the special foods prepared for New Year's. Since *ryori* means "cooking" in Japanese, department stores, when they first started offering premade New Year's foods, borrowed the term *osechi ryori* to give their boxed treats a luxurious image. It obviously worked; nowadays, few families make their own osechi ryori, but instead purchase it from department stores and caterers.

Tomiko withdrew several knives from the kitchen drawer and handed them out, along with aprons. She took the denim one, her mother tied on a white one, and I put on the black one printed with dancing pigs. "Do you need this?" Tomiko held out a small cutting board. I nodded and took it over to the wooden table where she and I sometimes ate breakfast. Then, having organized my ingredients, I began making two dishes from tea kaiseki class: the brown-and-coral sweet-and-sour salmon-kelp rolls and clams cloaked with golden sweet miso.

Tomiko and her mother set to work on the counter by the stove. And what a pair! Knives flashing, water rushing, and chopsticks clicking, they simmered dashi; braised mushrooms; grilled shrimp; seared tenderloin; slivered carrots; softened field yams; boiled black soybeans; steamed broccoli; hydrated wheat gluten; blanched snow peas; and pickled radish. In a matter of hours, Tomiko and her mother had prepared thirty-two dishes. I had finished two. But to my relief, they looked just like the ones from tea kaiseki class.

We carefully arranged all the foods in Tomiko's beautiful stacked lacquer boxes that she only pulled out for Oshogatsu. Called *jubako*, they were brick red inside and black outside with painted gold pine boughs adorning the tops and sides.

Jubako are a fancy form of *bento* (a compartmentalized boxed meal). Apparently, warrior lords invented them as a way to divide their spartan rations among their vassals. Allotments of rice, vegetables, and pickles were placed in small sectioned boxes made of wood and woven reeds. Over time, the boxes became elegant lacquer containers that commoners would fill with picnic foods to take to cherry-viewing parties, Kabuki theater performances (to nibble on between acts), or on long train rides. Today, you can buy casual bento in supermarkets, train stations, highway rest areas, and subway stations. Made of cardboard, Styrofoam, or balsa, they contain all kinds of cold cooked nibbles, such as braised vegetables, tofu, sushi, and at least two regional specialties that add a local flavor to Japan's own form of take-out food.

After garnishing the goodies in Tomiko's jubako with sprigs of pine, fern fronds, and shiny red nandina berries to symbolize purification, we placed the boxes in the unheated tatami room off the kitchen. Yasu had built this traditional Japanese room for Tomiko, who still hoped to teach flower arranging in it one day.

That night, Tomiko and her mother, Yasu, Toro, and I gathered around the television in the family room to watch the "Singing Battle Between the Red and the White Teams," a cherished New Year's Eve program starring Japan's hottest pop singers.

Yasu had already warmed up the television earlier that night, as he regularly did throughout the week. Despite Tomiko's disapproval, Yasu usually watched television before, during, and after dinner. He particularly liked game shows, often featuring male hosts egging on giggling teenage girls as they engaged in beat-the-clock-type competitions. Usually domestic in nature, they included such games as folding a pile of rumpled shirts or vacuuming a rug scattered with rice.

Ten seconds before midnight, we joined the television audience as they counted down the year of the rabbit. BANG! The television screen filled with red and white streamers and we all bowed and wished each other "*Akemashite omedetou gozaimasu* (The year is changing and darkness is giving away to light to begin a New Year. Congratulations)!"

As Yasu popped open a giant Kirin—the champagne of Japanese beers—Tomiko placed bowls of special buckwheat noodle soup at everyone's place, since the noodles represent long life. They are also said to bring prosperity, because in the past silversmiths and goldsmiths used to pick up the scraps of metal in their workshops with soba noodle dough. A salty seafood vapor wafted up from my soup bowl, holding a wobbly poached egg in a nest of gray noodles. A pink wheat gluten flower and sprig of Japanese chervil lay submerged in the hot dashi broth, along with two round slices of *kamaboko*, the springy sweet fish paste eaten all over Japan.

Most fish paste is fabricated from the flesh of white fish (usually shark) that is pureed, thickened with starch, then steamed until cooked through, before it is sliced and added to soups and other dishes. It is usually colored white.

But not that night. Tomiko had bought a special Oshogatsu fish paste at Nishiki market so that when we looked into our bowls we beheld an edible landscape of cresting azure waves against a rose horizon under an orange setting sun.

In honor of the New Year, Tomiko had also calligraphied everyone's name onto white paper wrappers of special Oshogatsu chopsticks. Made of willow wood, they tapered at both ends, like the cedar Rikyu-bashi used at a tea kaiseki. Under my name was a figure eight knot tied from threads of red, white, yellow, purple, black, silver, and gold. Above my name was a shiny gold kanji character that said "happy." In that spirit I began slurping down the hot noodles, while a young Japanese pop star wailed in the background.

Twenty minutes later, Yasu and I climbed into Tomiko's Honda with her at the wheel. Her mother had decided to stay home, so the three of us throttled off to Honen-in Temple, a small building secluded in the woods near the Ginkaku-ji (Silver Pavilion Temple).

Considered one of Kyoto's top tourist spots, Ginkaku-ji was built as a private villa for the shogun Ashikaga Yoshimasa, who moved into his residence upon its completion in 1483. Apparently more interested in aesthetics than politics, Yoshimasa devoted most of his time to admiring women, sniffing incense, and strolling through his lush garden.

To further enhance the view, the aesthete planned to cover his pavilion in silver leaf in honor of his grandfather, who had coated Kinkaku-ji (Golden Pavilion Temple) in gold leaf. But the villa never received its fancy foil. In 1945 Yoshimasa became a Zen Buddhist monk and five years later upon his death the villa became a Buddhist temple.

It is a Japanese tradition, even if you are Shinto, to visit a Buddhist temple on New Year's Eve to hear the tolling of the gong or bell. Polytheism is common in Japan. Most Japanese engage in Shinto rituals and observe Buddhist practices. Siddhartha Gautama, more commonly known as Buddha, claimed that all of life is suffering and the cause of suffering is desire (or ego attachments). But Buddha had a solution for ceasing the suffering in people's lives: follow the Noble Eight-Fold path. The path consists of eight equally important goals, including right understanding; right thought; right speech; right action; right livelihood; right effort; right mindfulness; and right meditation. And when a person finally embodied these praxes, he could reach nirvana (release from worldly engagement).

Since Buddhists believe that man has 84,000 desires, figuratively represented by the number 108, temple bells toll 108 times at midnight on New Year's Eve all over Japan. The theory is that if a Buddhist practitioner hears every toll, he can symbolically dispel all 108 desires from the past year.

The bell was ringing in the distance as we headed down the Philosopher's Path en route to the temple. This cherry tree–lined trail was named after the twentieth-century Kyoto University philosophy professor Kitaro Nishida (1870–1945). Known for his comparisons of Western and Zen philosophies, Nishida would regularly stroll this one-and-a-half-mile route to contemplate life.

The night was unseasonably warm. Most women wore ornate kimonos or fancy Western clothes; the men had on dressy slacks and sweaters. Perhaps in deference to me, Yasu and Tomiko had also worn blue jeans and tennis shoes. I had dressed for a walk in the woods.

After fifteen minutes of strolling down a sandy path lit with stone lanterns, we crossed the bridge over the canal and found our way through the bamboo groves to Honen-in Temple, where in a sort of roofed wooden corral hung the bell. People were yanking a thick rope attached to a smooth wooden log, sending it crashing into the hollow green metal vessel to release a loud bong. Tomiko and Yasu went first, pulling on the rope and then bowing and clapping to Buddha. They then stood back to watch me do the same. I hesitated, wondering if an Episcopalian should be doing such a thing. The thought evaporated when a bonze in black and yellow robes beckoned me forward to ring the bell. In seconds, we were hurrying off to the Kamigamo Shrine, where Yasu and Tomiko had gotten married.

Built in 679 and dedicated to Raijin—the god of thunder—the massive complex houses two glittering cones of silvery-white sand said to represent mountains upon which the god could rest. After passing under a huge orange gate, a symbolic form of Shinto purification, suddenly we heard a shout.

"Konbanwa!" It was Mr. Omura, dressed in an elegant black sweater and charcoal slacks. He trotted under the entrance gate to join us along the expansive gravel path. "Happy New Year," he wheezed, accepting a lit match from Yasu. He inhaled, then turned away and blew out a stream of smoke. When I asked him if he had come with family, he laughed.

"Too many people to drag away from their noodles." He ground out his cigarette in the gravel. "Hold on," he said, then disappeared into the dark.

While we waited for him in the courtyard, several Japanese stepped up to a wooden box topped with wooden slats that looked like a giant hibachi. They tossed in coins, then tugged on a multicolored cotton rope, thick as a tree trunk, to sound a bell. After clapping twice to summon the resident *kami* (god) they bowed their heads in worship. Money and prayers at a Shinto shrine were originally offerings of thanks to the particular god (of sun, rain, thunder, etc.) in exchange for a blessing bestowed upon the worshipper's crops. Nowadays, the god's blessing can be bestowed upon anything.

"Here," said Mr. Omura, slightly out of breath as he handed me a paper charm. I thanked him, then looked at Tomiko and Yasu.

"You tie it to the tree and make a wish," said Tomiko. I stepped over to a pine tree fluttering with hopes and attached my talisman. I closed my eyes and wished for something that would come true in August 1991, then tied the paper to a branch.

It was nearly 1:30 when we waved good-bye to Mr. Omura and headed back to the car. Just as we passed under the orange gate, Tomiko stopped and reached into her jean jacket pocket.

"This is for you," she said, handing me a small red brocade bag. Inside was a tiny white ceramic rabbit with a purple cord looped around its neck.

"For good luck," said Yasu, grinning. I thanked the couple in the politest form of Japanese that I knew, then placed my hands in a prayer position and bowed deeply. But the sentiments felt inadequate.

So breaking all rules of Japanese etiquette, I gave them both a huge American hug.

Year-Crossing Buckwheat Noodles (Toshikoshi Soba)

These are the nutty buckwheat noodles that families all over Japan enjoy on New Year's Eve to bring them good luck and a long life. Although recipes vary from family to family, this special soup always includes soba in a base of dashi. *Kamaboko is available in Japanese markets, often in the freezer section. If you buy the fish cake frozen, thaw it before slicing. For an added punch, sprinkle on some* shichimi, *a seven-spice mixture containing cayenne pepper available at any Japanese market.*

One ¾-pound bunch spinach, rinsed, tough stems removed
5 cups dashi (page 48)
5 tablespoons soy sauce
1½ tablespoons sugar
I tablespoon mirin
Twelve ¼-inch-thick slices kamaboko (fish cake)
4 large eggs
8 ounces dried soba
4 sprigs mitsuba (Japanese wild chervil)

I. Bring a small amount of lightly salted water to a boil in a medium shallow saucepan. Add the spinach, cover, and steam over low heat until the leaves have collapsed and just wilted, I to 2 minutes. Drain, form the spinach into a bundle, and lightly roll in a clean tea towel to remove excess water. Cut the spinach bundle into four pieces.

2. Pour the dashi into a large saucepan and bring to a boil. Add the soy sauce, sugar, and mirin and bring to a simmer. Add the sliced fish cake.

3. Using the same saucepan used to cook the spinach, poach the eggs until soft in the middle. Keep warm.

4. Bring a medium pot of water to a boil. Add the soba and cook according to package directions until al dente. Drain.

5. For each serving of soup, use a two-prong carving fork to twirl one fourth of the soba into a coiled nest. Place in a large soup bowl and add a bundle of spinach. Gently arrange an egg over the noodles and then arrange several slices of fish cake near the egg. Carefully ladle the broth around the noodles and garnish the soup with a sprig of mitsuba.

Makes 4 servings

13.

Putting
on the Obi

cold snap occurred overnight, so that when I awoke
on New Year's Day the gray tile rooftops outside my window were
fuzzed with a thin layer of snow. It was hardly a day for swimming, but that is what Yasu had in mind, as he did every January
1, when he drove to a lake in northern Kyoto to join his swimming club in a Shinto purification ritual. About forty students
ranging in age from seven to seventy would meet at the lake and
paddle through the icy water until their instructor told them to
stop. The plunge had been scheduled for noon, to allow plenty of
time for New Year's visits and breakfast.

Like families all over Japan, that morning we tucked into a
special New Year's breakfast soup called *ozoni*. Although recipes
vary from region to region, they all contain mochi because the
pounded rice dumplings symbolize the breaking of "bread" with

the New Year's deity Toshigami-sama. The rest of the ingredients in the soup, aside from the dashi base, vary according to what is fresh and regionally available. So around Hiroshima, for example, cooks add oysters, prawns, and saltwater eel caught from the nearby Inland Sea to their ozoni, while natives of Tokyo toss in nubbins of chicken, sliced fish cake, and spinach-like greens. For those living in Kyoto, the ozoni always includes lots of sweet white miso.

At Tomiko's suggestion, I chose one of the rice dumplings we had brought back from the Omuras'. The ones blended with bulgur seemed most appropriate for breakfast, so I placed one in my red lacquer bowl. Tomiko ladled the thick golden soup over the grain-flecked paddy, then dropped in a pinch of feathery bonito flakes. They fluttered on the surface and then wilted, adding a cured fish tang that nicely cut through the soup's heavy sweetness. Within minutes, the mochi at the bottom of my bowl had melted, so I lifted it up in long noodle-like strands, which I wound around my chopsticks.

"Don't choke," Tomiko cautioned everyone at the table. Every year in Japan several people die eating the mochi in their ozoni. Although freshly made mochi poses less of a hazard, the commercial versions soften into thick gluey ropes that lodge in people's throats.

After carefully finishing our soup, we all climbed into Yasu's truck to drive to the lake. On the way, we stopped at his widowed mother's house so he could pay his respects, a common New Year's Day tradition. Given the strained nature of their relationship, I was advised to stay in the truck, while Tomiko and her mother accompanied Yasu. No sooner had I waved them off than they were marching back to the truck from the perfunctory joyless visit based on filial piety.

Shortly before noon, Yasu's truck pulled up the muddy dirt path toward the small placid lake surrounded by pines. Many of the swimmers had already arrived and were milling around a worn wooden building in various degrees of undress. Yasu waved and chatted with several swim mates, while a group of spectators began to build a small fire in an old oil drum to warm up the swimmers after their dip. When it spat and crackled, Tomiko and I hurried over to thaw our fingers over the rippling heat.

Suddenly, the instructor pulled up in a white Nissan. Clearly, he wasn't going to swim with his students. He had on a natty russet wool coat, flared tan tweed pants, and hazelnut suede shoes that carried him in a purposeful direction over to the dock. As the rest of the students slipped off their clothes, the instructor lowered the thermometer into the water. The girls in their navy-blue one-piece suits stood trembling under the eaves of the building. The boys and men in their diaper-soft thongs broke out in goose pimples. Some tucked their palms under their armpits to warm up; others clasped their hands together, as if shaking dice.

"Thirty-six degrees," the instructor exclaimed with a wry smile. Cheers rose up through the chatters. The year before the swimmers had been forced to crack the ice to get into the water.

The adults and children walked single file down the dock's wooden stairs and silently slipped into the frigid water. There was no yelling, hollering, or even squealing from the children. At one point, Yasu began to move across the glassy surface holding his head above the water and one arm high above his head, as if carrying an imaginary sword. He was imitating an old samurai swimming art known as *suieijutsu*, which developed as a way for a samurai to cross a body of water in his armor. Yasu's swimming club had also mastered the ability to move silently through the water, a useful samurai technique that enabled the warriors to approach enemy territory making no more noise than the sound of small waves gently lapping the shore. Its application to contemporary life was the mental and physical discipline required to master the art.

Finally, the instructor called his students from the lake. Shuddering and blue, they emerged from the water, whereupon mothers and wives lunged forward to swaddle their loved ones in towels. Several swimmers dashed over to the oil drum, where they stood in bare feet and terry-cloth capes waving their fingers over the orange flames. While Tomiko rubbed Yasu's sinewy body with a bath towel, he pressed a cigarette between his purple lips. Minutes later, he tossed the butt into the drum and put on his blue jeans, white turtleneck, and red down vest. After waving farewell to several friends, he bowed to his instructor and climbed into his truck.

By the time we returned home, the ashen sky had become smudged with black. My watch read almost 5:30. After days of preparation and anticipation, the osechi ryori hour had finally arrived.

Tomiko took off her padded jean jacket and then whispered to her mother, who nodded and smiled at me. "Come upstairs," said Tomiko, "I have a surprise for you." She looked excited as she always did when introducing me to something new. We climbed the wooden stairs to her bedroom, leaving her mother setting the table and Yasu watching a game show.

"This is for you to wear," said Tomiko, gesturing to a gorgeous red-, white-, and green-plaid kimono spread across her bed. She was beaming.

"Where did you get it?" I whispered, stroking the thick cotton.

"I bought it for my flower arranging classes. And this one's from my wedding." From the open wardrobe she pulled out a shimmering pale peach kimono covered with ivory and watery blue chrysanthemums—the family crest of the Imperial Household. The fine silk looked as fragile as a sheet of phyllo dough.

In a matter of seconds, I realized why wearing a kimono was no longer practical for modern-day life. It was impossible to put on alone! At first I thought I would go into my bedroom and simply fold the kimono around myself like a bathrobe, but it proved much more complicated.

Tomiko opened her bureau drawer and pulled out a light cotton underkimono. "This goes on first," she said, shaking out the folds. I removed my clothes, keeping on my bra and underpants for modesty's sake, then put on the thin white robe. Tomiko secured it with numerous strings. She eased my arms through a sort of undercoat and cinched the cotton cords snug round my rib cage and waist. Over that, she placed a heavy stiff collar that extended over my shoulders, not unlike what football players wear. Then she helped me into the actual kimono. The ponderous fabric slumped over my shoulders and bunched around my feet. She hoisted it up, creating a fold in the middle, then strapped on the obi to hold the pleat in place. She knotted a red cord around the obi and yanked it tight in the back to stay secure. My breasts were flattened and I could only take short shallow breaths.

Because the obi cut into my sternum, Tomiko helped pull the little split-toed white socks over my feet. With the tight tube of kimono around my legs, I took baby steps into my room to put on lip-gloss and the gold bracelet John had given me for Christmas.

Several minutes later, Tomiko met me at the top of the stairs in her wedding kimono. She was totally transformed. Out of her blue jeans, loose shirt, and bulky sweater, she radiated femininity.

The kimono elongated her torso and created a smooth cylinder from neck to toe, the hallmark of a beautiful Japanese figure. A striking navy obi with red, yellow, white, and turquoise chrysanthemums hugged her waist. A flirtatious cream collar peeked out from under the pale peach robe. The sleeves were just high enough to expose a sensual swatch of skin above her wrist. When she moved her arm, the inner fold revealed an erotic flash of scarlet and white silk.

"Kirei, kirei," murmured Tomiko's mother as we entered the family room. She had changed for the occasion into a puce sweater and brown wool skirt. Yasu still had on his clothes from swimming, including the down vest.

"Nice," he said, with a nicotine grin. "Pretty Japanese ladies."

As Tomiko and I sank to our knees on floor pillows, her mother filled our sake cups with an amber-green liquid. Called *toso*, it was a traditional New Year's elixir made from sweet rice wine seasoned with a Chinese herbal-medicine mixture called *tososan*. Meant to ward off the evil spirits, the drink was honeyed, warm, and laced with cinnamon and peppery sansho.

To display the contents of the stacked lacquer boxes, Tomiko's mother had arranged the various layers in the center of the table. The top layer always contains the traditional sweet dishes and hors d'oeuvres, while the second layer holds steamed, boiled, and vinegared offerings. The third box consists of foods that have been grilled or fried.

Since not everything fit into the lacquer boxes, Tomiko's mother had placed a long rectangular dish at everyone's place holding three different nibbles. The first one was a small bowl of herring eggs to represent fertility. Waxy yellow in color, they had a plastic pop and mild saline flavor. Next came a miniature stack of sugar- and soy-braised burdock root cut like penne pasta and tossed with a rich nutty cream made from pounded sesame seeds. Called *tataki gobo* (pounded burdock root), the dish is so named because the gobo (root) symbolizes the hope for a stable, deeply rooted life, while the homonym for tataki (pounded) also means "joy aplenty." The third item consisted of a tiny clump of intensely flavored soy-caramelized sardines that tasted like ocean candy. Called *tazukuri*, meaning "paddy-tilling," the sticky fish symbolized hopes for a good harvest, since in ancient times, farmers used chopped sardines along with ash for fertilizer.

After these tidbits, we switched to regular hot sake and began eating from the various boxes. With our special New Year's chopsticks, we picked up fat shiny black soybeans cooked in clear sugar syrup to bring us good health. We bit into salt-grilled shrimp with long whiskers and sucked out the savory head juices. The shrimp represented one's hope to live long enough to have lengthy whiskers like an old man and a curled back like many of Japan's elderly (who suffer from osteoporosis due to the lack of calcium in their diet).

We crunched on a sprightly salad of shredded daikon and carrots tossed with vinegar and sugar and then sampled various vegetables, which, honestly, looked incredibly unappetizing. Having marinated in a potent sugar-soy bath that would preserve the vegetables for several days, the carrot flowers, broccoli florets, and snow peas had all turned dirty shades of rust-green and olive-brown.

After more sake, we dipped into salmon roe for fecundity, followed by salmon and kelp rolls. We also had slices of rare beef that had been seared in a drip of soy, plus grilled duck and pickled lotus root rounds, representing the root of the lotus flower that blooms in the lake of the Land of Happiness where Buddha lives. Each morsel lay nestled in separate sections of the various lacquer boxes.

"Have some *tai* (sea bream)," said Tomiko, passing me a container holding several slices of the coral-red fish, eaten because it sounds like *medetai*, meaning "auspicious." Her pale powdered cheeks had become flushed from the sake. She fanned herself with her palm. *"Atsui* (hot), no?" She looked at Yasu.

"Most Japanese ladies no drink alcohol," said Yasu, turning to me. "Makes face too red." He rubbed his cheek with his fist and laughed. I looked at Tomiko, who smirked, then bit into a huge slice of beef.

I was the first to stop eating. Not because I was full, but because the obi had begun to choke my waist. I excused myself to go to the bathroom. Where to begin? I tugged on the back of the obi and felt a slight ease of pressure. Then I reached inside my kimono sleeves to loosen a cord or two. I pulled, twisted, wrenched, and yanked until I had eased open the obi, just enough to accommodate another piece of eel, some pickled mackerel, and a bite, which I immediately regretted, of sea slug, a slimy, wet, bony sea creature.

By the time we had finished another round of sake, fresh strawberries, and a cup of brewed green tea, the obi had tightened its vise-like grip. Is this what geisha and *maiko* (apprentice geisha) have to put up with night after night? I wondered. Women must withstand such discomfort in this culture, physically and emotionally. As much as I encouraged my female students to pursue their interest in medicine and law, they would always shrug and say it was not the way. Wives tolerated their husbands' philandering by quietly telling themselves it was their way. No wonder Tomiko preferred our Western way of thinking, which offered women much more freedom.

Not wanting to offend Tomiko, I kept on the torturous kimono to wash and dry all the dishes. We all bowed goodnight to each other and headed upstairs, except for Tomiko's mother, who planned to sleep on the couch in the family room.

Such relief to undo the obi! I peeled off the kimono and various undergarments until I was down to my underwear. Pink cord marks curled around my ribs like serpents. Lying in bed, trying to rub away the cord marks, I attempted to recall all we had eaten but rolled over and fell asleep before I got to dessert.

14.

Two Birthday
Gifts

For the next several weeks Kyoto became a frozen world of black and white. The snow had arrived. The Kamo River hardened into a windswept bolt of silvery ice. Shrine and temple courtyards became empty white expanses dotted with shivering trees and snow-cloaked lanterns. The temperature dipped into the teens. The sky lost its color. Everyone around me, it seemed, was suffering.

First, John wrote to tell me his grandmother had died. Then a harrowing letter arrived from my best friend, Margaret, describing how she had been assaulted in the entryway of her Boston condominium on Christmas Eve.

Even Tomiko seemed sluggish and down. She had taken to sleeping longer in the morning and napping on a small electric rug in the family room off the kitchen. Often after returning home from teaching, I would find her curled up on the floor in the dark. "Maybe she's pregnant," my mother wrote.

When I called Stephen shortly after New Year's to wish him well, he had bad news of his own: he had suffered a stroke.

"It was all the booze and cigaress," he said with a slur.

"Is there anything I can do?" I asked, reeling with disbelief. He was only thirty-nine.

"Nah, I'll be fine. I have trouvvle walking, but I have a cane. Juss have to do some physical therapy."

"Are you going to tea kaiseki class this Saturday?" I doubted he would but still wanted to ask.

"Yeah, I think so. Less meet at the café near school. If I don't show up after thirty minutes, juss go to class."

Stephen did, indeed, show up. We met beforehand to discuss the recipes that he, once again, had translated. He explained that since it was January, everything we would make would be red and white, the two congratulatory colors in Japan. I forgot to ask why.

Sure enough, we added crimson azuki beans to the miso soup. The marinated scallop dish received a red carrot and grated radish garnish. The wanmori was embellished with pink and white shrimp. The chopstick wash was enhanced with ivory pine nuts and rose pickled plum. Even the "insisting dish" conveyed best wishes through thin slices of coral-colored smoked salmon brightened with lemon juice and spicy scarlet sprouts.

After class, I assisted Stephen with some of his errands, since he still used a cane to walk and had no strength in one arm. We stopped by the dry cleaners to pick up David's kimonos, the corner market for some dishwashing liquid and Diet Cokes, and finally the hardware store for a new broom that wouldn't catch on the fine weave of the tatami in their tearoom. Just as I was getting ready to head home, Stephen mentioned that he and David had decided to throw another *chaji* (a kaiseki meal followed by a formal tea ceremony).

"You're welcome to help," he said, leaning on his cane in his sitting room. "Only this time you can show up at a more civilized hour." He wiped his nose, sighed, and dropped into a chair.

"Come by around ten. The chaji won't begin till early evening." He leaned back and closed his eyes. When I asked him the date, he replied it was scheduled for the next Saturday, my birthday. "That okay?" he asked, his eyes opening.

I smiled and nodded. Then told him to take care of himself, and wished him farewell.

It was to be a fifteenth-century-style Zen Tea kaiseki, considered the precursor of Rikyu's modest style, which meant the meal would be composed of one soup and two side dishes.

Stephen was already working in the kitchen when I called from the outside gate. A woman named Joyce, who was studying tea, came out to let me in.

Stephen still appeared pale and his face looked drawn. His arm quivered and the limp made it difficult to get around the kitchen. Yet, despite his limitations, he had managed to pick up all the ingredients for the chaji, as well as buy lunch for everyone.

For the next several hours, Joyce and I slivered vegetables and helped Stephen prepare the sweets. We pulled out all the tea kaiseki serving dishes and utensils and arranged them on the tatami in the order we planned to use them.

Choosing appropriate wares for a tea kaiseki requires knowing about their various characteristics and paying attention to the season at hand. Evoking a sense of warmth in winter months and coolness in the summer months is essential. So at a July tea kaiseki, for example, raw fish often arrives on a bed of cracked ice in a glass or chilled metal dish. In January it would likely show up in a stoneware vessel glazed in dark earthy tones.

But variety is also important, which is why wood, lacquer, porcelain, glass, metal, and stoneware are used throughout the meal. Not only do they add visual appeal but a tactile one as well, since soup is drunk directly from lacquer bowls, rice bowls are cradled in the palm, and serving receptacles and utensils are picked up, passed, and admired.

The Japanese also know that unrelieved simplicity or ornamentation becomes tedious. That is why, for example, after a succession of black lacquer and plain stoneware, a striking red sake bottle embellished with flowers will arrive. It provides a refreshing contrast and, because it is unexpected, makes a lasting impression.

"I'm going to get lunch," announced Stephen, hobbling outside to retrieve three cardboard bento boxes of sushi he'd left chilling on the back doorstep. I jumped up to help, but he waved me away. "It's part of my therapy." He returned balancing the sushi boxes in the crook of his good arm. I filled three water glasses and carried them over to where Stephen and Joyce were sitting on the tatami counter area inside the kitchen.

"You guys know what *sushi* means, don't you?" asked Stephen, lifting off the lid of his bento box. I looked at Joyce.

"Sure," she said, putting down her water glass. "Fish on vinegared rice."

"Wrong," said Stephen, popping a shrimp in his mouth. "*Sushi* means 'vinegared rice.' *Nigiri zushi* is the correct term because the verb *nigiru* means 'to grasp, or hold tight,' as in a rice ball, and the Japanese spell and pronounce sushi with a *z*. So nigiri zushi means 'stuff over vinegared rice that you can grasp.' Seafood is the most popular topping, although there are others, like omelet and *natto.*"

I loved natto. Most foreigners despise the slippery brown fermented soybeans, saying they smell like stale sweat socks. But when you mix the beans with raw egg and scallions and spoon them over hot sticky rice, they taste like a combination of syrupy espresso and a ripe runny cheese.

"The second style is maki zushi," said Stephen, dipping his tuna into soy. "*Maki* means 'to roll' and this style of finger-food is made by spreading vinegared rice over nori, filling it with stuff, and then rolling it up and cutting it into rolls. If you ask for a hand roll, then you get a cone of nori packed with all kinds of good stuff." His eyes sparkled with excitement.

"And you both know the pickled ginger is to cleanse your palate between different bites of fish, right?" We both nodded.

"And you know never to add wasabi to soy when eating sushi?"

"What do you mean?" I asked, quickly swallowing a huge slab of yellowtail.

"You only add wasabi to soy when you're eating sashimi," said Stephen, "because the chef has already smeared wasabi over the rice for nigiri zushi or maki rolls."

"Then why does the chef give you a cone of wasabi when you order sushi?" asked Joyce.

"It's like putting salt and pepper shakers on the table at a fancy dinner party," answered Stephen. "It's a formality."

"And if you do add wasabi to your soy when eating sushi—" I started to ask.

"The chef thinks you're shit," butted in Stephen, chuckling. "That's because he's seasoned your food perfectly, and you're telling him otherwise."

I cringed, thinking of all the sushi chefs I had insulted over the years.

"And," said Stephen, "when you go to a zushi bar, if you're going to drink sake, order it before dinner. Because sake is based on rice and the Japanese consider drinking it with sushi to be redundant." He wiped a dribble of water from his chin with his shirtsleeve.

"Kind of like ordering a side of bread to go with your sandwich?" asked Joyce.

"Uh-huh," said Stephen, eating a pinch of pickled ginger.

After lunch we went out for coffee at a nearby café, since David was running errands and would not return for several more hours. Then the three of us trooped back to Stephen's house to rest.

Around 5:30, Stephen and I went into the kitchen to prepare the final sauces and garnishes, while Joyce changed into a majestic ice-blue kimono embellished with snow-white pine swags. Since it had begun to turn dark, David, now back, placed candlelit lanterns along the stone path.

The particular type of tea ceremony that Stephen and David were hosting goes by the name Yobanashi, or "evening talk." It is usually held in winter. To warm up the guests and stimulate conversation, Stephen filled four small mugs with hot *amazake*, a thick fermented rice drink made with the fermenting agent koji. For a nip of heat, he grated fresh ginger into each cup.

"Here," said Stephen, passing me an extra mug. I had first tasted amazake at a teahouse in Nara with Tomiko and her mother the day after New Year's. It was creamy and sweet and tinged with the flavor of sake. Stephen's version was like sipping a warm ginger frappé.

We prepared the first tray, beginning with the miso soup.

When properly made, miso soup for a tea kaiseki can be likened to a fine wine. The first taste strikes the palate with a burst of flavor, followed by deeper savory notes. It is the "finish" that matters. The chef wants the flavor reverberations to be so hauntingly delicious, the guests will yearn for more. Seconds are almost always served.

The secret to creating such a tantalizing flavor lies in blending together different kinds of miso. In winter, for example, a small amount of savory red miso combines with the rich white variety. As the days become warmer, more and more red miso is incorporated to balance the heavy sweetness of the white. At the height of summer, only salty varieties are used to create the lightest possible lingering sensation.

To give his soup depth, Stephen stirred red and white miso together before smearing it over the flattened underside of a wooden pot lid. He held the cap of miso over a gas flame, moving the lid in circles, until the soybean paste bubbled and charred all over. He kept scraping and turning the blistered paste with a knife until it became thick and concentrated, then whisked it into a pot of heated dashi. To achieve a satiny consistency, he poured the soup through a small woven bamboo sieve several times before ladling it into the bowls.

Miso soup served at a tea kaiseki fills roughly one third of the bowl, not two thirds, as in restaurants. The amount is supposed to equal three sips, which are supposed to be interspersed with bites of rice. Proper form in the tearoom calls for guests to take one bite of rice, a sip of soup, more rice, then more soup, until the soup is gone (but never the rice, to avoid having the host feel obliged to serve more). If guests request a second bowl of miso soup, they receive double the amount of the first serving, approximately six sips.

Unlike the miso soup served in restaurants, however, which contains lots of little goodies, like seaweed and diced tofu, the miso soup served at a tea kaiseki usually features one central ingredient that breaks the soup's surface. Depending upon the season, you might encounter a square of bean curd, a ball of wheat gluten, or a wheel of daikon radish simmered in dashi until butterscotch sweet. These central ingredients are usually cooked separately before being placed in the soup bowl and crowned with a seasonal garnish, such as fall chestnut, peppery spring shoot, or fragrant summer herb.

Stephen chose spinach-like greens as his focal point, which he blanched in water, squeezed dry, and mounded into the center of each bowl. He carefully ladled the miso soup around the greens and garnished them with a blob of mustard that he pushed off the tip of a butter knife with his finger. When the guests opened the lid of the soup, they would stir the fiery condiment into the broth to add a charge of heat.

Although Japanese cooking aims to spotlight the natural flavors of ingredients, zesty accents often appear to provide contrast. A blast of pungent wasabi counterposes the oily richness of raw fish. A shake of spicy herbal sansho cuts through the fatty succulence of grilled eel. And a dab of stinging yellow mustard offsets the mild sweetness of boiled greens.

Joyce and I placed the matching black lacquer covers over the bowls and set them in the bottom right-hand corner of each tray. Black lacquer is favored in tea kaiseki for its ability to trap heat, as well as its elegant luster. The exception is when cinnabar lacquerware is used to serve vegetarian tea kaiseki, a carryover from the olden days when tea kaiseki featured vegetarian temple food in August to avoid the risk of meat and fish spoiling in the heat.

The cinnabar wares were chosen to mimic the everyday red lac-querware the monks use for their vegetarian temple food.

Stephen scooped the rice into the shape of the figure 1 and placed it in the black bowl. He chose the linear shape because at David's tea school it represents *ichi*, meaning "one," and refers to the number one place of honor rice holds in Japan. Aside from being a staple food, rice symbolizes life and all beginnings. Each tea school shapes its rice differently, however, in order to set itself apart. At Mushanokoji our tea kaiseki teacher, Sen Sumiko, told us to form the rice into a small ball, since the round shape repre-sents a vestige of the *mosso*, the rounded implement used in Zen monasteries to measure out cooked rice.

Joyce and I placed the lacquer lids snugly over the rice bowls. One of the pleasures of removing the lid is to see the pearls of condensation that have gathered underneath; it evokes the purity of early morning dew.

At the top of each tray, Stephen placed the mukozuke, a small dish of sea bream sashimi tossed with light Kyoto-style soy sauce, a bit of dashi, and zesty yuzu juice. Unlike restaurant sashimi, which arrives with a separate saucer for wasabi and soy sauce, raw fish at a tea kaiseki comes seasoned in advance with a delicate dressing that harmonizes with the rest of the meal's sub-tle flavors. A bit of dashi or sake usually lightens the soy sauce, while a squirt of citrus adds brightness.

In keeping with the tea kaiseki philosophy of serving hot foods in heated dishes and cold fare in chilled ones, we had soaked the stoneware in cold water (and likewise had warmed the miso soup bowls in hot water). The wet ceramic would provide natural refreshment, like a rock at the beach dampened by waves.

In the center of each tray, we placed a small welcome dish.

It was a sort of pâté of abalone liver lightened with dashi. Rare and unusual foods seldom appear at a tea kaiseki because they belie the meal's "simple" nature and might unnerve the guests if they had never eaten them before. Nevertheless, each person received a teaspoon of the pâté, which I placed on a spicy, mint-like *shiso* leaf and garnished with nori filaments.

After wiping dry the Rikyu-bashi chopsticks, I laid them along the bottom edge of each tray. Stephen then signaled to Joyce that we were ready.

In traditional Japanese fashion, Joyce knelt with the first tray in front of her knees before partially sliding open the fusuma, which separated the tearoom from the kitchen. Joyce wasn't positioned to face the guests, but instead knelt with her right shoulder to the panel, so close to me I could touch her. After she pulled open the sliding door, she rose, stepped inside, and then sank down again onto her knees, whereupon she reached over to her left for the tray, slid it in front of her knees, then pushed the panel shut. Although I couldn't see what happened next, I knew from talking with Stephen and David that Joyce would stand up with the tray in one swift movement and carry it to David. He, in turn, would crumple to bent knees and slowly hand the tray to the principal guest, who would inch toward David to receive it with both hands.

When all the trays had been delivered in this manner, Stephen and I readied the wanmori, or climactic dish. In a large black lacquer bowl decorated with graceful gold brushwork I placed a dragon ball, a deep-fried round of juicy tofu stuffed with crunchy chopped carrots and lotus root. Stephen had purchased the golden balls at Nishiki market; we had simply placed them in his steamer to reheat them for the wanmori. He twirled hot-cooked soba around chopsticks to create a tight coil, then tucked the nutty noodle nests next to each dragon ball. I ladled a small amount of dashi over the noodles, after which Stephen grated a juicy white daikon radish over each bowl to resemble winter slush.

One of the many delights of an "evening talk" tea is the tease of hot and cold dishes, both visually and in terms of temperature. This interplay symbolizes the frigid weather outside in contrast to the cozy warmth of the tearoom.

Therefore, having just served a hot dish, Stephen and I prepared an "extra" offering that was light and cold. It was a refreshing snarl of slivered red carrot and chopped daikon tossed with vinegar, soy sauce, and water. When the guests had finished that, for contrast we grilled unctuous teriyaki-marinated butterfish for the yakimono and sprinkled it with tongue-numbing sansho. "Put five small pieces on the dish," instructed Stephen, as I divided up the fillet.

Food arrangement in Japan involves a multiplicity of factors beyond mere composition, including the auspiciousness of certain numbers. For some Japanese, serving one slice of any food is bad luck because *hitokire* (one piece) can also mean "kill someone." Four pieces are also avoided because *shi* (four) can also mean "death."

On the other hand, even numbers are yin, or dark and negative, while odd numbers are yang, or light and positive. As a result, most people tend to serve foods in clusters of odd numbers, such as three, five, or seven.

So based on Stephen's recommendation, I placed five pieces of the grilled butterfish on a single dish. But I didn't just spread them out on the plate. I overlapped them in the "piled-up" style, so that the burnished morsels would retain their heat and, when one piece was removed, the whole stack would not collapse.

Joyce delivered the fish along with a container of rice for extra helpings. Rice appears several times during a tea kaiseki. And each time it does the texture changes slightly. When it initially appears on the first tray, the grains are wet and soft because they have been skimmed off the top of the pot. The second time rice shows up it tastes more firm. By the third serving, after the grilled dish, the texture has become quite sticky. The final offering is the crusty shards stuck to the bottom of the pot that are served in warm salted water.

At this particular tea kaiseki, however, the grilled fish was the last course. The guests received no chopstick wash, no tray with tidbits from the mountains and ocean, no extra dish to go with more sake, no additional offering to use up leftover ingredients, no pickles, and no crusty brown rice bits mixed with salted warm water. The tea kaiseki was over.

David, who was now outside the tearoom, hovered by the sliding panel with one ear tipped toward his guests. Approximately five minutes later all chatter ceased. Suddenly, there was a *clack!*

In traditional tea kaiseki fashion, the guests had dropped their chopsticks on their lacquer trays in one synchronized movement to signal they were done. It was a subtle moment unbroken by the coarse call of human voices.

David gently slid open the panel to tell his guests he hoped they had enjoyed the modest meal. They responded with a soft chorus of "*Gochiso sama deshita* (Thank you for your hospitality)."

While Joyce cleared the trays, David set the charcoal in the brazier. All the guests spoke English, because I overheard them asking David all kinds of questions, such as: Where did the teakettle come from? Who made the incense container? Those were the kinds of set questions guests are supposed to ask the tea master at that point in a chaji. Sometimes I wondered if people ever strayed from their script. ("Say, David, how was your trip to Tokyo?" "Oh, fine, thanks for asking.")

I suspect the reason for limiting conversational topics in the tearoom is to set the tone for the ceremonial tea to come. After all, when you're headed on the path to nirvana, why take a detour to Tokyo or elsewhere?

Back in the kitchen, Stephen, Joyce, and I began to arrange the sweets on small plates. In keeping with the traditional kinds of confections fabricated in the fifteenth century, each guest received a whole dried persimmon, a chestnut, and a shiny shiitake mushroom cap that had been "candied" in a braising mixture of soy, mirin, and sake. None of these treats contained refined sugar because it wasn't widely used in tea sweets until after the first Portuguese trading ships came to Japan in 1543.

After the guests had quietly eaten their sweets, David invited them outside for some brisk air and a stretch. This interlude would give David time to ready the tearoom before making the ceremonial bowls of tea. He would roll up the scroll and replace it with an arrangement of flowers in order to honor the Shinto belief that all living things manifest a divine spirit. He would also light incense to evoke the fragrance of Buddha's paradise. Time out of the tearoom would additionally allow the guests to reconnect with nature, thus further purging themselves of any material concerns.

The guests spoke in hushed tones in the garden, since listening is a delight and necessity in tea. Hearing the rustle of the wind through the trees is a highly pleasurable experience; so is the soft scratching of the tea master's broom as he sweeps clean the tatami. These sounds elicit a flow of emotions that go beyond the actual sound itself. To hear the leaves flutter suggests an awareness of the breeze. Where has it come from? Where will it go? Whose cheek has it brushed? Is it the same wind Sen no Rikyu heard?

The sweeping of the broom conveys a sense of purity. This religious symbolism would be repeated during the tea ceremony when David purified the tea bowl and wiped the tea utensils with a special cloth.

When David was ready to receive his guests, he gently tapped a bell, just the way a Zen master does to call the monks to meditation. The idea of not speaking is important in tea. Often, the guests and host use little signs and noises to express themselves. The gentle ring told the guests it was time to leave the chill of winter behind and return to the cozy warmth of the tearoom. In a way, the tea master is a kind of Zen priest facilitating his guests' journey to enlightenment. Had it been sunny out, David would have hit a gong, since its low yin tone complements the bright yang of day.

While David made thick tea and then thin tea for his guests, we cleaned up, whispering and washing as quietly as possible to avoid being heard through the panel.

Around 9:30, the swish of fabric and scuff of tabi on the tatami indicated that the guests were getting up. I could hear them softly thanking David for the incredible evening in genuine tones of appreciation. Thinking about it, the gathering must have been sublime. How could it not have been? Imagine tiptoeing off into the woods to gather in a small beautiful room with an intimate group of friends, then sharing an exquisite meal and a bowl of tea that holds the promise of transcendence.

Since it was late, I said my good-byes and pedaled home. Around 10:30, I pulled into Tomiko and Yasu's driveway, my legs still vibrating from the ride. The light in their family room shone out through the metal blinds, so I knew they were up.

Still chilled, I kept on my fleece jacket and sat with them in the family room eating a cold rice ball that I had picked up from a nearby 7-Eleven store. It was a triangle of sushi stuffed with sweet pickled gourd and wrapped in nori. I had grabbed it unknowingly from the store's many offerings, since I still couldn't read much kanji. Tomiko made coarse green tea to warm everyone up and pulled out a box of pine nut cookies from her snack cupboard. As we sipped, and nibbled, and talked about everyone's day, we had our own tea ceremony of sorts, which became the crowning touch to an extraordinary birthday.

The next day I continued my birthday celebration in a more raucous style. Tomiko had suggested I invite several friends from the Guesthouse for a "quiet" birthday dinner. So earlier that week I had called Jocelyn and Eric and a few others, hoping to convince perhaps five or six people to stop by. Instead, twenty people showed up bearing presents and eager to party to a cassette tape of mixed tunes my younger sister had made me for Christmas.

"What a feeeeling!" screamed Irene Cara from *Flashdance,* as Eric grabbed Jocelyn's hand. They bumped and twirled in the family room. Others joined in as Tomiko danced off to the kitchen to fetch a small griddle. Elbows knocked and hands snatched savory rice-stuffed tofu pouches I had re-created from tea kaiseki class.

"C'mon, stand up and dance," urged Opus. Beer bottles popped. Soon wheat noodles, onions, carrots, and shredded cabbage were sizzling away on the hot metal for *yakisoba.* I set down a platter of scattered sushi and Tomiko poured oyster and beef okonomiyaki batter onto the griddle. She shook her hips and smiled at Yasu, who lit a cigarette.

"Every little thing she does is magic," howled the Police, as we danced, ate, drank, and danced some more.

Around 1:00 in the morning, after the last of the guests had tootled off, I heard Tomiko groan in the back room. "I don't believe it," she said, coming into the kitchen carrying a shiny white box. "I forgot the cake." She looked crestfallen.

So we decided to have it ourselves with some sparkling wine that someone had brought. While Yasu poured the bubbly, Tomiko pushed pink candles into the velvety chocolate square decorated with fat ganache roses. I made a wish and blew out the candles, then cut through the cocoa-dusted frosting and into the rum-soaked center to slide out three pieces. They came from the portion of the cake where Tomiko and Yasu had asked the baker to write "Happy Birthday Victoria," which they sang to me.

Red and White Miso Soup
with Sea Greens

Wakame seaweed is available in both fresh and dried forms. Look for the dried slivered version that does not include the tough spine. In Japan, wakame often enriches miso soup and also makes a tasty salad tossed with a sprightly vinegar dressing.

¼ cup dried slivered wakame
3½ cups dashi (page 48)
3 tablespoons red miso
2 tablespoons sweet white miso (shiro miso)
½ pound silken tofu, drained and cubed
1 scallion, trimmed and thinly sliced

1. Place the wakame in a bowl and cover with hot tap water. Let soak until softened, about 10 minutes. Drain and set aside.

2. Bring the dashi to a simmer in a medium saucepan. Transfer about a cup of it to a medium bowl. Whisk in the red and white miso and then transfer the mixture back to the dashi in the saucepan. (This prevents the soup from having any lumps of miso.) Add the wakame and tofu and bring the mixture to a simmer. Divide the soup among four bowls and garnish with scallions.

Makes 4 servings

Fried Noodles with Vegetables (Yakisoba)

This hearty noodle-vegetable mix usually cooks on a griddle in Japan. A wok, however, makes a fine substitute. This is a good party dish when accompanied by various side salads. Despite the name of this dish, the noodles traditionally used in the recipe are not true soba, since they contain no buckwheat flour. Instead, they go by the confusing name of chukasoba, *also known as Chinese-style ramen. Curly, yellowish (although they contain no egg yolks), and slightly elastic, they are available in most Japanese markets. Ketchup might seem like an unusual addition, until you realize that the original version came from China. What's more, with the influx of Western ingredients to Japan after the Meiji Restoration in 1868, the Japanese began to incorporate condiments like ketchup into their personalized form of Western-style food.*

¾ pound fresh Chinese-style ramen noodles, or dried spaghetti
¼ cup oyster sauce

¼ cup dashi (page 48)

3 tablespoons mirin

I tablespoon ketchup

2 teaspoons Worcestershire sauce

2 tablespoons toasted sesame oil

2 cups thinly sliced green cabbage

I medium onion, peeled, halved, and cut into crescents

I medium carrot, peeled, trimmed, and thinly sliced

I red bell pepper, cored, seeded, and thinly sliced

One 4-ounce boneless, skinless chicken breast, cut into small
  strips

¼ pound medium shrimp, peeled and deveined

2 scallions, trimmed and thinly sliced

I. Cook the noodles until al dente. Drain, rinse under cold water, and set aside.

2. Blend together the oyster sauce, dashi, mirin, ketchup, and Worcestershire sauce in a small bowl. Set aside.

3. Heat the oil in a wok. Add the cabbage, onion, and carrot and stir-fry for 3 minutes. Add the red pepper and chicken and stir-fry for a minute. Stir in the shrimp and cook for a minute more. Finally, add the noodles and reserved sauce mixture. Continue stir-frying the noodles until they are hot and glossy. Garnish with the scallions before serving.

Makes 4 to 6 servings

15.

The Ways of Tea

Between the end of winter and approach of spring, all those classes at my Japanese language school began to sink in. Without quite realizing it, I started translating street signs, restaurant menus, and doors marked "Lady's Room." I even found I could carry on simple conversations with strangers, telling them who I was, why I had come to Japan, and that I still didn't know how long I would stay.

I also was learning more and more about the enormous varieties of chaji, or formal tea ceremonies with kaiseki meals, that tea practitioners hold, thanks to those classes at Mushanokoji, as well as David and Stephen.

Nowadays, tea masters tend to be the most educated members of the tea world. They also tend to be male. Many Japanese women study tea as a way to enhance their personal résumé, much the way they might study calligraphy or flower arranging. Men, on the other hand, pursue the way of tea as a spiritual art form, in part because men are the only ones who can attain the prestigious title of Grand Tea Master.

Tea guests often come from the same social sphere as tea masters, since they must also understand the intricacies of tea in order to follow proper tea etiquette. And because of that, tea guests tend to be Japanese.

Most modern-day tea gatherings, like the ancient ones, are held to celebrate an occasion, such as a special birthday, a holiday, or a natural event, like the first snowfall.

Although there are an infinite number of variations that can occur within each chaji, seven principal types exist, beginning with the most common one, the noon tea gathering. For this standard chaji, held during any season, guests arrive shortly before noon to enjoy a tea kaiseki meal (which serves as a kind of lunch), followed by a moist sweet, a bowl of thick tea, a dry sweet, and then a bowl of thin tea.

During the frigid winter season, tea masters often host "daybreak" or "evening chat" chaji. The "daybreak" chaji begins around 4:00 in the morning and includes a tea kaiseki meal but is devoid of raw fish, since fresh seafood would be too difficult to obtain at such an hour. The meal also frequently eliminates the yakimono (grilled course) because of the labor involved.

The "evening chat" chaji usually commences in the late afternoon and then spills into evening. I had assisted Stephen and David with such a tea gathering on my birthday back in January.

A fourth type of chaji is called the "morning" tea. Generally held in the summer, it begins around 5:45 in the morning, before the weather becomes too hot and humid. Often generous amounts of white ash cover the gray ash in the brazier to evoke the cooling image of a mountain of snow or frothy waves breaking across a sandy beach. Again, because of the timing, as well as the heat, raw and grilled fish do not appear at this early morning tea kaiseki meal. Instead, tea masters serve cooling foods, such as noodles served over slippery clear chunks of ice in glass or cold metal dishes.

Another type of chaji occurs when a second group of guests, who for whatever reason could not attend the original tea ceremony, ask to see the tea utensils used during the event. While the second group of guests waits for the first group to leave the teahouse, an assistant of the tea master serves the second group an abbreviated tea kaiseki. It usually consists of some sake, a bowl of miso soup, some rice, and the hassun holding delicacies from the ocean and mountains. To speed things up, the assistant often serves the second group of guests their moist sweet outside the tearoom, so once they enter it, they can immediately enjoy a bowl of thick and thin tea before viewing the tea utensils.

For the "no-time" chaji, improvisation is the name of the game. A true tea master supposedly remains ready to prepare tea on any date, anywhere, and at a moment's notice. Such chaji are often held to honor a friend who arrives unexpectedly from a distant place. To facilitate the ceremony the tea master often invites only fellow tea practitioners so they can help with various duties, such as arranging the flowers in the alcove and putting together an impromptu tea kaiseki meal.

The last type of chaji is the "after meal" tea, primarily held during busy times of the year, such as over Oshogatsu, or shortly after breakfast. Because of the timing, the meal tends to be a sort of mini tea kaiseki, often featuring just the wanmori, or climactic dish, and the tray holding tidbits from the mountains and ocean, plus some sake.

It gradually became clear that the most influential factor determining the character of each type of chaji was the time of year in which it was held. Kyoto has twenty-four seasons, not four. These seasonal shifts stem from Japan's adoption of the old Chinese solar calendar that began with the winter solstice and measured the year by twenty-four sekki, or seasonal divisions. Tea masters recognize these ever-changing cycles of nature at every tea event in myriad ways, including the flowers they choose for the alcove, the scene or sentiments they decide upon for the hanging scroll, and the foods they offer during the tea kaiseki.

Given that the twelve-month cycle of tea begins in November (because according to the old Japanese lunar calendar the spring tea leaves that had been placed in sealed jars to mature are finally ready to grind into an emerald-green powder), one of the first (and most famous) tea gatherings held during this month is called the Kuchikiri. It celebrates the *kiri* (cutting) of the paper seal over the tea jar's *kuchi* (mouth) to retrieve the young tea leaves, which the tea master grinds to a fine powder in the presence of his guests, while they enjoy their tea kaiseki meal. Tea masters honor the new tea year by replacing the tatami in the tearoom, putting new paper panels on the shoji screens, and erecting fresh green bamboo fences in the garden of the teahouse. They additionally open the sunken hearth that had been closed for the previous six months (during which time the tea master made tea with a portable brazier to avoid overheating the tearoom). As I had experienced in my first tea kaiseki class, the tea kaiseki foods served during a November chaji would likely incorporate the celebratory colors of red and white and also feature ingredients at their peak, such as turnips and daikon radish, coldwater fish, potatoes, chestnuts, mushrooms, and persimmons.

The first Saturday in March, I helped Stephen cook for an

"after-meal" chaji that he and David were hosting for eight foreign women enrolled in the one-year tea program at David's tea school. The theme of the gathering was Girl's Day, a holiday originally involving the placement of dolls near the heads of infants to absorb any negative spirits or energy. Over time, the figures evolved into elaborate costumed dolls that little girls would display inside their homes. Nowadays, young girls all over Japan dress up in pink and red kimonos to enjoy special rose-and-petal-pink candies, cakes, and sushi. The women had been invited to show up at 10:00 in the morning.

Since the weather was unseasonably warm, a helper named Mark had sprayed the stones of the roji. I was concerned this might make the women slip. "No, it will force them to slow down so they can focus on their surroundings," said Stephen. "I want them to be like bowerbirds, noticing all the jewels along the path and taking the time to enjoy them." Mark would wet the stones once again before the middle break (after the women had finished their meal) and one last time before they left the teahouse to go home. In addition to making the stones slick, the water would imply purity (as well as coolness had it been hot).

Because this tea kaiseki would be served so soon after breakfast, it would be considerably smaller than a traditional one. As a result, Stephen had decided to serve each mini tea kaiseki in a round stacking bento box, which looked like two miso soup bowls whose rims had been glued together. After lifting off the top dome-shaped cover the women would behold a little round tray sporting a tangle of raw squid strips and blanched scallions bound in a tahini-miso sauce pepped up with mustard. Underneath this seafood "salad" they would find a slightly deeper "tray" packed with pearly white rice garnished with a pink salted cherry blossom. Finally, under the rice would be their soup bowl containing the wanmori, the apex of the tea kaiseki. Inside the dashi base we had placed a large ball of fu (wheat gluten) shaped and colored to resemble a peach. Spongy and soft, it had a savory center of ground duck and sweet lily bulb. A cluster of fresh spinach leaves, to symbolize the budding of spring, accented the "peach," along with a shiitake mushroom cap simmered in mirin, sake, and soy.

When the women had finished their meals, we served them tiny pink azuki bean paste sweets. David whipped them a bowl of thick green tea. For the dry sweets eaten before his thin tea, we served them flower-shaped refined sugar candies tinted pink.

After all the women had left, Stephen, his helper, Mark, and I sat down to enjoy our own "Girl's Day" meal. And even though I was sitting in the corner of Stephen's dish-strewn kitchen in my T-shirt and rumpled khakis, that soft peach dumpling really did taste feminine and delicate.

16.

Through the
Looking Glass

$\mathcal{S}$everal friends decided to visit that spring, including John, who planned to arrive at the height of cherry blossom season. In anticipation of his trip, I began to search for an elegant ryokan where we might stay, since I was still living with Tomiko and Yasu. The famous traditional Japanese inns, like Tawara-ya, host to such luminaries as Marlon Brando, Alfred Hitchcock, and Jean-Paul Sartre, and the two-hundred-year-old Kinmata, known for its sublime restaurant kaiseki meals, were considerably beyond our budget. So my focus switched to more modest options.

That was until an American friend named Betsy called to ask if I wanted to join her on a three-day modeling assignment in Osaka. I had met Betsy shortly after I arrived, having looked her up at the suggestion of a good friend who had gone to college with her. Betsy had been studying fabric design in Kyoto for the past two years and occasionally took on modeling jobs to earn some money, since she had the requisite blond hair, slim figure, and wholesome American smile desired in Japanese print and television ads.

"All they told me is that they needed two Americans to model eyeglasses for this new store," said Betsy.

"Model what?"

"Eyeglasses," she replied, giggling. "It's for the store's grand opening. Do you want to do it?"

I paused. It certainly sounded intriguing—modeling, being with Betsy, and getting paid generously to do so. "Why not," I said, laughing.

Which is how Betsy and I found ourselves early one Saturday morning riding the fast-train to Osaka dressed like New Yorkers. We had been told to "wear something nice" so had agreed that we would both show up in black skirts, sweaters, tights, and heels.

Our boss for the two-day assignment was a gentleman named Mr. Morimata. He told us he would meet us at the station and drive us to the store.

"Elizabeth Green-san?" inquired a small Japanese man in a teal business suit as we stepped off the train.

"Pleased to meet you," answered Betsy in Japanese. She bent into a deep bow, then introduced me to Mr. Morimata, who after more bows and handshakes led us out of the station to his silver Mercedes idling alongside the curb.

Almost two hours later, Mr. Morimata pulled up to the corner entrance of a busy pedestrian mall. "Your Yeux," he said proudly, pointing to the sliver of storefront sandwiched between a camera shop and a French bakery. Men and women in navy, white, and red uniforms were tying clusters of red and white balloons to the store's sign and lugging flower arrangements into the showroom.

Just as Mr. Morimata stepped out of his car, a fleet of staff members bounded over. "Herro!—Mice to meet you!—Wercome!—Herro!—Good Moaning!" They fluttered about Betsy and me as if we were movie stars. We returned their greetings with smiles and bows and then headed into the store.

Glass and chrome shelves lined the sky-blue walls of the shop, sporting hundreds of different eyeglasses. Some of the pricey designer frames lay arranged like the petals of a flower under waist-high, plastic, bubble-topped display cases.

Mr. Morimata breezed over with a young man sporting an oversize pair of elaborate gold frames.

"The Americans," Mr. Morimata announced, gesturing to Betsy and me. We introduced ourselves. The assistant bowed, pushing the glasses up the bridge of his nose as he lifted his head.

"Mr. Watabe will help you get ready, okay?" We nodded as Mr. Morimata excused himself.

"Follow me," said Mr. Watabe, briskly walking toward the back of the store. "What time is the grand opening?" I asked, scooting along behind him.

"Twelve," he responded over his shoulder. I glanced at my watch. It read almost 11:15. We would have plenty of time to get made up before the show, no doubt scheduled for the noon lunch rush.

Suddenly, Mr. Watabe stopped. "These are for you," he said, pointing to a clothes rack. Suspended from the metal pole were two dresses made of rough green cotton the color of surgical scrubs. Next to them hung two frilly white starched pinafores. I looked bug-eyed at Betsy. She pressed her lips together to suppress a laugh.

"These won't do?" I gestured at our skirts and then looked up at Mr. Watabe. He shook his head. "But we were—"

He cut me short. "Girl's room upstairs." He pointed to the staircase. "Come down when ready. But soon." He tapped his watch. We nodded, then lifted the garments off the rack and mounted the stairs, struggling to stifle our hilarity.

But it was impossible, particularly when we put on the dresses. Mine barely scraped over my rib cage. When I finally managed to yank it down, what was supposed to be the waist hung at my sternum.

"I think my dress is too small," I squeaked. Betsy looked at me in mock horror. I noticed her dress hung loose.

"Here, let me try to zip it," she said, giggling. After considerable tugging, there was a shrill *zzzzuuuuuup*, and suddenly the rough fabric pulled taut across my chest. I took a few quick breaths and rolled my shoulders, hoping to stretch the material. It didn't budge. The Peter Pan collar cut into my neck, while the bands around the puffed sleeves clamped around my upper arms like blood pressure cuffs.

Well, at least we'll get to wear cool glasses, I thought, tying Betsy's pinafore sash into a big bow. After brushing our hair and dabbing on lip-gloss we headed downstairs with Betsy looking "cute" and me feeling like a big fat Alice in Wonderland.

The curious thing about our baby doll outfits was that many Japanese men found them alluring. It was Betsy who clued me in on the sexual psyche of the Japanese male, or at least a good number of them.

Apparently, many Japanese men have a "thing" for young girls. They find their virginal innocence erotic. And Japanese women know it. They dress up like little misses, in knee socks, short skirts, and bow-covered sweaters and shoes.

Nowadays, Japanese men are getting the real thing, a Japanese female friend explained. "Originally it was high school students, but now businessmen are dating girls in junior high school," she said with concern. When I asked her what these young women got out of the deal, she paused.

"I think these girls feel flattered and grown up when they go out with these businessmen. The men probably have lots of money and take them to fancy places. But, you know," she said, shaking her head, "it is sad and kind of sick because I don't think these girls really understand what's going on."

The practice goes by the name *enjo kousai* (paid dating). The men tend to be middle-aged, lonely, and often unhappily married and pay extravagant sums (often several hundred dollars) to teenage girls to go out with them. The girls think that being young is a marketable novelty that can buy them the designer clothes they could never ordinarily afford. In their minds, they are working to obtain these purchases, albeit by selling their sexuality.

A more discreet way for some of these Japanese men to live out such fantasies is to buy certain comic books collectively called *manga*. On my train rides from Osaka back to Kyoto after a night of teaching, I would often see businessmen flipping through manga as thick as telephone books, showing rape scenes, samurai slicing off women's breasts with their swords, and teens in sexually compromised positions.

Vending machines offer another way for men to fulfill their desires. In strategic areas of Tokyo, for example, machines sell used schoolgirl uniforms, often accompanied by a picture of the student. It is said they also dispense soiled underpants.

So, I suppose, wearing baby doll scrubs was the "Your Yeux" way of luring men into the store. As for modeling glasses, that never happened. Instead, Mr. Watabe handed us trays of juice and coffee and told us to curtsy and pass them around. We handed in our pinafores late Sunday afternoon.

That evening on the train ride back to Kyoto, Betsy made an announcement.

"I'm going to get married," she confided, beaming. I could only imagine it was to the Japanese man she had been dating. Yet it seemed they hardly knew one another, let alone spoke the same language.

"Is it Toshi?" I asked, tentatively.

"Yes, and the reason I'm telling you now is because I'm leaving my apartment the first week of April. I thought you might want it."

I gasped, then congratulated her on her exciting news. I even gave her a hug, right there on the train. As for the apartment, I could not believe my good fortune. I had seen the six-tatami studio the previous autumn when she had invited me over for brunch. The tan stucco apartment building lay nestled on a small lane not far from Shirakawa-dori, a shady tree-lined street in an area northeast of the city called Sakyo-ku. I fell in love with the neighborhood the first time I saw it because it reminded me of Paris. It wasn't so much the architecture that gave Sakyo-ku its European air, but the gray brick sidewalks that flanked Shirakawa-dori and the strip of sycamore trees running down the median.

The second-floor studio was flooded with sunshine. It had an adorable Tinkerbell-size kitchen and a cozy adjoining room with a waist-high cupboard embellished with bamboo leaves built into the wall that held Betsy's clothes and futon during the day. One window looked out over the leafy treetops, while the other lay hidden behind a beautiful cedar wood and ivory paper screen.

Living in an authentic Japanese apartment had been a dream since college. Tomiko and Yasu had generously hosted me for almost five months. I knew English Fun World was expanding and they could use another classroom.

So without even hesitating, I told Betsy I would take it. She and I agreed she would introduce me to her landlady, an older Japanese woman, to whom I would bring a gift of imported English biscuits to sweeten the relationship. I would pay the woman the equivalent of a month's rent in "key money," which I would not get back. On April 9 the apartment would be mine.

The timing could not have been better. John was arriving the following week.

17.

Garlic Thunder
Comes to Kyoto

John carried two red roses all the way from New York to Osaka and handed them to me the moment he walked out of baggage claim. They were limp but had survived the twenty-two-hour trip. We hugged in a noisy crowded reception area, then wheeled his bags to the airport curb to catch the number eight bus to Kyoto.

There was a polite distance between us at first—the kind of emotional wound licking that comes from being apart from someone you care for deeply. We had known each other for seven years, having met the second day of freshman week in college. John was one of the brightest and most sensitive people I had ever encountered, yet it would take five years before we even kissed.

Our friendship began with a talk about medicine. His father was a surgeon and I was thinking of becoming a doctor. Over time, our relationship deepened as we swatted squash balls, shared life philosophies, and treated each other to dinners out. John was the first person with whom I ever ate duck.

Yet, despite his gorgeous hands, huge smile, and warm Italian nature, I was scared of him. Anyone called "Garlic Thunder," a nickname his roommates gave him because he loved to consume large amounts of oily, garlic-laced food, would have to wait for my affections. And wait he did—through freshman year and sophomore year, plus the year I spent in France, junior year, and finally senior year.

The kiss occurred one spring night, two weeks before graduation. We were at a party off campus and had gone down to a nearby beach to take a walk. There had been an undercurrent of romance for the past several weeks. It was dark. The waves pounded against the sand. A chain-link fence stood at the end of the beach and we were heading toward it. Suddenly, there was nowhere else to go. It was as if the fence was telling me my time was up—that there was no reason to keep fighting my heart. So I listened. And turned around.

Slowly John came toward me and pushed me gently up against the metal links. Then he placed his lips on mine. All my defenses fell away. By morning we were a couple.

From that time on, we were inseparable. He became my best friend, and I his. He called me "Sweetbread" (and "Sourdough" when I got on his nerves), while I called him "Johnnycakes." We both moved to New York and began working in advertising. We each had our own apartment, although I am not sure why, since every night we shared the same pillow.

Two years later, I had become a monster and was thinking about running away to Japan. He began to wonder if law school was what he wanted, instead of advertising. Washington, D.C., seemed like a good place to go. I didn't expect him to join me on my journey to the east; he didn't expect me to follow him to the nation's capital. So we took a break. Now, after six months of separation, we were groping along, each knocking gently on the other's heart, hoping to be let in.

Since my new apartment had no shower, the first thing we did after plunking John's bags down on the tatami was to visit the sento, or public bath. For most Westerners, the concept of a Japanese bath consists of a quiet pine-paneled room in a traditional inn where you scrub yourself clean before slipping into a smooth teak tub with a carefully designed view onto a miniature garden.

The sento offers a spontaneous view into the life of the neighborhood. In many ways these public baths function like local taverns where friends meet and exchange news and gossip. But instead of doing it over beers, they do it while scouring each other's backs and lounging about in tubs of hot water.

In the winter, the sento serves another purpose: it is a way to keep warm at night. After soaking in the scalding-hot tub, families scurry back to their unheated homes and bury themselves under the quilts on their futons.

John's introduction to public bathing took place with me on the female side of the bath and him on the men's side. Although I cringed at the idea of shouting instructions over the cement partition that stopped just short of the ceiling, I decided it would be more embarrassing for him to blunder about in Japan's highly codified water world.

"First undress and put your clothes in the basket sitting on the shelf," I hollered. Silence. "Cakes, are you there?"

"Yes. I can't find the basket."

"Look behind you. Now, do you see it?"

"I think so."

"Let me know when you're naked." Long silence. "Cakes, are you undressed?"

"I feel funny. All these men are staring at me."

"They're probably jealous. Do you have your soap?"

"Yes."

"And my bowl and shampoo?"

"Yes."

"Okay, next you're going to go through the door and into the bath. Then you'll want to fill the bowl with hot and cold water. Just press down on the spigots, red for hot and blue for cold, and dump the bowl over your head."

"Sounds pretty primitive. These are the same people who invented the Walkman?"

"I know. Next, wash and then rinse yourself, including your hair. Then put all your stuff in the bowl and go soak in any one of the tubs. Call if you need help."

"Okay, here I go," he announced.

By the time John emerged from the bath it was nearly 6:20. Given his jet lag, we decided to have dinner in. I had made a sort of Japanese antipasto to accompany a bottle of French Bordeaux I had bought in the food hall of Daimaru department store. So while John sat on a blue cotton cushion hunched over the low unfinished wooden table sipping red wine from a small glass tumbler, I presented him with a succession of nibbles: chili-speckled rice crackers and peanuts; boiled edamame tossed with coarse salt; chewy strands of dried calamari; and chilled steamed asparagus that I had bought fresh that morning at Nishiki market. For a taste of home, I sautéed pudgy slices of herb-flavored wheat gluten, soft as gnocchi, in garlic butter with sliced shiitake mushrooms. Dinner ended with snappy red grapes and imported coconut sables that broke into buttery splinters in our cupped palms.

Later, under the opalescent moonlight, we lay on my futon and held each other. As we reestablished our closeness, the ache of separation gave way to the relief of finally being together, once again.

For the next several days, my view of Kyoto came through John's eyes, a funny, joyful, and occasionally stinging vision. For so long I had imagined having him in Kyoto. Now the time had come for reality to live up to fantasy.

One day we strolled down the Philosopher's Path, which proved as enchanting as I had hoped in the fragrant pink bloom of spring. Since ancient times, the Japanese have heralded the arrival of the cherry blossoms because they symbolize the ephemeral beauty of life.

But it isn't just the three or four days of open flowers that stirs the senses. It is their arrival and departure. Looking at a bud about to burst open offers the pleasurable anticipation of rebirth, while the soft scattering of petals on the ground is often considered the most beautiful stage of all because it represents the death of the flowers.

Another day I took John to one of my tea kaiseki classes to watch the making of a traditional picnic to celebrate the arrival of the cherry blossoms. While he sat on a stool near my cooking station, Stephen and I cooked rice in water flavored with kelp, sake, and light soy, then packed it into a wooden mold shaped like a chrysanthemum. After tapping out the compact white flower, we decorated it with two salted cherry blossoms.

We wrapped chunks of salted Spanish mackerel in brined cherry leaves and steamed the packets until the fatty fish turned milky in parts. We also made cold seafood salad, pea custard, and chewy millet dumplings, which we grilled over a charcoal burner until brown and sticky enough to hold a coating of ivory Japanese poppy seeds.

In between these cherry blossom–related events, I took John to famous temples and shrines, the Imperial Palace, and numerous gardens and villas. I also led him down the winding back streets of Kyoto. Many resemble Venice, in that we could practically touch the houses on both sides of the street by simply stretching out our arms. Walking down a small lane toward sunset one evening, we came across several old wooden homes so blackish brown they almost looked charred. Dishes clattered in someone's kitchen. We smelled grilling chicken from a neighbor's dinner. Someone laughed and we turned around, only to realize it came from indoors. We mistook the wail of a bird for a baby and realized that this was the kind of place where there could be no nocturnal moans.

Not surprisingly, it took several days and nights for us to establish our mutual rhythm. John's exuberant manner often clashed with the reserved conformist one I had developed in this fragile world of paper screens and unspoken rules. This was no more apparent than at dinner one evening at a nouvelle kaiseki restaurant in the Gion called Hanakanzashi (Flowered Comb). I had never encountered restaurant kaiseki and thought John might enjoy this unique form of cuisine, which I had come to learn differed dramatically from what I had been studying at the tea school.

First of all, restaurant kaiseki is all about the food, whereas tea kaiseki focuses on the tea. In a restaurant, joviality and entertainment set the tone for the kaiseki meal, which is based on sake. At a tea kaiseki, which is based on rice, solemnity and ritual set the tone for that final spiritual moment culminating in the drinking of whipped green tea. And while both meals aim to offer freshly prepared local ingredients with an acute sensitivity to the seasons, they contrast significantly in their order, style, and content. We splurged on a taxi from my apartment to the Gion, where upon our arrival the driver pointed us in the direction of an office building and sped off. After riding the elevator up to the fifth floor, we turned left and walked into a hushed gray dining room.

Hanakanzashi was arrestingly spare. Emptiness of space is a fundamental aesthetic in Japan used for visual, aural, and emotional effect. In a vast raked garden, for example, a few carefully placed rocks inspire contemplation. In Noh and Kabuki theater stillness between the action, or a silence inserted between spoken lines provokes introspection.

In Japanese food arrangement, chefs consider empty space a dynamic entity. Bowls are never filled to the brim. Serving dishes never come to the table heaped with food. The blank expanse creates a pleasing balance, framing the ingredients in a way that is tantalizing, not overwhelming. It is similar to Japanese ink paintings, where the effect of open white space serves to amplify the black and create a balanced whole.

"Whenever I go to a Western museum I get a headache," said a Japanese friend. "There is simply too much stimulation, too many paintings on the wall."

A young woman in a white kimono accented with purple iris escorted us to our seats, tall cushioned chairs that pulled up to a smooth counter of polished red lacquer. Glistening under the dim overhead lights, it was a dramatic stage, upon which the chef would tell his story of spring.

The waitress behind the counter, an older woman in a rose and navy kimono, placed two black lacquer trays before us. Along the bottom sat a pair of willow chopsticks resting on a pink ceramic holder shaped like a cherry blossom. A small frosted glass of *umeshu* (plum wine) sat on a white paper coaster toward the top. The syrupy wine, actually made from small Japanese apricots, had a honeyed smoothness and a fruity finish that left behind a streak of warmth.

Several minutes later, the elderly waitress set down two rectangular white dishes holding the hors d'oeuvres. In restaurant kaiseki, they call this course the *hassun,* and it arrives either at the beginning or at the end of the meal. Confusion often arises because these tidbits do not come on the wooden tray that gives the tea kaiseki course its name. Yet both types of hassun feature foods from the ocean and mountains.

We began with two buttery sweet edamame and one sugar syrup–soaked shrimp in a crunchy soft shell. A lightly simmered baby octopus practically melted in our mouths, while a tiny cup of clear, lemony soup provided cooling refreshment. The soup held three slices of okra and several slippery cool strands of *junsai* (water shield), a luxury food that grows in ponds and marshes throughout Asia, Australia, West Africa, and North America. In the late spring the tiny plant develops leafy shoots surrounded by a gelatinous sheath that floats on the water's surface, enabling the Japanese to scoop it up by hand from small boats. The edamame, okra, and water shield represented items from the mountains, while the shrimp and octopus exemplified the ocean. I could tell John was intrigued and amused by this artistic (perhaps puny?) array of exotica.

Two pearly pieces of sea bream, several fat triangles of tuna, and sweet shelled raw baby shrimp composed the sashimi course, which arrived on a pale turquoise dish about the size of a bread plate. It was the raw fish portion of the meal, similar to the mukozuke in a tea kaiseki. To counter the beefy richness of the tuna, we wrapped the triangles in pungent shiso leaves, then dunked them in soy.

After the sashimi, the waitress brought out the *mushimono* (steamed dish). In a coal-black ceramic bowl sat an ivory potato dumpling suspended in a clear wiggly broth of dashi thickened with kudzu starch, freckled with glistening orange salmon roe. The steamed dumpling, reminiscent of a white peach, was all at once velvety, sweet, starchy, and feathery and had a center "pit" of ground chicken. The whole dish, served warm and with a little wooden spoon, embodied the young, tender softness of spring.

Steamed foods do not show up at a tea kaiseki. Nor do fried foods, our next course, because the heavy oils are said to linger on the palate, thus marring it for the tea to come. What makes restaurant kaiseki unique is that it does not have to worry about the rules, social considerations, or type and order of courses that guide a tea kaiseki. Nor does it have to concern itself with the ultimate spiritual purpose of the meal.

Our *agemono,* or "deep-fried thing," was tempura, the lacy batter-fried style of cooking that came to Japan in the latter half of the sixteenth century via Spanish and Portuguese missionaries and traders. The dish was so named because it was originally sold at stands on *tempura* (temple grounds).

At Hanakanzashi, our tempura came in the form of a crunchy flaxen flounder for two that fell apart under the gentle prod of our chopsticks. But instead of serving the fish with the traditional tempura dipping sauce of dashi, soy, mirin, and grated daikon (which helps the body digest oily or fatty foods), the chef offered a tiny dish of salt seasoned with peppery tongue-tingling sansho.

For the yakimono out came a vivid red plate holding one of my favorite dishes, a disc of supremely soft deep-fried eggplant that had been "buttered" with thick sweet miso paste, then run under the broiler. Four peas, which sent John into spasms of laughter, decorated the top, while a pickled pink stalk of ginger and a fresh shiso leaf garnished the plate. "It's all very beautiful, but a little precious, don't you think?" he asked, holding up a pea. I agreed, but added that it was only if you view it through Western eyes.

Our final course before dessert was a flower of rice topped with tilefish, salted cherry blossoms, and a cherry leaf. Had we splurged, we would have also received a *suimono,* meaning "thing to drink," usually a clear soup flecked with things like spinach, tofu, and seaweed. We would have also encountered a *sunomono,* meaning "vinegared thing," often a tiny tumble of fish or vegetables tossed with rice vinegar and soy. Finally, we would have been offered either a spring *takiawase,* meaning "foods boiled or stewed together," or a wanmori (the apex of a tea kaiseki meal) featuring seasonal ingredients, such as a cherry blossom–pink dumpling of shrimp and egg white served in a dashi base accented with *udo,* a plant with a white stalk and leaves that tastes like asparagus and celery, and a sprig of fresh sansho, the aromatic young leaves from the same plant that bears the seedpods the Japanese grind into the tongue-numbing spice always served with fatty eel.

Since we had chosen a more modestly priced menu, however, dinner finished with pickles—eggplant slices and crisp cucumber crescents—and dessert. Sometimes lavish restaurant kaiseki meals offer fruit, followed by a sweet, such as a small slice of cake. Our dinner sort of combined the two. On a kiwi-green plate sat a ball of what I can only describe as "chewy" lemon sherbet. Perhaps it had been blended with mochi? Then there were two large grapes, the tops of which had been scored like a cross and pulled back at the corners. "Oh, I'm stuffed, I couldn't possibly finish these," snickered John, pointing to the tiny purple orbs. For a man known to down thirty or more pieces of sushi in one sitting, this meal had been "elegantly spare," bordering on ridiculous.

"I'm still hungry," he said, back out on the street, not realizing that visual satiation was all part of the feast. Granted, I am almost half his size, but to me, any more food would have left us suffering. I tried to explain how these small offerings had been majestic, opulent, and extravagant in their own way. I felt as though I had visited a museum, heard a fascinating lecture, opened several gorgeously wrapped gifts, and consumed the essence of spring in Kyoto, all while sitting at a striking red lacquer counter in the heart of the geisha district with my best friend. John nodded, then suggested we look for a bar.

Much more to his liking was dinner at a local *robatayaki,* which I took him to several days after our visit to Flowered Comb.

In traditional Japanese homes, the *robata* is the large square sunken fire pit in the middle of a tatami room. Families used to cook in these pits, which also heated their homes, since central heating did not exist. As a concession to modern times, people still dangle their legs in the fire pit, only instead of drawing on spent coals for heat, they warm themselves from a hot bulb encased in a wire net hanging from the underside of a special table, usually draped with a thick blanket.

Since *yaki* means "to grill," a robatayaki is a sort of Japanese tapas bar where you gather around the "fire pit," or grill in the center of the restaurant to drink and gorge on finger-foods prepared with no nod to Zen minimalism. The atmosphere is smoky and robustious.

The evening began with two huge Kirin beers and a dish of chicken sashimi. (Is there even a Japanese word for salmonella?) Served in smooth pink slabs, oddly enough the raw chicken tasted like fish. More of a textural than taste experience, we found it frighteningly easy to eat. After that, there was no stopping us. Off the grill came smoky chicken-scallion skewers; grilled baby squid; charred pork-wrapped asparagus rolls; and rounds of flame-licked lotus root. We tucked into flinty cooked spinach doused with rich sesame cream; nibbled on edamame; and sucked down cold custardy tofu splashed with soy and topped with shredded nori and scallions. Then we ordered a borderline revolting, yet popular Japanese snack: grilled sparrow heads. These tiny crunchy craniums were totally bald and burnished with a Japanese "barbecue sauce" of soy, sugar, sake, and mirin. As long as we closed our eyes, they were delicious.

And then we were full. We paid the bill and stumbled home via the sento. While I scrubbed off the accumulated oil and soot from our down-home country dinner, John fought off sleep on a bench outside. With beer still on our breaths, we fell into my futon.

><

The next morning I whisked John off to a modestly priced *onsen* (hot springs resort) in a small fishing village on the Kii Peninsula west of Kyoto. He looked pleased but apprehensive. "Is it going to be like the public bath?"

"No, no," I assured him, "*total* luxury."

Because of Japan's volcanic nature, there are over two thousand natural hot springs dotted throughout the country, along with numerous man-made ones. Both types offer the same therapeutic release from the stresses of work, family, or the fast pace of a city.

For the Japanese, communal bathing combines the Shinto element of purification with the social and physical pleasures of immersing oneself in a soothing pool of water with friends. The type of onsen you choose depends upon your personal preference and budget: they can be as small as a Jacuzzi, or as big as a pond; made of teak wood, or fabricated from stone; filled with water as clear as vodka, or as cloudy as milk; feel lobster-pot-hot, or pleasantly warm; and smell fresh as rain, or sulfurously foul.

Although many onsen are situated outside in gorgeous natural settings—in the mountains, by a river, or in rocky caves by the sea—some lie indoors with fanciful themes. At the Arita Kanko Hotel in the western area of Honshu, for example, you can slip into a hot tub located inside a cable car that chugs up a mountain to give you a breathtaking view of the coastline—in the buff.

The type of onsen that John and I were headed toward advertised seaside delight. Meaning: we would spend the night in a traditional Japanese inn and sample local delicacies caught from the cold salty waters of the Kii Peninsula. I could just imagine us in a gorgeous outdoor bath pushing a floating tray of sake back and forth to one another, a scene reproduced in so many resort brochures.

The train ride was promising. After gliding by a lovely stretch of pine-studded mountains, we dipped down to the Japanese coast and sped past numerous quaint port towns. The sun shone bright and only a few wispy clouds drifted across the pale blue sky. We could practically feel the salt spray on our cheeks.

Then we arrived at our destination. To our dismay and ultimate amusement, we had arrived at the Jersey Shore of Japan. From the window of our small tatami room our "ocean view" included an industrial sewage facility. A coin-operated TV glared at us from the corner of the room, next to a coin-operated safe. The final touch was the dirty Band-Aid near the bathroom. We immediately decided to stay only one night instead of the intended two.

A walk around the fishing village found us holding our noses as we passed leathery charcoal triangles of drying shark fins strung up on clear fishing reel. In an attempt to escape the stench, we wandered into a nearby hotel, which had just begun the formal process of welcoming a busload of Japanese tourists. Before we knew it, we had been swept down a corridor of Japanese well-wishers, only to have our picture taken by the tour's photographer.

Back at the inn, we decided to venture into the waters. After all, that was one of the reasons why we had traveled to the Kii Peninsula. As is typical with most onsen, the baths are segregated by sex. Clad in nothing but our bathing suits and casual cotton kimonos, we gingerly tiptoed down the questionably clean tile stairs and into our separate soaking pools. Mine was empty. And for good reason. The rock grotto–like pool bubbled up a sulfurous gas, as if it had just gobbled down a barrel of azuki beans. The tan rocks wore a slick coat of greenish algae and the windows were streaked with a mysterious scum. I was in and out in less than ten minutes, ready to hit the shower and wash off the slime.

Not surprisingly, John was already in the shower when I burst into our room. We could only imagine what lay in store for dinner.

To our surprise and delight, dinner was stupendous. Served in our room at the low polished wood table, it exuded a freshness and artistry we had not seen since leaving Kyoto. The sashimi— sea bream, squid, and skipjack—tasted as clean as a freshly sliced apple. Rusty-red miso soup had a meaty fortifying flavor enhanced with cubes of tofu and slithery ribbons of seaweed. The tempura, served in a basket of woven bamboo, shattered to pieces like a well-made croissant. Hiding inside the golden shell was a slice of Japanese pumpkin, a chunk of tender white fish, an okra pod, a shiitake mushroom cap, and a zingy shiso leaf.

Pale yellow *chawan-mushi* also appeared in a lidded glass custard cup. With a tiny wooden spoon we scooped up the ethereal egg and dashi custard cradling chunks of shrimp, sweet lily buds, and waxy-green ginkgo nuts.

In a black lacquer bowl came a superb seafood consommé, along with a knuckle of white fish, tuft of spinach, mushroom cap, and a tiny yellow diamond of yuzu zest. A small lacquer bucket held several servings of sticky white rice to eat with crunchy radish pickles and shredded pressed cabbage. A small wedge of honeydew melon concluded the meal.

After taking away our dinner dishes and trays, a maid came in to make up our futons, which she pushed together with good intentions. A little too squeamish about our surroundings to do anything more than read, we fell asleep at 7:30, thus bringing a rapid close to what had been a most unusual day.

Our romantic getaway ended early that next morning when we hurried to catch the first train back to Kyoto. From there, we headed off to Hong Kong and China, where we spent the next eight days laying siege to our senses with an explosive array of sightseeing, walking, shopping, dancing, and eating endless amounts of oily, spicy, garlic-laced food.

Then John was gone. He had flown into my life, shared my little nest, and soared off. I had no idea when I would see him again.

Sizzling Chicken and Scallion Skewers (Yakitori Negima)

Burnished brown from the soy-mirin marinade, these sweet and savory chicken-scallion tidbits make a terrific hors d'oeuvre. In Japan, you can find these skewers at robatayaki, as well as yakitori restaurants and stands, casual after-work snack shacks recognizable from the red lanterns out front and tantalizing clouds of smoke billowing off the grill.

30 wooden skewers, soaked in water for at least 30 minutes
    before using
10 scallions, trimmed and cut into six 1-inch batons
1 pound boneless, skinless chicken breasts, cut into 30 bite-size
    pieces
¼ cup soy sauce
¼ cup dashi (page 48)

½ cup mirin

2 tablespoons sugar

Sansho powder for sprinkling

I. Thread each skewer with one piece of scallion (speared crosswise), one piece of chicken (speared crosswise), and one more piece of scallion. Wrap the "handle" portion of each skewer with foil. Continue threading the remaining skewers in this order. (The skewers may be prepared up until this point and stored in the refrigerator, covered, for up to 6 hours.)

2. Combine the soy sauce, dashi, mirin, and sugar in a small saucepan. Bring the liquid to a boil, reduce the heat to low, and simmer until it has reduced to ½ cup, about 15 minutes. Transfer this "barbecue sauce" to a small wide-mouth jar and let cool.

3. When ready to cook, place the skewers on a grill or broiler rack. Grill or broil the skewers for approximately 30 seconds on each side, making sure to watch them carefully to prevent the skewer tips from burning. Dip the skewers in the barbecue sauce, letting the excess drip back into the jar. Grill or broil on one side for 30 seconds, then dip the skewers into the jar of barbecue sauce again, and grill or broil on the other side for 30 seconds, or until the meat is juicy and just cooked through. Slip off the foil handles, arrange the skewers on a platter (like the spokes of a wheel), and sprinkle with the sansho. Serve warm.

Makes 30 skewers

Cold Seasoned Tofu

Custardy cold tofu makes a wonderfully restorative dish when the weather turns warm. It is served in Japanese taverns and robatayaki, as well as at home, usually along with a variety of other dishes. Fresh tofu, sold in most Japanese markets, tastes much creamier than commercially made versions and is worth seeking out. Splurge on good soy sauce, which varies in quality and price. The inexpensive versions tend to taste flat and quite salty. The pricier ones have a rounder, more full-bodied flavor that in a dish like this you can truly appreciate.

I-pound block silken tofu, chilled

I teaspoon grated fresh ginger

I scallion, trimmed and thinly sliced

8 teaspoons soy sauce

2 tablespoons shredded nori (available in packages)

Drain the tofu and gently rinse under cold water. Cut the block into four equal pieces. Place each piece of tofu in the center of a shallow bowl or on a small plate. For each serving, place ¼ teaspoon of grated ginger in the center of the tofu. Sprinkle with scallions and drizzle with 2 teaspoons of the soy sauce. Garnish with a pinch of shredded nori.

Makes 4 servings

Egg and Dashi Custard (Chawan-Mushi)

In Japan this savory custard is considered a soup and thus is served with a small spoon. It makes a lovely light appetizer that you can serve warm in the winter months and cold in the summer months.

I cup dashi (page 48)
2½ teaspoons soy sauce
I teaspoon mirin
½ teaspoon coarse salt
4 shiitake mushroom caps, scored on top
One 4-ounce boneless, skinless chicken breast, cut into 8 pieces
8 medium shrimp, peeled and deveined
I tablespoon sake
2 large eggs
8 whole water chestnuts, each cut in half
4 sprigs mitsuba (Japanese wild chervil)

I. Bring the dashi, I½ teaspoons of the soy sauce, the mirin, and salt to a boil in a medium saucepan. Add the mushroom caps and simmer for 2 minutes. Remove the caps with a slotted spoon and let drain on a double layer of paper towels. Let the dashi mixture cool completely.

2. Place the chicken and shrimp in a small bowl. Add the sake and remaining I teaspoon soy sauce. Toss to mix.

3. Lightly whisk the eggs until blended, but not too foamy, in a large bowl. Add the cooled dashi mixture and whisk to combine. Pour the custard through a fine sieve to remove any bubbles.

4. Lay out four chawan-mushi containers or custard cups. Place 2 pieces of chicken, 1 shrimp, and 4 water chestnut halves in each cup. Ladle the dashi custard mixture over the ingredients. Place the remaining shrimp on the surface of each cup, along with the shiitake mushroom cap, scored side up.

5. Place the cups in a bamboo steamer over boiling water. Wrap the steamer cover in a clean tea towel (to prevent condensation from dripping onto the custards) and place it over the steamer. Steam the custards over low heat for 8 minutes. Place the mitsuba sprig over the tops of the custards and continue cooking for 2 to 3 more minutes, or until a toothpick inserted into the center of a custard comes out clean. Let the chawan-mushi cool for a few minutes before serving warm with a little spoon. Alternatively, let the custards cool completely and chill in the refrigerator until ready to serve.

Makes 4 servings

18.

Lounge Lady

In a matter of days, I had more or less settled back into my solitary existence in Kyoto. Although I missed John, I had soon forgotten the pleasures of a marble-tiled shower, maid service, and coffee in bed. I had also happily adapted to the calm serenity of Japan, which after the corrugated chaos of Hong Kong and China proved extraordinarily appealing.

The week of my return, I applied for a position as a "Native-speaking English Instructor" at the Global Celebrity Speechcraft office in Kyoto.

"The name of the company means nothing," admitted the gentleman who interviewed me. "But it's catchy, no?" I had to agree with him. It was one of the reasons why I had answered the ad in the newspaper.

To my delight and later dismay, I was hired on the spot. I had beaten out several other candidates for the privilege of teaching conversational English to the soon-to-be members of this English conversation club. A rather generous salary was negotiated. Hands were shaken with the company president in lieu of a contract. But when I thumbed through the latest issue of the *Kansai Time Out*, instead of being listed as the Global Celebrity Speechcraft office's new "English Instructor," I had been crowned their "Lounge Lady."

My English conversation "salon" ran from 6:00 to 9:00 every Wednesday and Friday night. Club members would drop by at their convenience and join the conversation in session. I was told (and paid), however, to begin work at 5:00.

This was worrying, since it meant I would be alone with my boss, Mr. Niwa. He was an extremely hyper man in his early thirties with mossy teeth, pockmarked skin, and a thick shock of greasy black hair that he would constantly flick out of his eyes with a fast jerk of his head. He also had a bizarre habit of jogging around the room—to let club members in, fetch photographs from his desk, or hurry to the back office to grab pens, pieces of paper, or whatever else caught his fancy.

Mr. Niwa never stated what I was expected to do during that hour. Nor did I ask. I had lived in Japan long enough to know such a question had no real answer. So I simply showed up and waited to see how the hour would unfold.

Usually, Mr. Niwa and I ended up chatting, which, frankly, was like giving an English lesson. Mr. Niwa spoke rapid, poor English and no two thoughts ever connected. But what did he care? I was a captive audience, who was being paid to laugh hard at his jokes and interject "wow!" and "really!" as he shared with me his feats, including climbing mountains, having his picture snapped with famous city officials, and master-minding the Global Celebrity Speechcraft language club.

One afternoon, after showing me his calligraphy set, he leapt out of his seat, saying he had something to give me. "Hold on," he said, grinning, then trotted out of the room. I sat waiting, wondering if it was a package of those special fish-shaped rice crackers he regularly rhapsodized about eating as a boy.

"For you," he said, winking, as he jogged back into the room, holding a large box wrapped in red paper with white ribbon. He placed the gift down in front of me. Then, flicking the black fringe off his shiny forehead, he sat down. Quite close. I smiled and told him he shouldn't have, and really meant it.

"I wanted to," he said, drawing his chair closer. I carefully undid the ribbon and wound it around my hand in a crisp efficient manner. Then, in a totally uncharacteristic fashion, I tore off the paper, hoping to shock and maybe revolt him. Instead, he looked aroused. I placed the shiny silver box in my lap and lifted off the cover. A thick layer of tissue neatly concealed his gift. His right foot was jackhammering the rug.

"What could this be?" I asked, peeling away the tissue. "Why, it's a sweater!" I stared at the vixen-red angora pullover. "How beautiful," I said, trying to hide my astonishment.

"Just your color," he murmured.

"How kind of you." I smiled.

"Try it on," he urged.

"No, no, no. I'll try it on at home." I glanced at my watch. It was 5:45.

"Oh, come on. I want to see Victoria-san in it." He gave me a naughty grin. Not wanting to offend him, I pinned the sweater up against my shoulders. It was huge.

"Perfect," I said, putting it down. "Thank you."

There was a knock. A student had arrived. Mr. Niwa cantered over to the door to let in a shy young woman. She apologized for arriving early.

"Oh, no, don't be sorry at all," I said, coming to my own rescue. I escorted the woman to the classroom and began asking her about her day, leaving Mr. Niwa to fold up the sweater and clean up the mess.

What I didn't realize was that long ago in Japan, it was customary to give gifts of clothing to those who worked for you. Lower-grade samurai would often receive a *haori* (three-quarter-length kimono-like coat that loosely tied at the chest) from their daimyo with the daimyo's crest upon it. When the samurai called upon his "boss," he was expected to appear in the crested haori. Mr. Niwa probably hoped I would wear his sweater to work. Had I known better, I would have. I think.

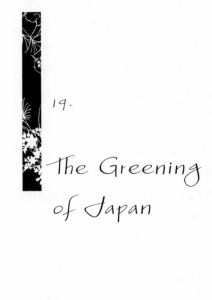

19.

The Greening
of Japan

Over the course of the next several weeks, late spring gave way to early summer. A faint floral sweetness permeated the air from the azaleas, begonias, roses, and purple irises that now edged the sidewalks and riverbanks around Kyoto. Emerald leaves fluttered from the ginkgo trees, lime-green spears shot out of young bamboo, and dark green ivy spilled over the railings of apartment buildings. Everything looked green, smelled green, and tasted of its essence.

Such was the topic of my first May tea kaiseki class. Tea gatherings held during this time of year emphasize green refreshment in anticipation of the heat. The foods become a cooling distraction for the senses.

But instead of making a formal tea kaiseki, we made what is called a *tenshin*, a small simple meal to enjoy before thin tea and occasionally thick tea. Tenshin originated in China and came to Japan via the Zen monasteries, where the snacks were served *after* the whipped green tea. Unlike a tea kaiseki, the food served at a tenshin (both in the monastery and in the tearoom) arrives all at once and often in a small stacked lacquer box, as opposed to appearing on trays in a succession of courses. When a tea ceremony includes a tenshin (or a similar sort of abbreviated tea kaiseki meal), the event is called a *chakai,* versus a chaji.

This all seemed quite confusing. Why have tea kaiseki and a tenshin? I asked Stephen after our teacher's lecture. What is the difference between a simple Rikyu-style tea kaiseki and a snacklike tenshin? Why don't tea masters just serve a few rice balls before the whipped green tea? Why so many names, rules, and foods?

"You must understand there are no set rules regarding tea kaiseki or tea," replied Stephen. "Every tea master has the freedom to do what he wants, within reason. The tea ceremony and the tea kaiseki will vary according to the season, the occasion, and the tea master's whim."

So what I realized was that a tea master tends to follow certain patterns for his tea kaiseki and tea ceremony, much the way a minister follows a certain format for his service. The church, like the teahouse, always serves as the gathering place. There will usually be hymns, prayers, a reading, and a sermon, the same way there will always be food and tea at a formal tea ceremony with a kaiseki meal. But depending upon the occasion, the service changes. A service for Thanksgiving, for example, will differ from one for Christmas, the same way a tea kaiseki and tea ceremony for an October moon viewing will differ from one to celebrate New Year's. And a church service can be very short—say, one prayer, a hymn, and a quick reading—the same way a tea kaiseki and tea ceremony can offer a tenshin and tea versus a full-blown tea kaiseki and tea.

"The biggest problem with tea kaiseki is its threatened loss of seasonality," said Stephen, closing his notebook. Historically, life in Japan revolved around the seasons and the year was regulated by the lunar calendar. Each month commenced with the dark nights of the new moon, which became full around the middle of the month.

In general, the New Year began at a time that now approximates our February, which meant the foods during that time corresponded with the beginning of spring. That explained why my February tea kaiseki classes had focused on foods for spring and not winter.

The special opening of the sealed tea jar, for example, which marked the beginning of the new tea year, used to be determined by the yellowing of yuzu citrus fruit in late October, not by a set date, which is currently November. What shifted the seasonality was Japan's switch to the Gregorian calendar in 1873, shortly after the Meiji Restoration. Suddenly, all the food, flowers, weather, colors, and numerous other seasonal aesthetics involved in the tea ceremony and tea kaiseki fell slightly off track.

"In the olden days most tea kaiseki were based on vegetables," said Stephen. "You would serve certain vegetables at certain kinds of tea kaiseki because that's what was seasonally available. Now everything is available." He sighed. "And the seasonality is becoming increasingly contrived."

As I sat there, I wondered if tea (and kaiseki) had become an endangered species. Aside from the seasonality issues, I had come to learn most tea masters no longer cooked their tea kaiseki meals. Instead, they hired fancy caterers to assume the role. What's more, some of the symbolism had changed.

"In the olden days," said Stephen, "the garden outside the teahouse was a miniaturization of an idealized world free from the devastation of earthquakes and fires. But things are different now." The garden still exists, but instead of escaping earthquakes and fires, tea guests are escaping phones, faxes, and work-related stress.

Mrs. Hisa, the elderly woman who had introduced me to Mushanokoji's tea master, nodded in agreement. "In ages past," she added, "sometimes tea kaiseki would last all day and into the night. It was an extremely relaxing affair." She smiled and closed her eyes, as if savoring the thought.

"But who has time for that in today's world?" she asked, abruptly opening her eyes. "Plus, the younger generation can no longer sit on the tatami." Kneeling with your feet beneath your bottom requires years of practice to prevent the legs and toes from falling asleep. The samurai were said to have invented this position so that in an emergency, they could rapidly rise and brandish their swords. Nowadays, most Japanese can only kneel for short periods of time because they're so used to sitting in chairs.

Stephen sighed again and then looked at his watch. "We should get cooking." Most of the class had already begun preparing foods for their tenshin. It was nearly 1:30. So Mrs. Hisa, Stephen, and I got up from our chairs and headed over to the only free cooking station. Setting down our recipes, we began to make cooling green foods.

While Mrs. Hisa steeped fresh fava beans in sugar syrup, Stephen dry-fried baby chartreuse peppers. I made a salad of crunchy green algae and meaty bonito fish cubes tossed with a bracing blend of soy and ginger juice. Mrs. Hisa created a tiny tumble of Japanese fiddleheads mixed with soy, rice vinegar, and salted baby fish.

For the horse mackerel sushi, Stephen skinned and boned several large sardine-like fillets and cut them into thick slices along the bias. I made the vinegared rice and then we all made the nigiri sushi. After forming the rice into triangles, we topped each one with a slice of fish and then wrapped it in a long oval piece of fresh bamboo grass, as if folding a flag.

Last, we made the wanmori, the heart of the tenshin. In the center of a black lacquer bowl we placed a succulent chunk of salmon trout and skinned kabocha pumpkin, both of which we had braised in an aromatic blend of dashi, sake, and sweet cooking wine. Then we slipped in two blanched snow peas and surrounded the ingredients with a bit of dashi, which we had seasoned with soy to attain the perfect whiskey color, then lightly salted to round out the flavor.

Using our teacher's finished tenshin as a model, we arranged most of the dishes on three polished black lacquer rectangles, first lightly spraying them with water to suggest spring rain. Then we actually sat down and ate the meal. To my surprise, the leaf-wrapped sushi, the silky charred peppers, candied fava beans, and slippery algae did taste cool and green. More so than I ever could have imagined. We ate a little too fast. And left sooner than I had planned. Had I known that would be my last tea kaiseki class, I would have lingered.

Along with the greening of May came the rain. Then the clouds disappeared and a soft pale lightness fell over the city, as if Kyoto had broken free of its tethers and lifted up toward the sun. The mornings were as dewy and verdant as a glass of iced green tea. The nights folded into pencil-gray darkness fragrant with white flowers. And everyone's mood seemed buoyant, happy, and carefree.

When I wasn't teaching or studying tea kaiseki, I would ride my secondhand pistachio-green bicycle to favorite places to capture the fleeting lushness of Kyoto in a sketchbook. With a small box of Niji oil pastels, I would draw things that Zen poets had long ago described in words and I did not want to forget: a pond of yellow iris near a small Buddhist temple; a granite urn in a forest of bamboo; and a blue creek reflecting the beauty of heaven, carrying away a summer snowfall of pink blossoms.

Sometimes, I would sit under the shade of a willow tree at the bottom of my street, doing nothing but listening to the call of cuckoos, while reading and munching on carrots and boiled egg halves smeared with mayonnaise and wrapped in crisp sheets of nori. Never before had such simple indulgences brought such immense pleasure.

With the rainy season over, the swollen Kamo River offered up its riverbanks to couples and families, who strolled along the embankment, and to lovers, who found privacy late at night behind the dark bushes. On the western side of the river, between Gojo and Oike Streets, restaurants set up outdoor dining platforms for *yuka* (floor dining). Unique to Kyoto, these wooden extensions evolved during the sixteenth century, so diners could enjoy the gentle breezes blowing off the water.

Cool green foods became the natural choice in restaurants and teahouses. Matcha, the powdered green tea used for the tea ceremony, flavored ice cream, jewel-like gelatin cubes, and sweet whipped cream eaten in parfaits and layered with grapes, pineapple chunks, and chewy white mochi balls. There were Japanese-style snow cones, huge hills of shaved ice drizzled with green tea syrup, along with green tea–flavored mousse and tea-tinted sponge cake.

Matcha flavored savory items too, including green tea noodles served hot in dashi soup, as well as chilled and heaped on a bamboo draining mat with a cold dipping sauce of dashi, mirin, and soy. There was green tea–flavored wheat gluten and the traditional Kyoto-style dish of white rice topped with thin petals of sashimi that you "cooked" at the table by drenching it with brewed green tea from a tiny teapot.

One afternoon in late May, I decided to cool off with the famous hot weather dish of *nagashi somen,* meaning "flowing somen noodles." In the small town of Kibune, a thirty-minute train ride north of Kyoto, I found the outdoor restaurant Hirobun, known for this eccentric specialty. After locating a free cushion on the tatami-covered wooden platform that extended out over the rushing river under a canopy of green leaves, I knelt down in front of a silver metal gutter filled with flowing water. The waitress brought me brewed green tea, then set down chopsticks and a bowl of cold dashi seasoned with soy sauce, scallions, sliced shiitake mushrooms, and a runny poached egg.

No sooner had I split open the chopsticks than a knot of thin white noodles flew by in the silver gutter. "For you!" shouted the noodle maker, leaning out of her wooden hut, where the noodles began their journey. I snatched the strands from the rushing water just before they sailed by and dunked them in the dashi. They were glassy and cool and bits of buttery yolk clung to the salty strands. Suddenly, a tangle whizzed past me. A party of Japanese women farther down my row looked over and giggled. Another noodle knot zipped by. More hands over mouths. I managed to grab the next nest of somen and was dipping it in the sauce when—whoosh!—off sped another white clump. Determined to rescue the rest of lunch, I seized several more bunches, not sure when to stop, since two new diners had sat down beside me. "Yours!" yelled the noodle maker, pointing to me. So I plucked three more snarls of somen from the gutter before retiring my chopsticks.

There were other ways to counter the early summer blaze. Packs of teenagers would set off strings of firecrackers by the Kamo River late at night, then whoop at their cooling luminescent glow. Fans fluttered everywhere and the ding-a-ling of wind chimes hanging outside people's windows provided welcome sensory refreshment.

As I gave myself up to this exotic sensual world, it pulled me back to my grandmother and to the Kyoto she had described and I had sentimentalized: a faraway place where moss, soft as chenille, carpeted temple gardens; mock orange perfumed the air; and sunsets over the Tatsumi Bridge in the Gion created a fairyland of kimonos, hushed voices, and geometric shadows of dark and gold. It was the Japan of my imagination, rife with mystery, beauty, exoticism, and grace. Only it no longer existed. Reality had taken its place.

Green Tea Soba with Shredded Vegetables

Matcha (powdered green tea) colors and flavors these noodles, which are served cold in this summer dish heralded for its ability to revive flagging appetites. Traditionally, the dish is made with buckwheat noodles and served on either a round flat basket (called a zaru*) or a box-like slatted tray, which enables the noodles to drain completely. Wasabi paste is available in tubes in most Japanese markets.*

14 ounces dried green tea soba
I cup dashi (page 48)

⅓ cup soy sauce

⅓ cup mirin

1 cup matchsticks of English cucumber

1 cup bean sprouts

¼ cup shredded nori (available in packages)

2 teaspoons wasabi paste (available in tubes)

2 scallions, trimmed and thinly sliced

1. Cook the noodles according to package directions until al dente. Drain and refresh under cold water. Drain well again and chill in the refrigerator until cold.

2. Blend together the dashi, soy sauce, and mirin in a small bowl. Chill this dipping sauce in the refrigerator until cold, about 2 hours.

3. When ready to serve, mound equal portions of the noodles onto four plates. Decoratively arrange a portion of cucumbers on one half of the noodles and bean sprouts on the other. Place a tuft of shredded nori in the center.

4. Pour the dipping sauce into four small bowls. For each person, arrange the wasabi paste on one side of a tiny dish and the scallions on the other. To serve, let each person blend some scallions and a little wasabi into their dipping sauce before dunking mouthfuls of the noodles and vegetables.

Makes 4 servings

Green Tea-Cooked Salmon over Rice

This cook-at-the-table Japanese dish is called ochazuke, *which loosely means "tea rice." It evolved as a way to clean out the rice bowl at the end of the meal, since meals in Japan traditionally end with a cup of brewed green tea. The rice and toppings come to the table along with a small pot of tea, which you pour over the fish to cook it. You can eat the dish with chopsticks and simply pick up the bowl when you wish to sip the tea broth.*

2 cups hot cooked rice (page 32)
4 ounces sushi-quality salmon fillet
2 tablespoons loose Japanese green tea (such as sencha)
2 tablespoons salmon roe
1 teaspoon toasted unhulled white sesame seeds
2 tablespoons shredded nori (available in packages)
Coarse salt
Wasabi (available in tubes)

1. Prepare the rice.

2. Remove the skin from the salmon and then cut the fillet into thin matchstick-like slices.

3. Place the loose tea in a small teapot, then add 2 cups boiling water.

4. While the tea steeps, heap the cooked rice into two large bowls. Arrange the salmon over the rice so that it forms a thin (not thick and clumpy) cap. Scatter the roe over the salmon, followed by the sesame seeds. Garnish each serving with a pinch of nori.

5. To serve, let each person pour half of the tea over the rice to cook the salmon. Season with coarse salt and wasabi to taste.

Makes 2 servings

Green Tea Ice Cream

Matcha (powdered green tea), which is available in select tea stores and Japanese markets, adds marvelous flavor and brilliant emerald-green color to homemade ice cream, which in Japan signals the arrival of warm weather. Enjoy the ice cream plain, or topped with chunks of melon, pineapple, and bananas and a dollop of whipped cream.

3½ tablespoons matcha

3 large eggs

1 cup sugar

Pinch coarse salt

1¾ cups heavy cream

2 cups 2 percent milk

1. Place the matcha in a small bowl. Add ¼ cup boiling water and whisk until the matcha has completely dissolved. Let cool.

2. Whisk together the eggs, sugar, and salt in a large bowl until well combined. Place the cream and milk in a medium saucepan and bring just to a simmer. Gradually whisk the hot cream mixture into the egg mixture. Whisk in the cooled matcha mixture to form the ice-cream base, then transfer it back to the saucepan. Cook the ice-cream base over medium heat, stirring

constantly, until the mixture coats the back of a spoon, about 5 minutes. Pour through a sieve into a large bowl and let cool. Place the ice-cream base in the refrigerator until cold, about 2 hours, before freezing in an ice-cream machine according to the manufacturer's instructions.

Makes 4 cups

20.

Letting Go

It began as an ordinary June evening. I arrived home after a day of teaching and changed into a white T-shirt and pair of worn black pants. Then I opened a beer.

The late afternoon sun poured into the tatami room like liquid caramel, lighting up the walls with a bronzy glow. One of the most poetic aspects of a traditional Japanese home is the play of sunlight throughout the interior during the day. Light and dark shadows shift along the tan stucco walls. Brightness and coolness enter and exit rooms, casting long and short beams of color upon the polished wood planks. Paper screens filter an artistic array of yellow, ivory, and white light onto the tawny straw mats.

A gentle breeze blew in from the window, ruffling the pages of the *Newsweek* I was using as a coaster. I pushed open the screen wider to gaze at the view: a cool forest of trees, dappled with rocks, plunging down to a rushing creek.

After taking a sip of beer, I began thinking about the fabulous new teaching position I had just been offered. A friend of Mr. Tsuki, the head of The New School where I taught, had recently opened the Japan Health Sports Academy in Kyoto. The friend needed several language teachers to round out his fitness program and Mr. Tsuki had given him my name. After a cursory interview, I had been offered the job, which came with a generous salary and the use of the gym and indoor pool.

The job also came with a twelve-month contract, which got me thinking about how long I wanted to stay in Kyoto. Now that I could finally speak Japanese, my world had expanded. The tofu maker down the street knew my name. The women at the sento had begun to chat with me. And the children around the neighborhood waved back when I walked by. Luck had brought me into the welcoming embrace of a Japanese family and the elite world of Mushanokoji. Teaching had helped me make friends and understand the culture. I loved the food. Adored the weather. And lived in what felt like a tatami paradise. In short, it seemed life could not get any better.

But then I thought about Stephen and David, who considered Kyoto their home. They knew the rules, had mastered the language, but still lived in a cultural limbo. Because they were not Japanese, Japan would forever remain a place where even the nature of secrets is a well-kept secret.

To most foreigners this sort of existence is intolerable. Unable to live on the fringe, they begin to despise the very place they once embraced. I could not bear the thought of that happening to me.

What's more, if I remained in Kyoto for another year, John might not be there when I finally returned. That evening I realized I had two choices: I could stay in Kyoto and gorge myself on all that lay piled on my plate, or I could leave slightly hungry with the desire to return.

I decided to let go of it all and leave Japan.

Suddenly, a tremendous sense of bliss washed over me. At that moment I realized I was taking home far more than I was leaving behind: I had become Japanese in my thinking. Through tea kaiseki I genuinely had come to believe that when you leave a meal, moment, or place not quite completely satisfied, you cherish it that much more because it was ephemeral and left you wanting.

That is how I wanted to remember Kyoto. So before I was ready to say good-bye, I left.

21.

"Welcome Back to Kyoto"

Thirteen years would pass before I returned to Japan. After I left Kyoto, I corresponded with friends from the Guesthouse, as well as Tomiko and Yasu. But over time our letters tapered off, as we all became busy with our own lives.

In the fall of the year after I returned, John and I continued to date. He worked in New York, while I job-hunted from my parents' home outside Boston, eventually landing a job in television production with the hope of working on a cooking show. Although there was distance between us, it had shortened. John and I lived for those moments when he or I would step off the train.

Almost a year later, when he was accepted to law school in Boston, we came face to face with our future: Should we commit ourselves and live together or continue to date and have separate apartments?

"I won't be easy to live with," warned John. "You know what I'm like as a student." I did know. We would rarely see one another. How long could this situation last? I wondered. How long could I last? After weeks of deliberation, we decided to share an apartment. If we could endure Japan, and then this, hope lay ahead.

By the spring of John's second year of law school, hope had given way to certainty. He proposed and I accepted. We married the summer he graduated from law school in August 1991.

Over the years, I thought a lot about Kyoto, especially in the beginning. Fragments of my time there would emerge from the shadows, stay with me, then retreat and disappear. For a while, I contemplated working for a Japanese organization. But in the end, I decided against it, sensing I might feel frustrated having to conform to certain conventions.

As I concentrated on producing and editing, the memories of that year faded. I thought less about Tomiko. Less about Stephen, Mushanokoji, and tea kaiseki. For a while, I even stopped eating sushi.

Then there came this pull. As I segued from a career in television production to one in writing, I began to think more about Japan, the food, and especially tea kaiseki. With the exception of the author of the out-of-print picture book *Kaiseki Zen Tastes in Japanese Cooking,* no one to my knowledge had shared this extraordinary culinary art form with the Western world. There were books about tea that touched upon tea kaiseki, but no one had explored it from the culinary side. And the handful of articles that attempted to explain tea kaiseki focused on the lavish party-style restaurant kaiseki that focuses on sake, not tea.

Whenever I talked with Japanese friends in America, I was

surprised to learn that some had never heard of tea kaiseki. And those who had heard of tea kaiseki knew very little about the ritual. Even among those Japanese who lived in Kyoto, their knowledge seemed limited.

In many ways, a tea kaiseki resembles a haiku, where the tea master is the poet and nature his muse. Each morsel of heartfelt prose has the power to move the diner in astonishing ways. But unless you know that the carp in your wanmori symbolizes the brave heartiness of boys, or a sweet white rice dumpling represents the perfection of enlightenment, how can you interpret the poem? Every ingredient means something, whether it captures the season, celebrates a festival, or acts as a fetish to prevent disease or bring good luck. But only the highly trained members of Kyoto's tea world truly understand and appreciate such profundity.

Since this population was aging rapidly, my desire to chronicle this kind of cooking became significant. Then it turned into a passion.

There was one vital component of tea kaiseki that I had not explored, however: its origins in Kyoto's Zen temples. Buddhist monks had first practiced the tea ritual in Japan and their vegetarian temple food, called shojin ryori, had inspired tea kaiseki. The two characters that form the word shojin mean "spirit" and "to progress." The idea is that by preparing and consuming simple, seasonal, unadulterated foods, a Buddhist monk can better progress along the path to salvation. The process of cooking offers a way to learn self-discipline, humility, and focus, much like meditation. The frugal dishes help the monks break their bonds with the fleshy pleasures of the material world.

Having never tasted Zen temple food, I made arrangements

to do so. I would return to Kyoto to close the *enso,* the Zen term for the circle of infinity, simplicity, beginnings, and endings.

The cherry-red Fiat chugged and strained up Mount Hiei in the heavy August afternoon heat, then dropped down to a shady shelter of cedar trees surrounding a sleek concrete building. I got out, thanked the driver, then dragged my rolling red suitcase toward a sliding glass door.

I had arrived at Enryaku-ji Temple, one of the major centers of Japanese Buddhism, founded by the priest Saicho (767–822) in 788. Overlooking the city of Kyoto, the temple was built at the request of Emperor Kammu to protect the city from evil forces. Enryaku-ji eventually became a threat to the capital itself when it became a wealthy complex of more than 3,000 sub-temples with a growing clan of warrior monks, ready to fight anyone who challenged their power and authority. Angry at the temple's impertinence, Japan's leader at the time, Oda Nobunaga (1534–82), sent his army to burn the entire complex and slaughter every monk. Over time, the complex was rebuilt to its present form of 125 sub-temples.

"Konnichiwa," said the gentleman at the front desk as I stepped inside the temple's guest quarters. No sooner had I finished checking in than I started to worry. Aside from not knowing the rules, I had never "sat." Buddhists meditate for several hours at a time as a way to still the body and mind. The purpose is to clear your head of all of life's niggling details (like, should I have grilled salmon for supper or chicken Caesar salad?), so you can be in the moment. For only when you are balanced internally and externally can you possibly reach enlightenment.

What's more, posture matters. Ideally, you pretzel your legs into a full lotus and sit with your spine erect and your head held straight. And this is where the scary part comes in: If you slump or fall asleep, the head monk could whack you on the back with a stick! It's all part of the discipline. What if I got hit? Would I yell "shit!" like I sometimes did at home when I bumped my leg on a table? Would they kick me out? And what about meals? I had heard monks eat very little and very fast. Would I take too much food, or hold up the whole temple if I lingered over my pickles and rice? And how about sleeping? Would I have my own room? Or would I be sent to my futon before sunset in a great hall filled with chanting monks?

I should have known better. Finding salvation is serious business in Japan, particularly at Enryaku-ji, where the monks live in quiet separation from potentially curious visitors like me. Hence, the guest quarters.

A maid led me up to my room on the fourth floor, which easily rivaled the finest Japanese inn. Twelve tatami lined the floor, upon which sat a low wooden table surrounded by six large raspberry-and-gray-flowered floor pillows. A private toilet and shower stood to the right of the door, to the left was a cupboard that held my rolled up futon. A decorative alcove in the far right corner hid a telephone and small safe.

The walls were bare, save for a cream paper and wood screen along the room's back wall that when opened revealed a small balcony overlooking the sage peaks of Mount Hiei and nearby Lake Biwa. The Japanese love to take advantage of what's called a "borrowed view." And for good reason: If Mother Nature can be your artist, why pay for Picasso?

Equally as lovely as my bedroom was the private tatami room on the first floor that I had been assigned for dinner. It had an airy lightness accentuated by a large window overlooking a garden of bonsai. There must have been at least ten similar rooms situated next to mine, all set aside for the same purpose.

At 6:00, I slid open the screen. A polished sepia wood table sat in the middle of the room holding a black lacquer tray set with over a dozen bowls and plates filled with shojin ryori. There was no written menu. The kitchen prepared and served two meals a day, breakfast and dinner, and guests ate what the kitchen determined was freshest. All the dishes were vegetarian because of the religion's "no killing" tenet. But unlike the Chinese-style version of Japanese Buddhist temple food called *fucha ryori*, showcasing mock versions of the forbidden seafood, meat, poultry, and game, the food on my tray tasted just the way it looked, tantalizingly natural.

Evening meals at a Zen temple, I came to learn, still carry the name yakuseki and, like the "medicinal" sustenance that they once were, consist of simple vegetarian fare, such as some mixed cooked vegetables, miso soup, rice, and pickles. A more generous spread, like the one that lay before me, was saved for feast days or special occasions.

Clearly, the kitchen had considered my visit a special occasion. And it was. In front of me lay the origins of tea kaiseki, simply prepared vegetarian dishes using peak seasonal ingredients from the temple. And like tea kaiseki, the foods perfectly suited the oppressive heat of August, suggesting coolness through their color, temperature, texture, and flavor.

Because monks eat their meals from five nesting red lacquer bowls, my tray held five red lacquer bowls of food, plus several more dishes. The reason temples use red lacquer, not black, is the vestigial belief that the red pigment helps protect against food poisoning. The practice apparently stems from Taoist beliefs, in which cinnabar, the pigment originally used for red lacquer, was used as one of the ingredients in potions for immortality. The ancient Chinese also used cinnabar to embalm the bodies of the aristocracy.

My largest red lacquer bowl held a rainbow-colored mix of cold simmered vegetables. Shojin ryori features the five essential colors of blue/green, yellow, red, white, and purple/black. This concept evolved as a way to add visual interest to a cuisine that avoids meat.

The vegetable bowl proved to be not only a visual feast but a culinary one as well. In addition to two sticky steamed white field yams, there were several bright green stalks of a plant called coltsfoot, which tasted like parsley. There was also a succulent blackish shiitake mushroom cap, a sweet wedge of red-orange pumpkin, and a custardy square of tofu wrapped with soymilk skin. An edible peppery yellow chrysanthemum, the size of a button, added the fifth hue.

Another bowl held tempura because shojin ryori meals always include something that is deep-fried as well as grilled, steamed, boiled, and raw to add five different kinds of textural excitement to the meal. Beneath the crunchy batter crust lay a wedge of summer pumpkin, an okra pod, a tiny sweet plum, and several soft slices of sugar-preserved yuzu, the yellow citrus with the exotic pine-lemon flavor. But the dipping sauce was not the traditional mix of dashi and grated daikon radish that is eaten in restaurants and at home. Due to shojin ryori's taboo against eating animal flesh, the kitchen had omitted the fish flakes from the dashi in order to make it vegetarian. To beef up the flavor of the kelp and water, they had added dried mushrooms.

Because of the heat, the temple had also prepared a traditional summer dish of somen in a cold kelp broth. The slender snow-white noodles sat twisted in their bowl like a chignon with a "hair pin" of soy-marinated eggplant topped with spicy *myoga* shreds (Japanese ginger-like buds). The slithery noodles had a pleasing saltiness that accented the sweet gingery flavor of the slippery cool eggplant. I tried to imagine what the monks were eating on the other side of the compound and hoped it was something equally as flavorful and refreshing.

In lieu of meat, there were several kinds of high-protein wheat gluten on my tray. One version was in the form of a small yellow pillow stuffed with sweet miso "jam," kind of like a Zen ravioli, I thought, dipping another type seasoned with cinnamon in a sweet miso mustard sauce. As I chewed, the salty, sweet, and fiery flavors ricocheted around my mouth like a game of culinary pinball.

Flavor variety plays a pivotal role in shojin ryori cooking. In addition to the five different colors and cooking methods, every meal includes five different tastes: bitter, spicy, salty, sour, and sweet. (Shojin ryori also aims to include the sensation of *awai,* meaning "fleeting and delicate.")

This focus on five comes from China. In religious schools of thought, such as Taoism, there are five elements in the universe: wood and fire (which are yang), water and metal (which are yin), with the earth in the center. The Chinese believe the universe operates in terms of yin and yang, which together produce energy and all phenomena.

Because the temples served as the inspiration for tea kaiseki, every kaiseki meal also aims to include these same five flavors, cooking methods, and colors. An ideal wanmori, the zenith of the tea kaiseki, includes them all (along with five different textures, such as crunchy, soft, chewy, slippery, and soupy). Given the shadowy light in a teahouse, however, the five colors are often appreciated more in the mind than eye.

Probably the tastiest dish on my tray that night was the Zen temple staple "sesame tofu." Made from ground sesame seeds, water, salt, and the starch kudzu, the dense nutty square of custard came in a pool of soy topped with a spot of wasabi. It was satiny, rich, and as unctuous as a triple-crème cheese.

In the tradition of all monastery meals, I ended dinner with a small bowl of white rice, some clear soup (instead of miso), pickles, and a pot of brewed green tea. The soup, made from a lightly salted kelp stock, contained tiny pinwheels of hydrated dried soymilk skin that unfurled in the hot broth to look like miniature white roses. The pickles consisted of a few chewy kelp squares, a salty pickled plum, and popular yellow daikon radish pickles called *takuan*.

Takuan Osho (1573–1645) was the Zen monk said to have invented these pickles, which appear at every temple meal. The shape is the reason. Cut in rectangles to resemble *hyoshigi*, the paired wooden sticks that are struck together to mark the beginning of temple meditations, these beloved pickles nicely sponge up the juices from the monks' bowls. At the end of each meal the monks rinse their bowls "clean" with a swirl of brewed green tea, which they then drink, thus eliminating the need to waste dishwater and soap.

Tea kaiseki guests also always receive takuan pickles to sponge clean their bowls. For dishes that come before the pickle course, they wipe them clean with soft papers, which they carry in small packets tucked into the front fold of their kimonos. Leaving spotless bowls enables the guests to express their respect for the food. It also helps the tea master clear away dishes more easily, since sloshing soup bowls and stacked receptacles half filled with food could tumble onto the tatami.

Additionally, each tea guest carries a small leak-proof bag in his or her kimono sleeve in which to deposit unwanted food, such as bones or garnishes (although a thoughtful tea kaiseki cook will avoid such things). Again, the concept of letting nothing go to waste at a tea kaiseki stems from life in the temples, along with the concept of "pickle-wiped" spotlessness and purity.

Despite all that the temple had served me, I did not feel full. This made sense, since balance and harmony are essential to all shojin ryori meals. Rich foods, like the tempura, balance with fresh light foods, like the cooked vegetables. Also, portions are modest because the monks' evening meal is considered "medicine" and, thus, consumed in judicious quantities.

Since meditations are a major activity at Enryaku-ji Temple, I set my alarm clock for 6:00 the next morning to dress in time to join the monks in their prayers. To my relief, the services resembled nothing I had feared. They began at 6:30 in the cavernous Central Hall, billowing with incense and glowing with half a dozen candles and the famous "Inextinguishable Dharma Light" on the altar. Dharma, meaning "Great Law" in Sanskrit, refers to Buddha's teachings, and the trio of lamps at Enryaku-ji has been burning ceaselessly for the past twelve hundred years. Said originally to have been lit by the founder, Saicho, himself, they symbolize the legions of Buddhist priests who study at Enryaku-ji and then leave to "illuminate their surroundings" in the outside world.

According to Buddhist texts, right before Buddha died, he told his cousin Ananda, "As long as monks like you gather in a group, follow the rules, and train themselves, the Dharma will thrive. Be lamps unto yourselves. Holding fast to the Dharma, be your own refuge. Do not seek refuge beyond yourselves. In this way, you will overcome darkness."

Along with several other guests, I sat on a tatami stage behind the monks. We had cushions to sit on. We could slump. There were no sticks. Although I couldn't understand the services, the humming and chanting proved tremendously soothing. And in that cloud of calm, I headed back to the guest quarters for breakfast in the communal dining hall.

Compared to dinner, breakfasts at Enryaku-ji were meager. However, they were much more generous than the monks' lean offering of rice porridge, pickles, and brewed green tea. Each morning we received steamed white rice, thin miso soup filled with fronds of wakame seaweed, pickles, and a braised vegetable dish, such as cold string beans that had been simmered in vegetable stock and topped with ground sesame seeds.

After breakfast, I usually walked around the temple complex with the other visitors. Approximately 500 pilgrims venture to the temple each year to walk the grounds or stay overnight and chant with the monks. At the top of a long set of stone stairs sat Daiko-do, the Great Lecture Hall, where Enryaku-ji's monks have gathered for centuries to hear talks on Buddhist teachings. Behind the massive wooden door stood several life-size wooden statues of famous priests who had studied at Enryaku-ji and then left to establish various Buddhist sects. There was even a figure of Eisai, the man who had first brought powdered green tea and fine tea seeds to Japan.

Another morning I hiked up a rocky winding path to the summit of Mount Hiei. As my brown leather sandals crunched the twigs underfoot, I felt a sort of kinship with all the monks who had trod this same path. Unique to Enryaku-ji is the 1,000-day walk that the monks complete over the course of seven years.

During this holy journey, they save every pair of rope-and-cotton sandals that they wear to shreds.

On my second to last day, I finally had the chance to meet with a monk to learn about his life on the other side of the temple. Shortly after breakfast, twenty-nine-year-old Kosho stopped by the guest quarters in black cotton pants, a black kimono-like top, and straw sandals. As he spoke to me in English in the small sitting area off the front lobby, he exuded the most extraordinary sense of warmth, openness, and grace. He had nothing to hide and everything to give, which he did freely.

Kosho told me that monks at Enryaku-ji train anywhere from two months to twenty-four years. Some bonzes like himself, who have finished their initial studies, live off the mountain but commute to the temple each day for spiritual practice and meals.

He also mentioned that the temple relies on donations for all its food. Mochi is one of the biggest offerings, along with noodles, vegetables, and tofu. When times are lean, dinner can consist of spaghetti with ketchup. "Oishii," he said, grinning.

Driven by curiosity, I asked Kosho if I could visit the temple's kitchen and meet the cook. He kindly agreed and that afternoon stopped by the guest quarters in his shiny gold Toyota. From there, we zoomed through the woods to a small newly constructed temple on the south side of the complex, where we met the twenty-five-year-old cook. After serving us cups of brewed green tea, the cook ushered us into the kitchen, a small but well-equipped space with stainless steel counters, a gas stove, and large refrigerator.

In a Japanese monastery, the cook is often referred to as the *tenzo*. Usually the newest monk in training, he prepares all the meals for the complex. If he doesn't know how to cook, the elders teach him and share their recipes.

The tenzo's yakuseki that night consisted of a humble tofu-vegetable stew, steamed rice, miso soup, pickles, and green grapes. Kosho, who turned out to be a bit of a jokester, explained that garlic and onions are off limits in shojin ryori. "They ruin our breath when chanting," he said, with a smirk. I later found out the real reason alliums are forbidden is that they are considered mild aphrodisiacs, not exactly ideal fare for those who choose to be celibate.

It was still light when Kosho dropped me off at the guest quarters. Since it was his wife's birthday the next day, he told me he would not be showing up at the temple the next morning. "I hope that's all right?" he asked with concern in his eyes. I assured him it was and thanked him for spending so much time with me.

Later that night in my room, after another ethereal shojin ryori dinner, the phone rang. It was Kosho.

"I was just calling to make sure you found out everything you wanted to know about our cooking," he said. I assured my new friend I had, indeed, found what I had come looking for. I had tasted the origins of tea kaiseki at Enryaku-ji and at last experienced its spiritual roots.

My visit to Enryaku-ji Temple would not have been possible had it not been for the efforts and generosity of one person: Tomiko. Several weeks before leaving America, I had written her to say I was coming to Kyoto and hoped we might get together. We had been out of touch for so many years that I had no idea if she would respond to my letter or if it would even reach her. By the time I had left for Japan, I had not heard a word.

Then I arrived at the Japanese inn where I planned to stay

for a few days prior to visiting Enryaku-ji Temple. On a small red lacquer table in my six-tatami room lay a fax.

> *Welcome back to Kyoto, Victoria. It's so nice to hear from you. We'd love to see you. Please call me when you get to Kyoto. Until 7:00 P.M. I'm at the office. Talk to you later!*
>
> *Tomiko*

My eyes misted over as I read her words. She had gotten my letter.

I called her the next day and we agreed to meet for lunch that Friday. She would stop by the inn, which turned out to be seven minutes from her home by car. From there, we would drive to a restaurant, a small neighborhood noodle shop known for its homemade soba.

At 12:10, a cherry-red Fiat pulled over to the curb. Tomiko got out. She had grown her hair below her ears, but because of the heat swept it off her forehead with a black hair band. She seemed heavier and much more hunched over than I had remembered and as she crossed the street I noticed she almost limped in her high-heeled black sandals. A loose short-sleeve black blouse hung over the waist of her peg-leg cream pants and a long double strand of tiger's eye beads swung back and forth as she walked. "How are you?" she asked, smiling broadly.

So often in Japan communications rely on the nonverbal. In conversations, what you refrain from saying becomes most important. We hugged and then stood back and looked at each other. In a matter of seconds, thirteen years had collapsed in on themselves like a house of cards. We had no need for words. Tomiko's and my friendship simply picked up where we had left off.

She and I got together several more times during my stay in Kyoto, which looked pretty much the same as I had remembered. I awoke to the same dull thumping of housewives airing out their futons and still caught my breath as the magical light of dusk, shimmering, hazy, and golden, washed across dark temple doors and the dusky-sage tips of Kyoto's distant mountains. Even the Gion, home to most geisha, brought forth that familiar rush of anticipation, wonderment, and sense of secrecy, as the clop of wooden sandals echoed throughout the warren of twisting side streets.

Of course, there were a few changes, such as the three Starbucks filled with young Japanese sipping Frappuccinos, noshing on tuna-pumpkin sandwiches, and retrieving e-mail messages on their cell phones to the ubiquitous Michael Franks soundtrack. Several Gap stores had also sprung up, along with a Tiffany's and the glittering new Kyoto Station, a massive conglomeration of glass and metal grids resembling an atrium crossed with an airport lobby. Several indigents now made their home under the bridges of the Kamo River and the frumpy neighborhood near Tomiko's, once filled with cabbage patches and rice paddies, felt more like the Champs-Élysées with a Cordon Bleu gift shop, numerous boulangeries, and several Parisian-style clothing stores.

One night I stopped by Tomiko's home for dinner to see Yasu, who looked just the same, except his hair had turned gray. I even got together with Stephen, who was alive and well. Although he had changed addresses and no longer had a genuine teahouse on his property, he was still living with his partner, David, and hosting formal tea ceremonies for friends and tea students.

As I reacquainted myself with the city, I could not help thinking about how living in Kyoto and studying tea kaiseki had impacted my life. The rhythm of each day in Japan had taught me patience and the ability to make the best of almost any situation.

I also came to embrace good and bad, imperfect and whole, and light and dark. You have to know the bad to appreciate the good; the imperfect offers room for creativity and growth; and only by residing in the dark can you find the light. It was like learning Zen without becoming a monk.

But one of the most poignant messages that Japan pressed into my consciousness was to live each day as if there were no tomorrow. I saw that at Enryaku-ji Temple. In Buddhism, life is seen as fleeting, therefore every moment is sacred and should be appreciated to the fullest. The art of tea embodies this concept. Every tea ceremony becomes a unique occasion because you will never gather again with that same group of people on that day, during those hours, in your lifetime. The evanescence of the gathering, not unlike the brief flowering of the cherry blossoms, heightens the pleasure found in such pathos.

This kind of thinking brings grace and meaning to everything you do, including the mundane. In preparing dinner, for example, you can treat it as either a chore or a joy.

To me, cooking a meal is a gift you give to someone, including yourself. Tea kaiseki taught me that. Each dish becomes a creative expression of the heart, filled with kindness, compassion, and love. That is why the tea ceremony and tea kaiseki will ultimately live on. Both are art forms that despite the many challenges they face nourish the body and spirit.

In many ways, my return to Kyoto was like the second bowl of tea at a chaji. First there is the tea kaiseki to temper your hunger. Then comes the thick tea to lift you toward enlightenment. The second bowl of tea, made thinner and lighter, brings you back down to earth. And that is where I felt I had finally landed. Japan had raised me up to unexpected heights, made uncommon things possible, then set me down with a new way of looking at the world.

On the dawn of my departure, the elderly woman who ran the Japanese inn where I had been staying offered to help carry my bags to the street where I would meet the taxi to take me to the airport bus station in southern Kyoto. Her honey-brown dog, limping with age, followed her up the winding alley to where the taxi sat waiting. After helping the driver pile my bags in the trunk, I thanked the woman and gently stroked her dog one last time along its graying muzzle. Then I climbed into the car and sped away, turning around to wave farewell through the rear window.

There is an old Chinese custom in tea for the host to see his guests off by accompanying them to their destination in order to ensure they arrive home safely. It evolved from the concept that the host might never see his guests again, in the event of a war or natural disaster. The Japanese touch at a formal tea ceremony is to wait until the guests are out of sight, then retreat to the tearoom for a moment of reflection.

Just as the taxi rounded the corner, I spun around one last time. There, in the fragile morning light at the end of the street, were two tiny figures—still standing sentinel to see their guest off to the burning world of dust and passions, perhaps never to return.

Zen Temple Summer Somen with Gingered Eggplant

Cold noodles are a popular summer dish in Japan, especially in temples during August as part of the Obon, or All Soul's Day observance. The noodles are almost always served in chilled glass bowls to give a cooling sensation. Sometimes the somen are even topped with beautiful clear chunks of hand-chipped ice with a cold dipping sauce on the side. Here, slippery cool eggplant slices marinated in fresh ginger and soy sauce add a jolt of spiciness to the plain noodles.

1 slim lavender Asian eggplant
3½ tablespoons soy sauce
2 teaspoons grated fresh ginger
⅔ cup vegetarian dashi (page 265)
¼ cup sake
½ teaspoon sugar
¼ teaspoon coarse salt
4 ounces dried somen noodles
2 scallions, trimmed and thinly sliced

1. Trim the eggplant and cut lengthwise in half. Cut each half crosswise into four pieces.

2. Bring a small amount of water to a boil in a medium saucepan. Add the eggplant, skin side down, reduce the heat to low, and cook until just tender, about 4 minutes. The eggplant should be soft, but not mushy, when a toothpick is inserted into flesh. Remove the eggplant from the saucepan and drain, skin side up, on a clean tea towel. Cut each piece lengthwise in half.

3. Combine 1½ tablespoons of the soy sauce with the grated ginger in a small dish. Drizzle over the eggplant slices and chill in the refrigerator for at least an hour.

4. Combine the vegetarian dashi with the remaining 2 tablespoons soy sauce, the sake, sugar, and salt in a small saucepan. Bring to a boil, reduce the heat to low, and simmer for 4 minutes. Cool the mixture and then chill in the refrigerator until cold, about 2 hours.

5. Shortly before serving, boil the somen according to the package directions. Drain and rinse under cold water to cool. Transfer to a large bowl of ice water.

6. Using your fingers, or chopsticks, pick up one fourth of the noodles and twist into a neat coil. Place the coil in a glass bowl, tucking the ends under the coil. Arrange a portion of the gingered eggplant in the center of the noodles. Carefully ladle the chilled dashi mixture around the noodles. Sprinkle each serving with some scallions.

Makes 4 servings

Vegetarian Dashi (Konbu Dashi)

Given the Buddhist proscription against eating animal products, the fish flakes in traditional dashi must be avoided. As a result, temple cooks use shiitake mushrooms to add robustness to the kelp base. To avoid wasting the soaked mushrooms and kelp after you have used them in the dashi, cut them into thin slices and add them to noodle, rice, or vegetable dishes.

8 dried shiitake mushrooms

One 4-inch-long piece konbu (kelp)

Combine 10 cups water with the shiitake mushrooms and the kelp in a stockpot. Bring to a simmer, reduce the heat to very low, and simmer the stock for an hour, or until the liquid has reduced to 5 cups. Let the mixture cool. Pour the stock through a cheesecloth-lined sieve, saving the solids for another use.

Makes 5 cups

Zen Temple Sesame "Tofu" (Goma Dofu)

Traditionally, this sesame custard is poured into a special shallow square metal container and left to set. The firm custard is then turned out, cut into squares, and served in small bowls in a pool of soy sauce. Since most Western cooks do not have such a mold, six 6-ounce ramekins have been substituted. You can serve the goma dofu as a first course or side dish.

1 cup hulled white sesame seeds

3 tablespoons crumbled kudzu

⅛ teaspoon coarse salt

12 teaspoons soy sauce

Wasabi paste for garnish (available in tubes)

1. Place 2½ cups water and the sesame seeds in a blender. Cover and whip for 5 minutes to render the mixture as smooth as possible. Pour through a cheesecloth-lined sieve into a medium saucepan, pushing on the sieve with the back of a spoon, and

then squeeze the cheesecloth into a ball, pressing on the ball, until you have nothing more than a dryish paste in the cheesecloth. You should have about 2½ cups of sesame "milk."

2. Whisk the kudzu and salt into the sesame milk until the kudzu is completely dissolved. Whisk the mixture constantly over low heat for 10 minutes. It will thicken and bubble. Remove from the heat and pour into six small ramekins that have been rinsed with cold water (this will prevent the custard from sticking). Let them rest until firm, then cover with plastic wrap and refrigerate until cold.

3. To serve, gently shake the ramekins, or run a sharp knife around the edges to loosen the "tofu." Turn out onto small dishes (square if possible, since the Japanese like contrasting shapes). Spoon 2 teaspoons of soy sauce around the bottom of each "tofu" circle and top with a little squirt of wasabi.

Makes 6 servings

Author's Note

This book is a work of nonfiction. Everything that happened is true and the people, places, and situations are real. However, because I do not wish to invade people's privacy and portray them in a light different from how they possibly see themselves, I have changed the names of certain people and businesses to protect their identity. This does nothing to alter the story.

When it comes to chronicling the past, the question inevitably arises, "How did you remember so many details?" My answer is simple: e-mail did not exist, as we know it. If it had, I would not have written so many letters to my parents, siblings, friends, childhood pal Margaret, and John. They, in turn, would not have held on to my letters, nor written back so many, which I also saved. All our communications would have been deleted into a void.

Several other materials aided my memory, including the diaries I kept describing everyday life in Japan, as well as my feelings and thoughts. I also filled two notebooks with recipes and notes from my tea kaiseki classes at Mushanokoji. In addition, I took numerous photographs and saved scores of pamphlets, ticket stubs, brochures, booklets, and restaurant menus. For my return trip to Kyoto, I kept another diary and took dozens of rolls of film. I also met with several tea masters. These tangible reminders, combined with my own extensive research, enabled me to impart the flavors and details of what it was like to live in Kyoto and events and conversations that took place during my time there.

Glossary

Below are the meanings of important Japanese words or terms, or those that are first defined in the text and then appear more than once.

amazake—a creamy, white, naturally sweet fermented rice drink made with a fermenting agent; usually served warm in winter

azukebachi—literally, "entrusted bowl"; the name of the tea kaiseki dish made from ingredients left over from preparing the various courses of a tea kaiseki meal

azuki (*also* adzuki)—small crimson-colored beans used occasionally in savory dishes but primarily in confections

bento—a compartmentalized boxed meal

bonito—skipjack tuna, also known as oceanic bonito; dried and shaved to make flakes for dashi, as well as eaten fresh

bonsai—miniature trees or plants that compose an arrangement or garden

chaji—a formal tea ceremony that includes a kaiseki meal

chakai—a tea ceremony where only thin tea is served (after a sweet)

chakaiseki (*see* tea kaiseki)

chanoyu—literally, "tea's hot water"; the formal practice of preparing and consuming whipped powdered green tea

daikon—a giant white radish with a crisp fresh flavor and juicy texture

daimyo—a samurai lord

dashi—a pale brown stock made from shaved bonito fish flakes and kelp (called konbu, or kombu), steeped in water

donburi—a pottery bowl that is approximately three times as big as a rice bowl; also the name of the dish served in such a bowl, composed of rice topped with broth and goodies, such as egg and chicken

edamame—fresh soybeans usually boiled in the pod, lightly salted, and gently pulled out of the pod with the teeth

fu—wheat gluten; eaten fresh *(nama fu)*, grilled *(yaki fu)*, or dried (and hydrated)

furikake—a dry seasoning mix usually composed of nori flakes, sesame seeds, and freeze-dried granules of fish stock

fusuma—a removable sliding panel made from a wood frame grid covered on both sides by thick opaque paper or cloth, used to separate tatami rooms

futon—a cotton floor mattress

hana—flower

happi coats—traditional work jackets often made from soft cotton resembling short kimonos

hashiarai—literally, "chopstick wash"; a small portion of liquid (often hot water) flavored with a seasonal ingredient served at a tea kaiseki meant to clean the chopsticks and refresh the palate after the grilled course

hassun—several meanings, including square cedar tray upon which foods are served at a tea kaiseki; the name for the actual course of a tea kaiseki composed of something from the ocean and something from the mountains served on the cedar tray; the hors d'oeuvre course served during a restaurant kaiseki meal

herro—hello

honzen ryori—literally, "main-tray cooking"; formal court cuisine consisting of two or more soups and at least five side dishes distributed between one main legged tray and several smaller ones

iemoto—the male head of a particular house (or school) of traditional arts

jubako—stacked lacquer boxes usually used for holding special New Year's foods

kai—several meanings, including group; or bosom pocket, meaning the breast-pocket fold in a kimono

kaiseki (*see* restaurant kaiseki *or* tea kaiseki)

kanji—Chinese characters used in Japanese writing

Kansai—the area of Kyoto-Nara-Osaka-Kobe

kirei—beautiful

koji—a fermenting agent made by inoculating either beans or grains with the mold *Aspergillus*

konbu (*also* kombu)—kelp; mainly used to make dashi (along with bonito flakes); also steeped in hot water to make vegetarian stock (primarily for temple cooking) konomono—literally, "a thing for incense"; also pickled vegetables, as well as the name of the pickle course at a tea kaiseki

kudzu—a rocky white starch made from the tuberous root of the plant of the same name

matcha—a fine powder made from ground green tea leaves that is whipped with boiling water for the tea ceremony; also used to flavor foods, such as soba noodles, sweet dumplings, and ice cream

mirin—a sweet rice wine with a 14 percent alcohol content; it is usually used for cooking, although occasionally sipped as an alcoholic beverage (such as at New Year's when infused with an herbal-spice mixture)

mochi—pounded glutinous rice that is formed into cakes; eaten fresh or hard (in which case the mochi is either hydrated in water or stock until soft, or grilled and sauced or seasoned)

mukozuke—literally, "beyond attach"; the marinated raw seafood or vegetable dish at a tea kaiseki served on the first tray with the miso soup and rice

nigiri zushi (also nigiri sushi)—vinegar-seasoned rice ovals spread with a thin layer of wasabi and then topped with raw seafood or other ingredients, such as sliced omelet, cooked shrimp, or vegetables

nori—laver; usually dried and formed into dark green sheets

obi—the long wide sash worn around the waist with a kimono

oishii—delicious

okonomiyaki—literally, "cook what you like"; a Japanese-style egg-flour batter pancake filled with chopped vegetables and a choice of added seafood, poultry, and/or meat

osechi ryori—honorable seasonal cooking; currently refers to special foods prepared for the extended New Year's holiday and served in layered lacquer boxes

Oshogatsu—the New Year's holiday period beginning on the eve of December 31 and ending January 3

ozoni—a dashi-based New Year's Day breakfast soup containing mochi plus other regional ingredients

restaurant kaiseki—a formal restaurant meal that resembles aspects of a tea kaiseki but is based on sake instead of rice and aims to entertain versus spiritually enlighten

Rikyu-bashi—cedar chopsticks that are tapered at both ends and used exclusively for tea kaiseki

roji—a Zen term for "dewy path"; also the inner garden of the teahouse containing stepping stones, a waiting pavilion, and a stone basin; some teahouses have an inner roji and an outer roji

sabi—a complicated aesthetic concept that treasures the beauty in things that are rusted, aged, faded, and withered

sake—Japanese rice wine

samurai—a Japanese warrior (also known as *bushi*)

sansho—a tingly tongue-numbing green powder made from the ground dried seedpods of the prickly ash tree

sashimi—sliced raw fish or shellfish

seki—several meanings, including: gathering place; or stone

sekki—seasonal divisions derived from the old Chinese solar calendar

sensei—teacher

sento—public bath

shabu-shabu—a dashi broth–based dish, similar to fondue, in which thinly sliced beef and vegetables are dipped into the stock; the name of the dish is onomatopoeic for the sound the ingredients make when cooking

shiizakana—literally, "insisting fish"; an optional course, usually composed of seafood, served at a tea kaiseki if tea guests request more sake

shiso—also called perilla, it is a jagged-edged spicy green leaf from the mint family, often served with sashimi; red shiso, also referred to as beefsteak plant, is used to season pickled plums and various sweets

shogun—the head of the samurai government

shoji—translucent paper- and wood-paneled sliding screens, used as windows or doors

shojin ryori—vegetarian temple food

soba—thin noodles made from pure buckwheat flour or a mixture of buckwheat and white flour; they can also be flavored with powdered green tea

sushi (zushi in Japan)—the term for any one of the many preparations made from rice seasoned with vinegar (and often sugar and salt as well)

tabi—the formal white socks worn with kimonos that separate at the big toe to accommodate the thong of a sandal

tatami—woven rice-straw floor mats

tea kaiseki—a kaiseki meal based on rice that precedes a formal tea ceremony; in the ceremony, a moist sweet is served before a bowl of thick tea and a dry sweet is served before a bowl of thin tea

tenshin—a small simple meal served after the thin tea and occasionally the thick tea in temples, but before the whipped green tea at a tea ceremony; it originated in China and came to Japan via the Zen monasteries

tenzo—the cook in a Japanese monastery

udon—thick white wheat noodles

wabi—a complicated aesthetic concept that values a person, way of life, or thing that can be poor, sad, lonely, simple, elegant, or tranquil

wakame—a deep green seaweed with a soft ribbon-like appearance and mild flavor; mainly used in miso soup

wanmori—the climactic course in tea kaiseki consisting of exquisite cooked ingredients surrounded by a clear dashi stock that is lightly seasoned and delicately garnished

yakimono—literally, "grilled thing"; also the grilled course in a tea kaiseki meal

yakuseki—literally, "medicine stone"; the hot stones that monks placed in the breast-pocket fold of their kimonos to alleviate hunger pangs; later the term came to mean a small vegetarian temple meal; currently it refers to the small evening meal served in temples

yen—Japanese currency

yuto—the name of a tea kaiseki dish of warm salted water mixed with savory shards of the scorched rice loosened from the bottom of the rice pot; also the name of the black lacquer hot water pitcher in which the dish arrives

yuzu—a Japanese citron used for cooking (both the zest and the juice), predominantly when it is yellow and ripe, although sometimes when it is green and unripe

zushi (*see* sushi)

Recipe Index